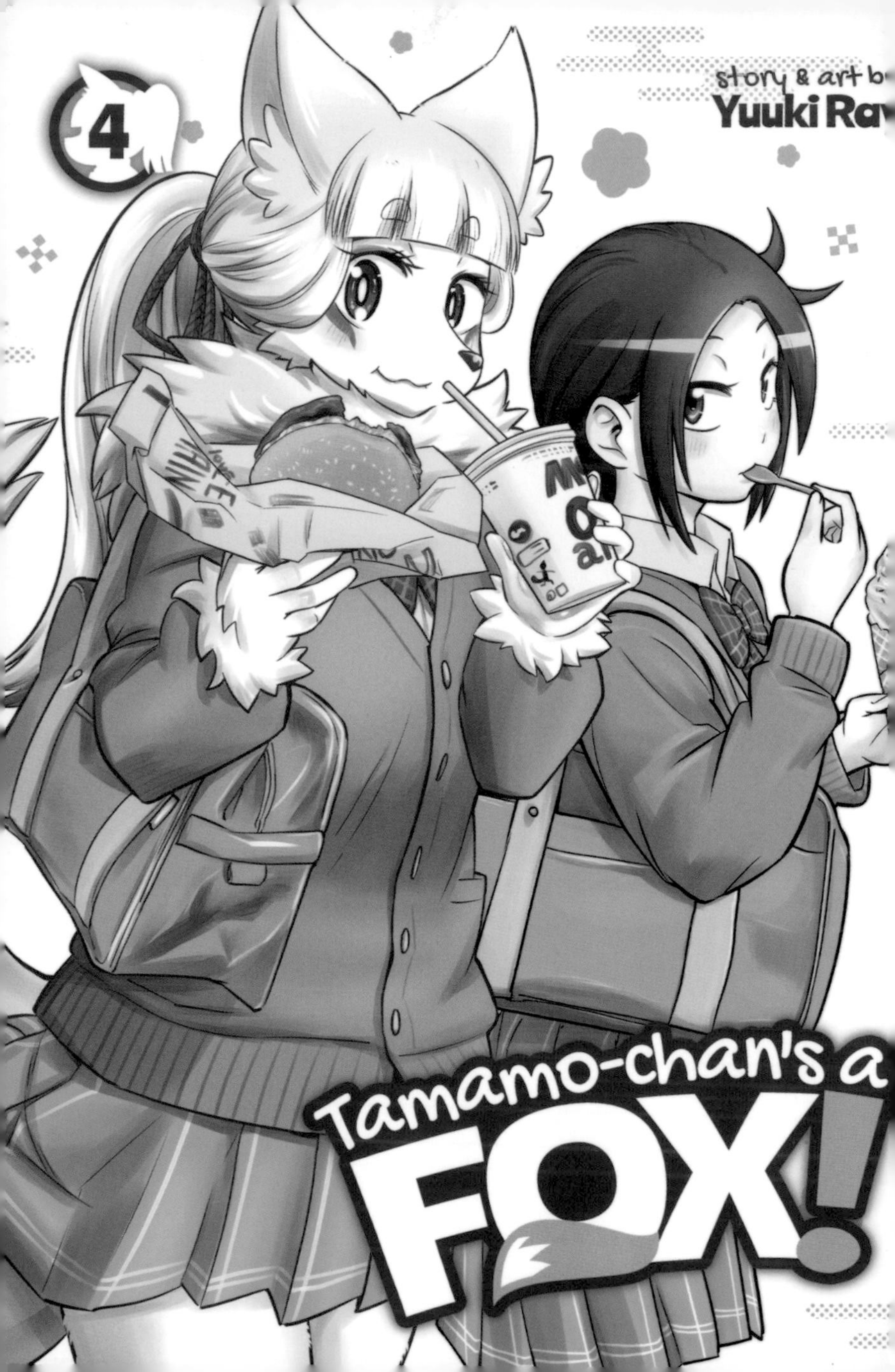
4
story & art b
Yuuki Ra
Tamamo-chan's a
FOX!

Tamamo-chan's a FOX!

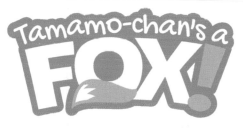

CONTENTS

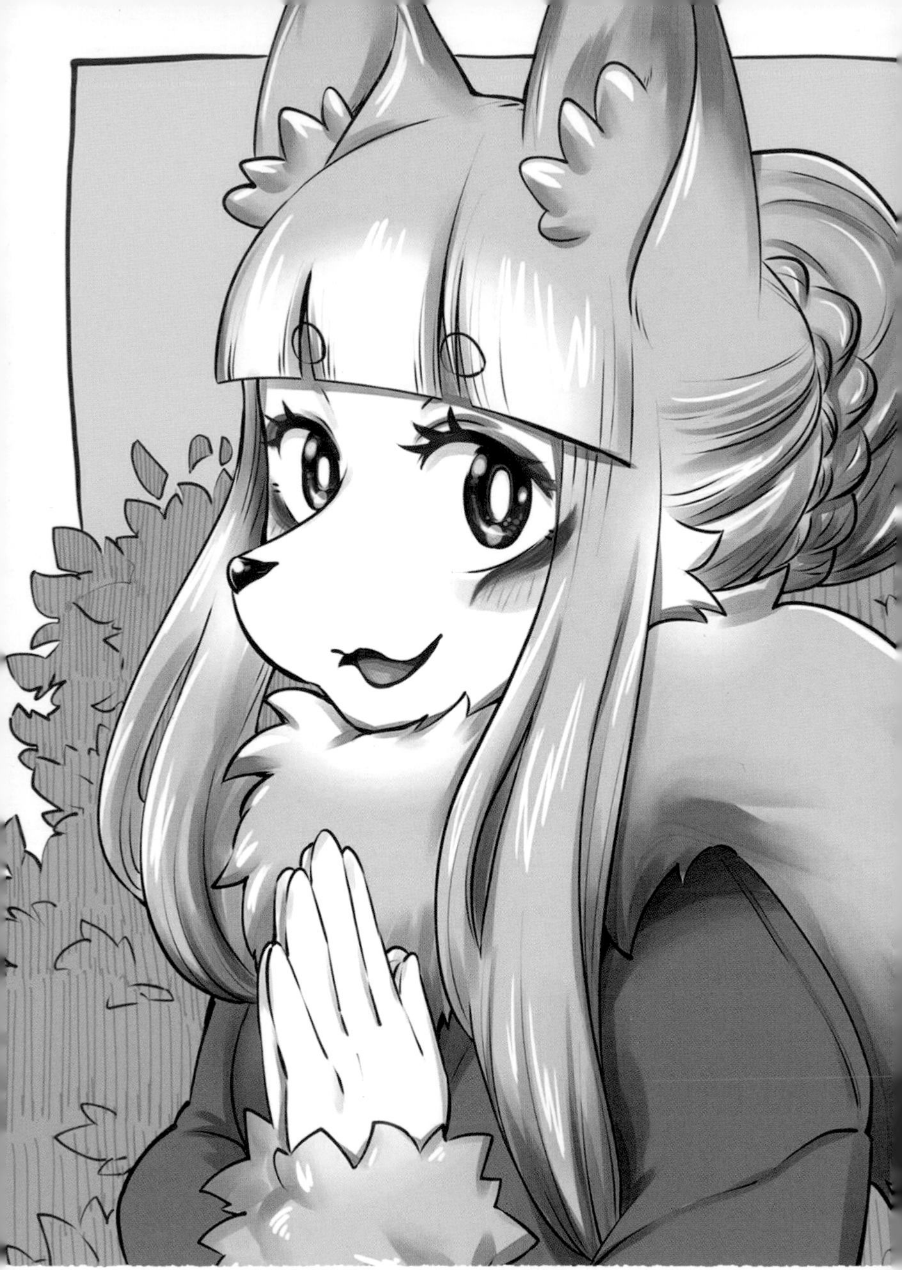

Tamamo-chan's a FOX! 4 story & art by Yuuki Ra

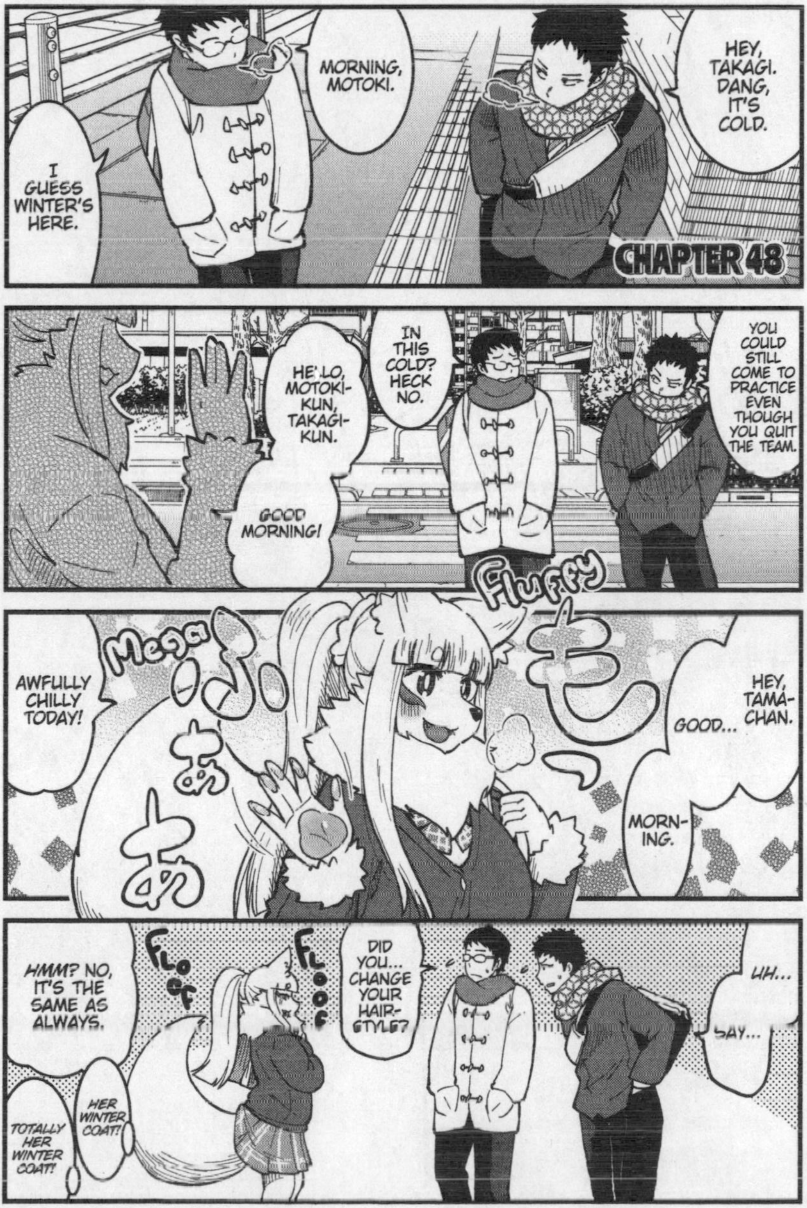
HEY, TAKAGI. DANG, IT'S COLD.
MORNING, MOTOKI.
I GUESS WINTER'S HERE.
CHAPTER 48
YOU COULD STILL COME TO PRACTICE EVEN THOUGH YOU QUIT THE TEAM.
IN THIS COLD? HECK NO.
HELLO, MOTOKI-KUN, TAKAGI-KUN.
GOOD MORNING!
Fluffy
HEY, TAMA-CHAN.
GOOD...
MORN-ING.
も
Mega ふ
あ
あ
AWFULLY CHILLY TODAY!
UH... SAY...
DID YOU... CHANGE YOUR HAIR-STYLE?
FLOOF
FLOOF
HMM? NO, IT'S THE SAME AS ALWAYS.
HER WINTER COAT!
TOTALLY HER WINTER COAT!

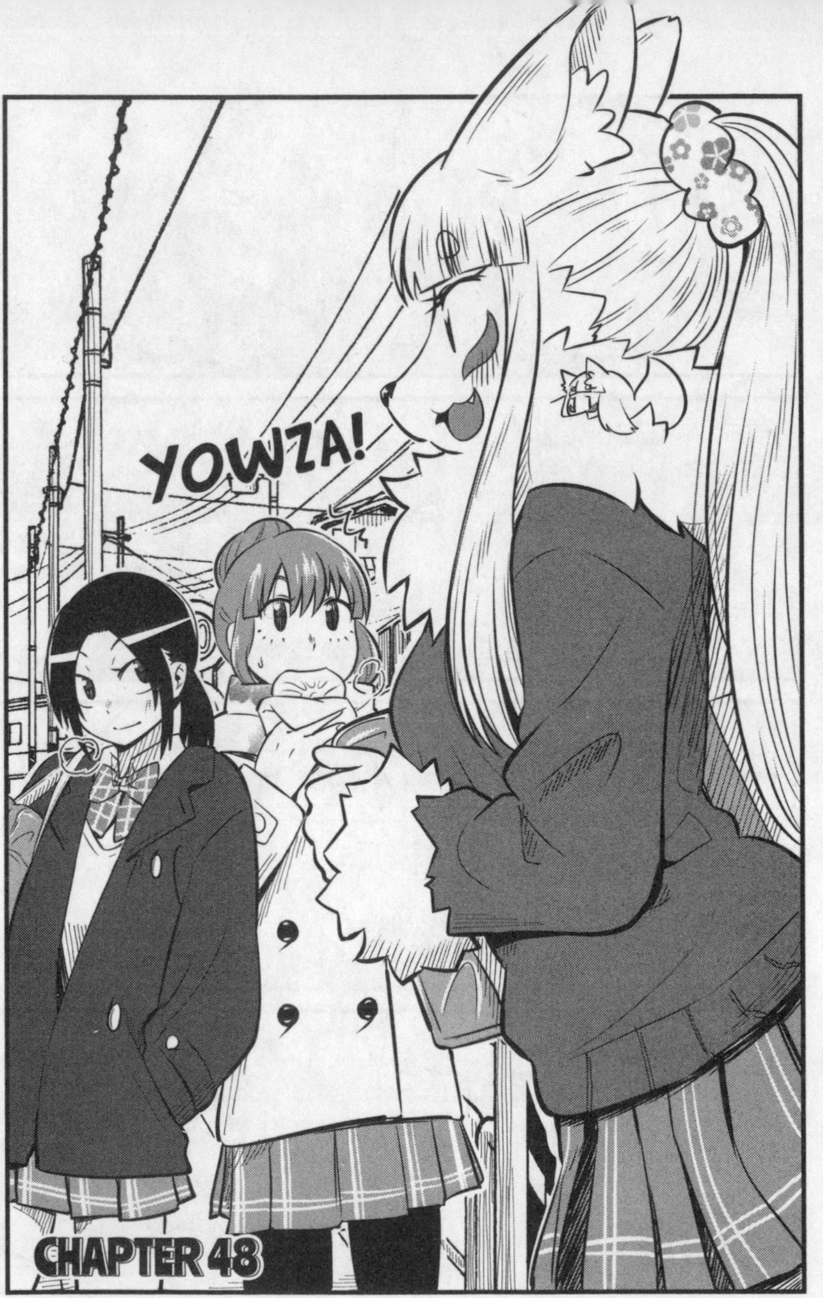
YOWZA!
CHAPTER 48

This high school girl could survive in the Arctic.

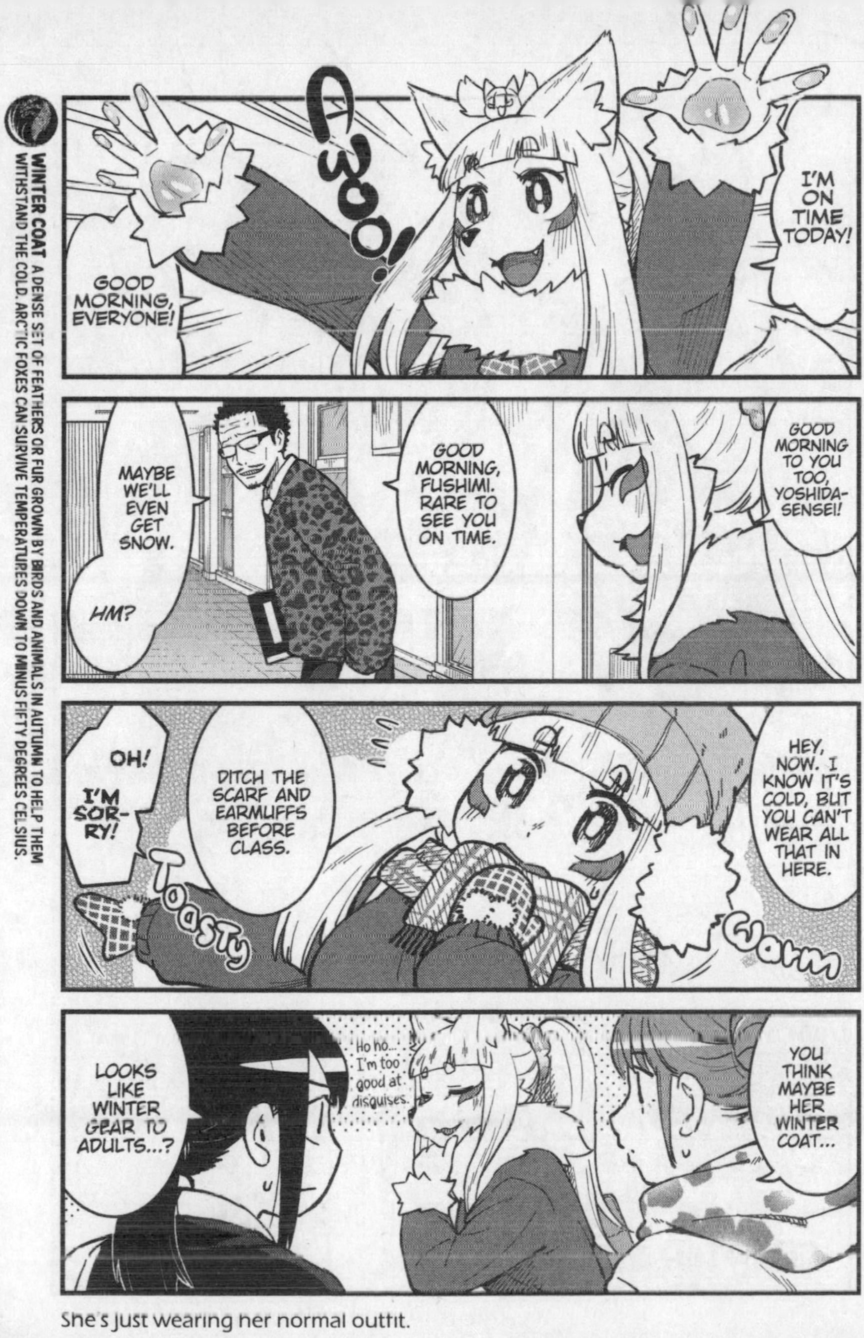
I'M ON TIME TODAY!
GOOD MORNING, EVERYONE!
GOOD MORNING TO YOU TOO, YOSHIDA-SENSEI!
GOOD MORNING, FUSHIMI. RARE TO SEE YOU ON TIME.
MAYBE WE'LL EVEN GET SNOW.
HM?
HEY, NOW. I KNOW IT'S COLD, BUT YOU CAN'T WEAR ALL THAT IN HERE.
Warm
DITCH THE SCARF AND EARMUFFS BEFORE CLASS.
OH! I'M SORRY!
Toasty
YOU THINK MAYBE HER WINTER COAT...
Ho ho... I'm too good at disguises.
LOOKS LIKE WINTER GEAR TO ADULTS...?

WINTER COAT A DENSE SET OF FEATHERS OR FUR GROWN BY BIRDS AND ANIMALS IN AUTUMN TO HELP THEM WITHSTAND THE COLD. ARCTIC FOXES CAN SURVIVE TEMPERATURES DOWN TO MINUS FIFTY DEGREES CELSIUS.

She's just wearing her normal outfit.

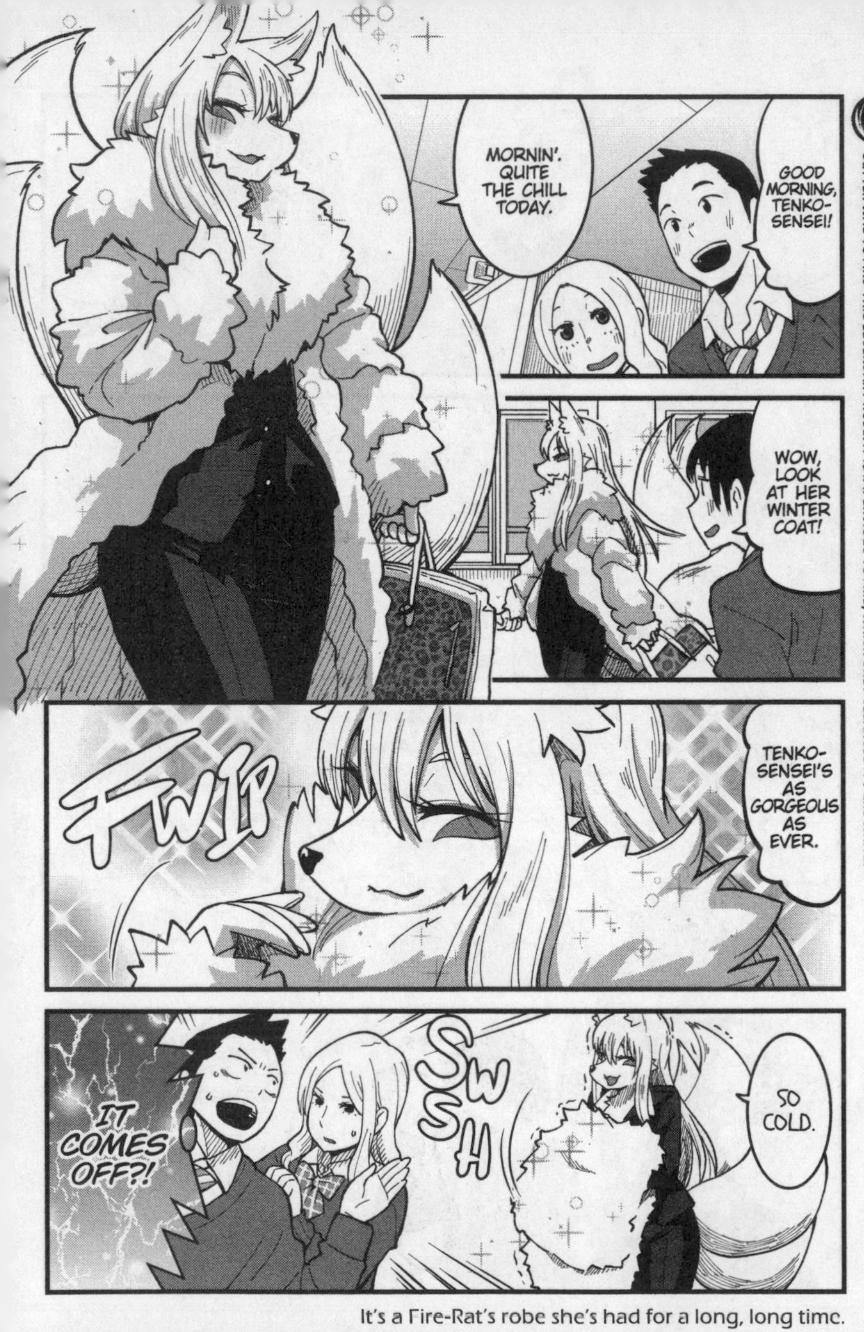
GOOD MORNING, TENKO-SENSEI!
MORNIN'. QUITE THE CHILL TODAY.
WOW, LOOK AT HER WINTER COAT!
TENKO-SENSEI'S AS GORGEOUS AS EVER.
FWIP
SO COLD.
SWSH
IT COMES OFF?!

ROBE OF THE FIRE-RAT ONE OF THE IMPOSSIBLE TASKS SET BY PRINCESS KAGUYA IN THE *TALE OF THE BAMBOO CUTTER* WAS TO FIND THIS LEGENDARY ROBE. IT IS IMPERVIOUS TO FIRE, WHICH ONLY CLEANSES IT PURE WHITE.

It's a Fire-Rat's robe she's had for a long, long time.

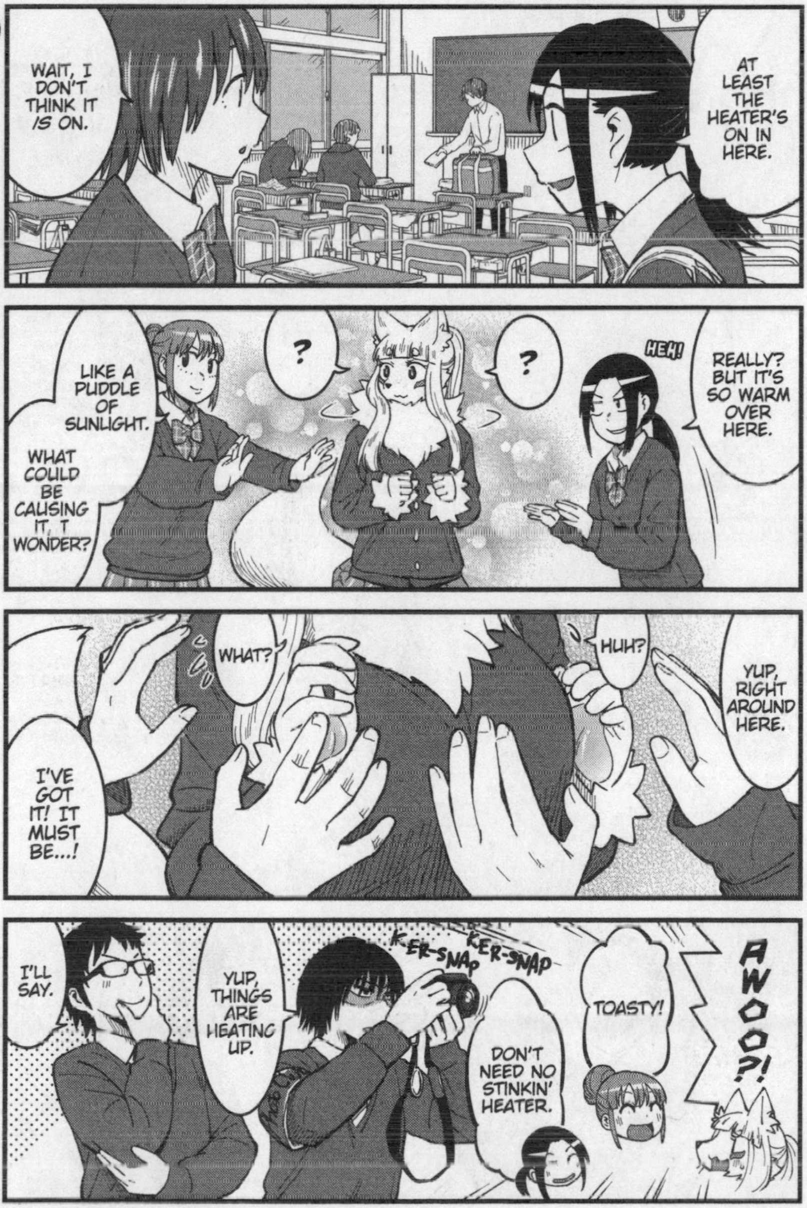
AT LEAST THE HEATER'S ON IN HERE.
WAIT, I DON'T THINK IT IS ON.
REALLY? BUT IT'S SO WARM OVER HERE.
HEH!
?
?
LIKE A PUDDLE OF SUNLIGHT.
WHAT COULD BE CAUSING IT, I WONDER?
YUP, RIGHT AROUND HERE.
HUH?
WHAT?
I'VE GOT IT! IT MUST BE...!
AWOOO?!
TOASTY!
KER-SNAP KER-SNAP
DON'T NEED NO STINKIN' HEATER.
YUP, THINGS ARE HEATING UP.
I'LL SAY.

SEASONAL CHANGE ARCTIC FOXES TURN WHITE WHEN THEIR WINTER COATS GROW IN, AS DO STOATS, GROUSES, AND RABBITS. THIS HELPS CAMOUFLAGE THEM AMONGST THE SNOW.

They just ruffled her neck fur.

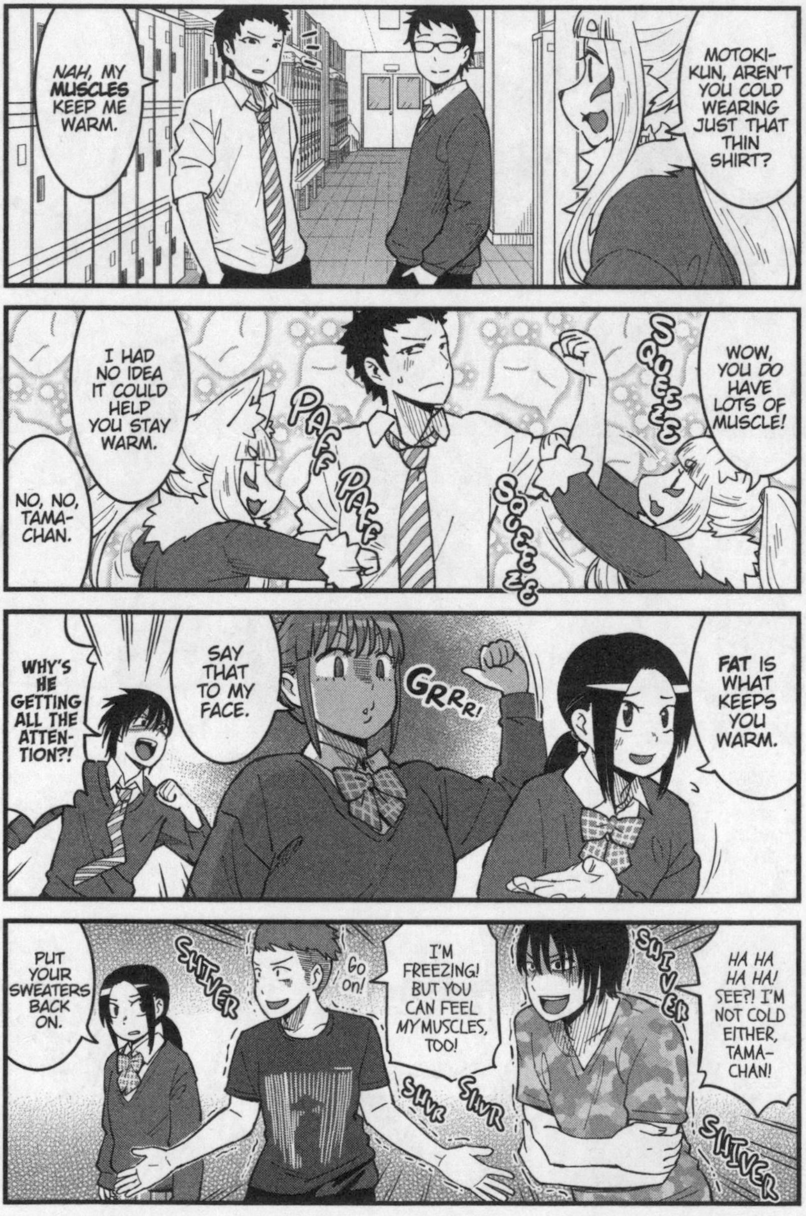
MOTOKI-KUN, AREN'T YOU COLD WEARING JUST THAT THIN SHIRT?
NAH, MY MUSCLES KEEP ME WARM.
WOW, YOU DO HAVE LOTS OF MUSCLE!
SQUEEZE
SQUEEZE
PAFF
PAFF
I HAD NO IDEA IT COULD HELP YOU STAY WARM.
NO, NO, TAMA-CHAN.
FAT IS WHAT KEEPS YOU WARM.
GRRR!
SAY THAT TO MY FACE.
WHY'S HE GETTING ALL THE ATTENTION?!
HA HA HA HA! SEE?! I'M NOT COLD EITHER, TAMA-CHAN!
SHIVER
SHIVER
I'M FREEZING! BUT YOU CAN FEEL MY MUSCLES, TOO!
Go on!
SHVR
SHVR
SHIVER
PUT YOUR SWEATERS BACK ON.

SUBCUTANEOUS FAT MAMMALS EAT HEARTILY IN THE FALL TO BUILD UP LAYERS OF FAT UNDER THEIR SKINS. MANY ANIMALS SURVIVE OFF THIS FAT AS THEY SLEEP THROUGH THE WINTER.

The boys were just fishing for compliments.

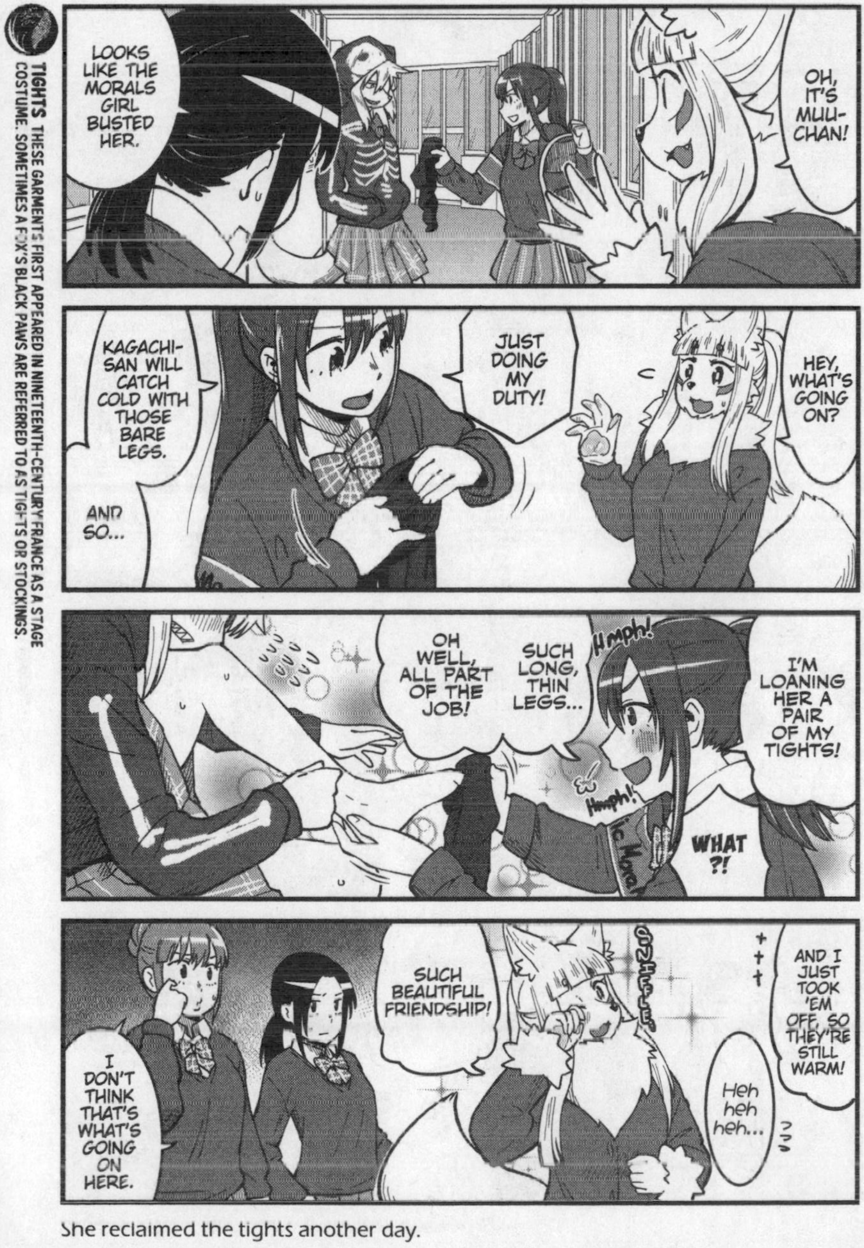
OH, IT'S MUU-CHAN!
LOOKS LIKE THE MORALS GIRL BUSTED HER.
HEY, WHAT'S GOING ON?
JUST DOING MY DUTY!
KAGACHI-SAN WILL CATCH COLD WITH THOSE BARE LEGS.
AND SO...
I'M LOANING HER A PAIR OF MY TIGHTS!
Hmph!
SUCH LONG, THIN LEGS...
OH WELL, ALL PART OF THE JOB!
Hmph!
WHAT?!
AND I JUST TOOK 'EM OFF, SO THEY'RE STILL WARM!
Heh heh heh...
SUCH BEAUTIFUL FRIENDSHIP!
I DON'T THINK THAT'S WHAT'S GOING ON HERE.

TIGHTS THESE GARMENTS FIRST APPEARED IN NINETEENTH-CENTURY FRANCE AS A STAGE COSTUME. SOMETIMES A FOX'S BLACK PAWS ARE REFERRED TO AS TIGHTS OR STOCKINGS.

She reclaimed the tights another day.

ACCURATE? THERE'S ALWAYS SOMETHING OFF ABOUT MIURA-SENSEI'S LESSONS. I LIKE LEARNING ABOUT MODERN SOCIETY, BUT...

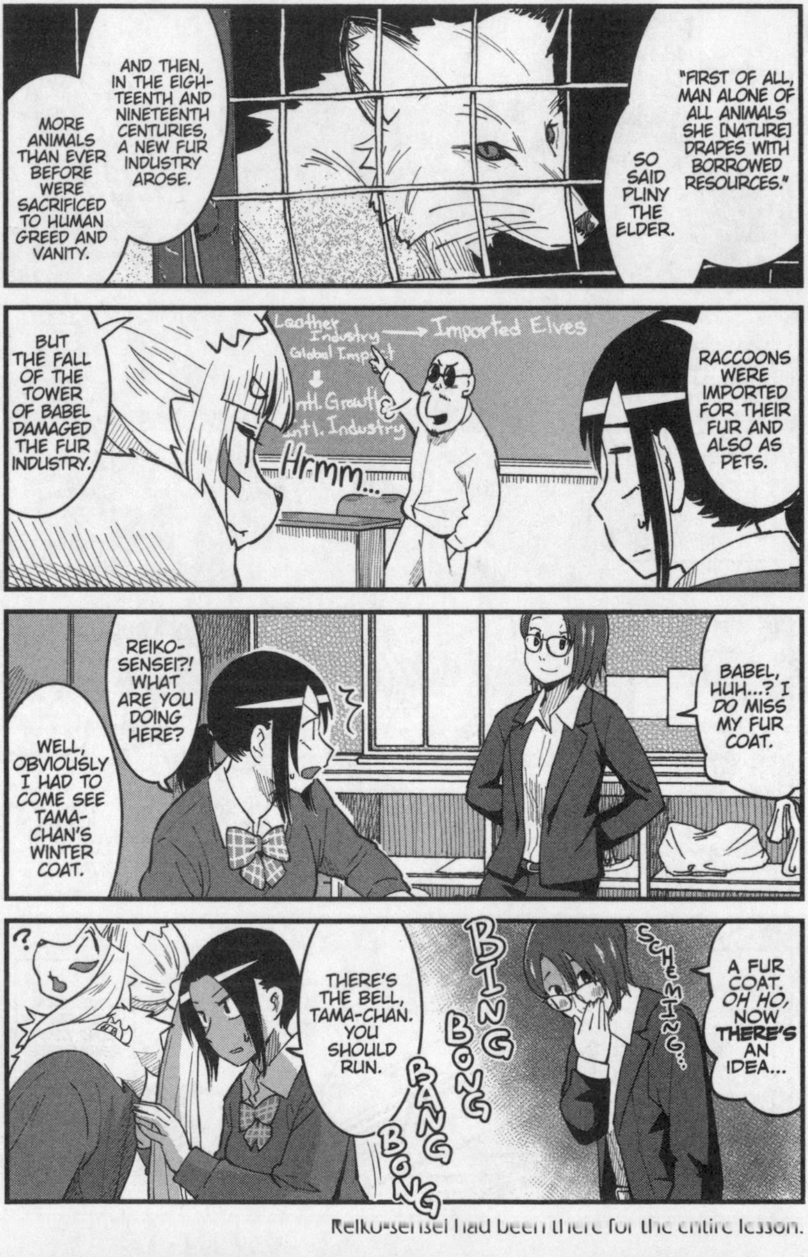
"FIRST OF ALL, MAN ALONE OF ALL ANIMALS SHE [NATURE] DRAPES WITH BORROWED RESOURCES."
SO SAID PLINY THE ELDER.
AND THEN, IN THE EIGHTEENTH AND NINETEENTH CENTURIES, A NEW FUR INDUSTRY AROSE.
MORE ANIMALS THAN EVER BEFORE WERE SACRIFICED TO HUMAN GREED AND VANITY.
RACCOONS WERE IMPORTED FOR THEIR FUR AND ALSO AS PETS.
Leather Industry → Imported Elves
Hrmm...
BUT THE FALL OF THE TOWER OF BABEL DAMAGED THE FUR INDUSTRY.
BABEL, HUH...? I DO MISS MY FUR COAT.
REIKO-SENSEI?! WHAT ARE YOU DOING HERE?
WELL, OBVIOUSLY I HAD TO COME SEE TAMA-CHAN'S WINTER COAT.
A FUR COAT. OH HO, NOW THERE'S AN IDEA...
SCHEMING...
BING BONG
BANG BONG
THERE'S THE BELL, TAMA-CHAN. YOU SHOULD RUN.
?

Reiko-sensei had been there for the entire lesson.

CHAPTER 49

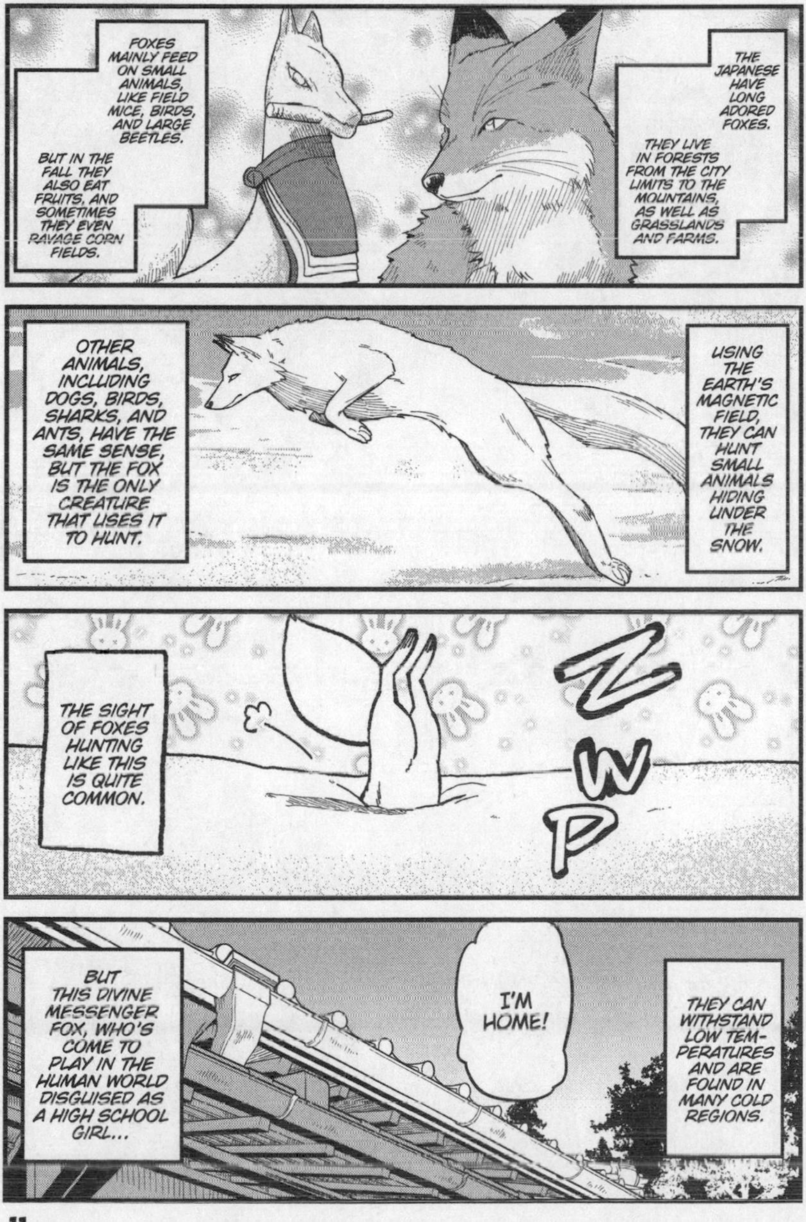

THE JAPANESE HAVE LONG ADORED FOXES.
THEY LIVE IN FORESTS FROM THE CITY LIMITS TO THE MOUNTAINS, AS WELL AS GRASSLANDS AND FARMS.
FOXES MAINLY FEED ON SMALL ANIMALS, LIKE FIELD MICE, BIRDS, AND LARGE BEETLES.
BUT IN THE FALL THEY ALSO EAT FRUITS, AND SOMETIMES THEY EVEN RAVAGE CORN FIELDS.
USING THE EARTH'S MAGNETIC FIELD, THEY CAN HUNT SMALL ANIMALS HIDING UNDER THE SNOW.
OTHER ANIMALS, INCLUDING DOGS, BIRDS, SHARKS, AND ANTS, HAVE THE SAME SENSE, BUT THE FOX IS THE ONLY CREATURE THAT USES IT TO HUNT.
ZWP
THE SIGHT OF FOXES HUNTING LIKE THIS IS QUITE COMMON.
THEY CAN WITHSTAND LOW TEMPERATURES AND ARE FOUND IN MANY COLD REGIONS.
I'M HOME!
BUT THIS DIVINE MESSENGER FOX, WHO'S COME TO PLAY IN THE HUMAN WORLD DISGUISED AS A HIGH SCHOOL GIRL...

CHAPTER 49

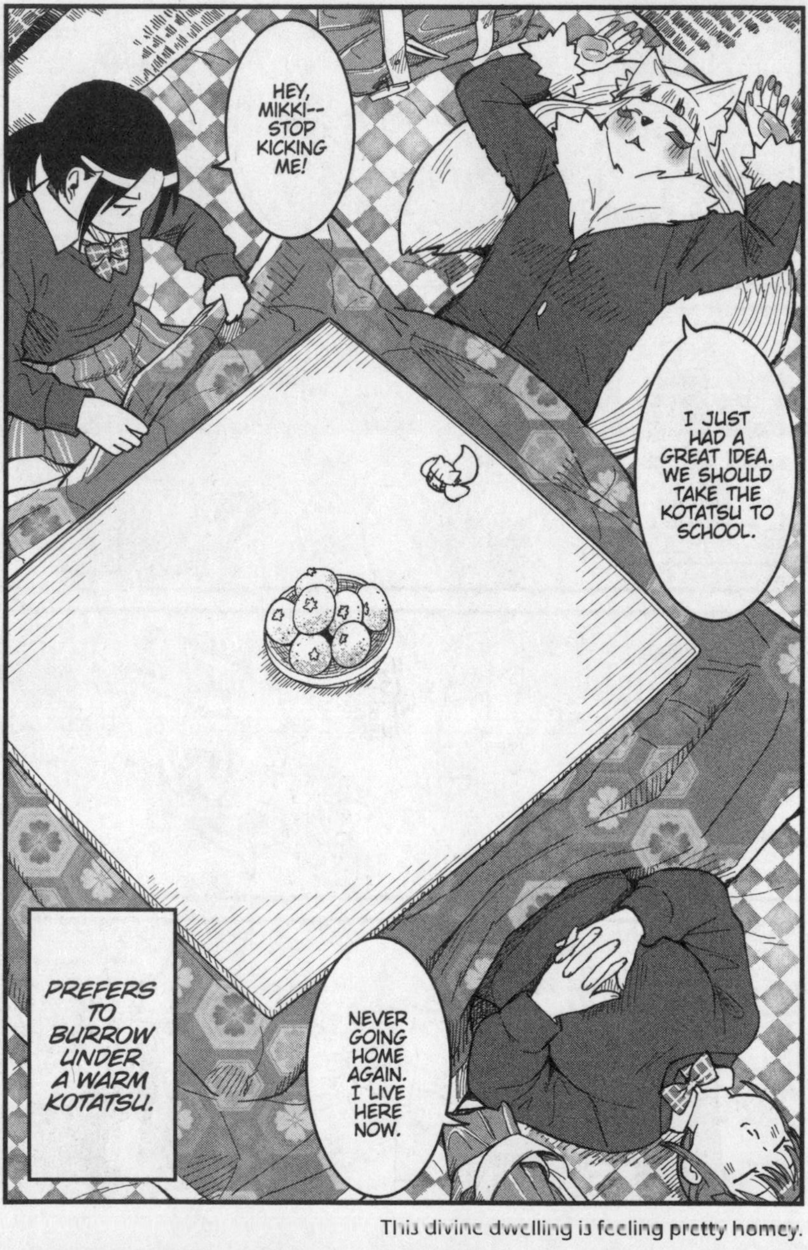
HEY, MIKKI-- STOP KICKING ME!
I JUST HAD A GREAT IDEA. WE SHOULD TAKE THE KOTATSU TO SCHOOL.
NEVER GOING HOME AGAIN. I LIVE HERE NOW.
PREFERS TO BURROW UNDER A WARM KOTATSU.

This divine dwelling is feeling pretty homey.

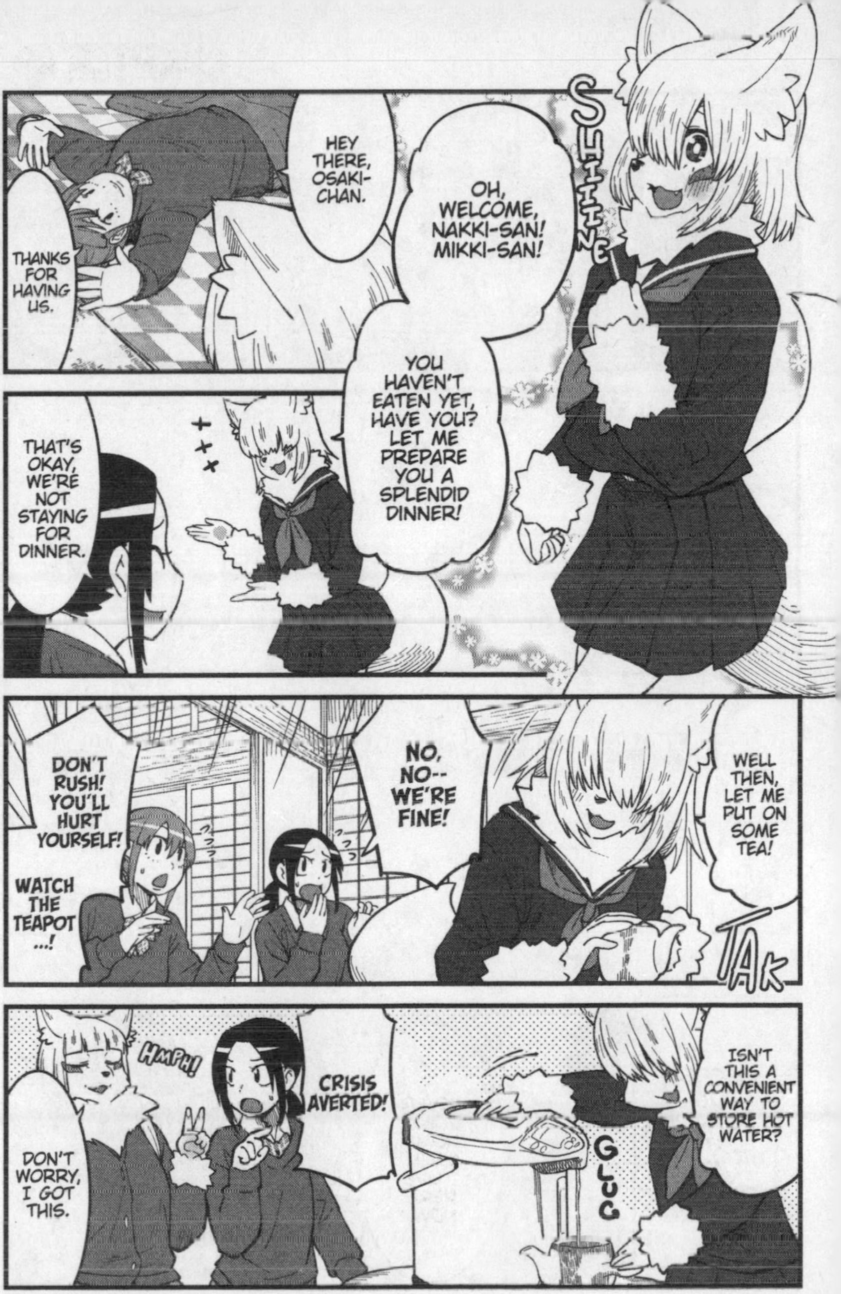
SHIIINE
OH, WELCOME, NAKKI-SAN! MIKKI-SAN!
HEY THERE, OSAKI-CHAN.
THANKS FOR HAVING US.
YOU HAVEN'T EATEN YET, HAVE YOU? LET ME PREPARE YOU A SPLENDID DINNER!
THAT'S OKAY, WE'RE NOT STAYING FOR DINNER.
WELL THEN, LET ME PUT ON SOME TEA!
TAK
NO, NO-- WE'RE FINE!
DON'T RUSH! YOU'LL HURT YOURSELF!
WATCH THE TEAPOT ...!
ISN'T THIS A CONVENIENT WAY TO STORE HOT WATER?
GLUG
CRISIS AVERTED!
HMPH!
DON'T WORRY, I GOT THIS.
A triumph of modern convenience.

KYUSU TEAPOTS IN ANCIENT CHINA, *KYUSU*POTS WERE SMALL POTS USED FOR HEATING LIQUOR. WHEN THEY WERE INTRODUCED TO JAPAN IN THE LATE EDO PERIOD, THE JAPANESE USED THEM FOR LOOSE LEAF SENCHA GREEN TEA.

REPAIR DUE TO MY CARELESSNESS, I'M ALWAYS PESTERING TAMA-NEESAMA TO DO THINGS LIKE RE-PAPERING THE SCREENS OR BUYING NEW CROCKERY.

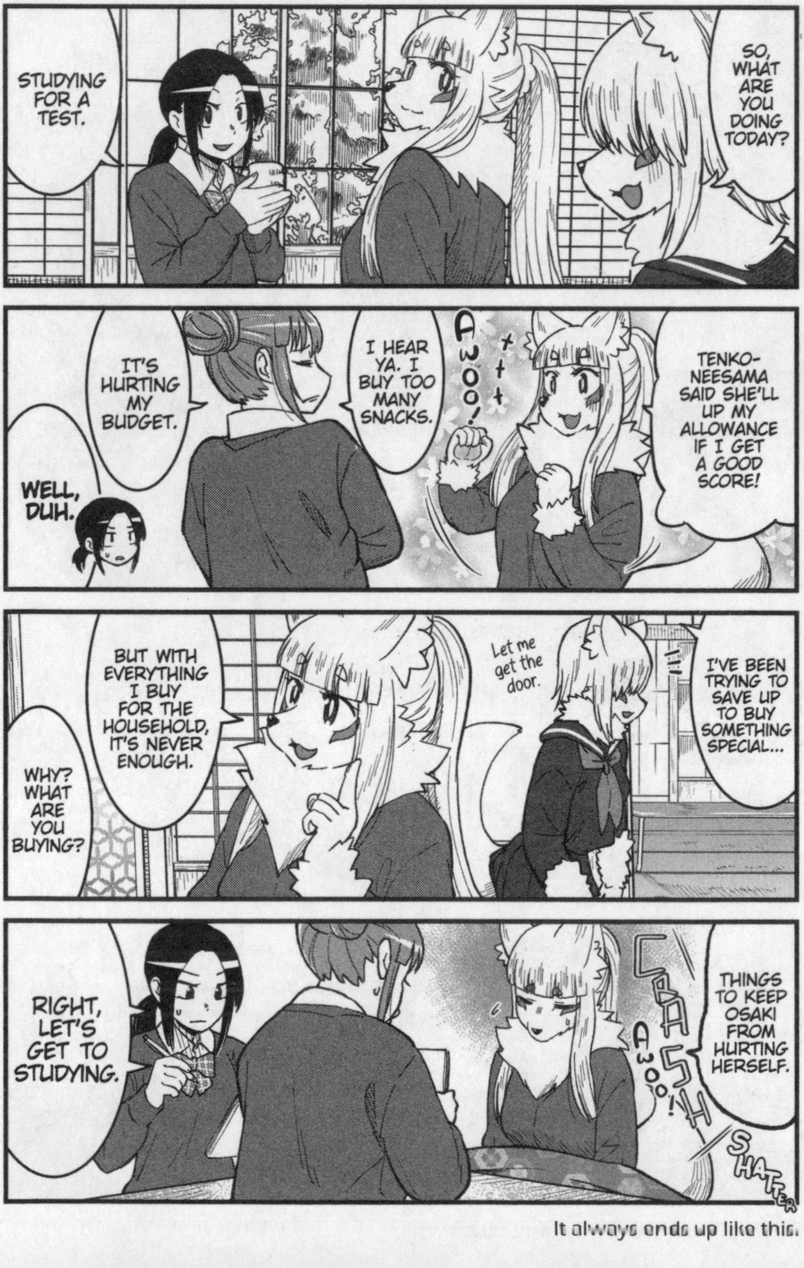
SO, WHAT ARE YOU DOING TODAY?
STUDYING FOR A TEST.
TENKO-NEESAMA SAID SHE'LL UP MY ALLOWANCE IF I GET A GOOD SCORE!
AWOO!
I HEAR YA. I BUY TOO MANY SNACKS.
IT'S HURTING MY BUDGET.
WELL, DUH.
I'VE BEEN TRYING TO SAVE UP TO BUY SOMETHING SPECIAL...
Let me get the door.
BUT WITH EVERYTHING I BUY FOR THE HOUSEHOLD, IT'S NEVER ENOUGH.
WHY? WHAT ARE YOU BUYING?
THINGS TO KEEP OSAKI FROM HURTING HERSELF.
CRASH
AWOO!
SHATTER
RIGHT, LET'S GET TO STUDYING.

It always ends up like this.

TEST PREP I'M HERE TO EXPERIENCE THE WORLD AND PART OF THAT IS REALLY KNUCKLING DOWN ON MY STUDIES! TWO PLUS TWO EQUALS...FOUR?

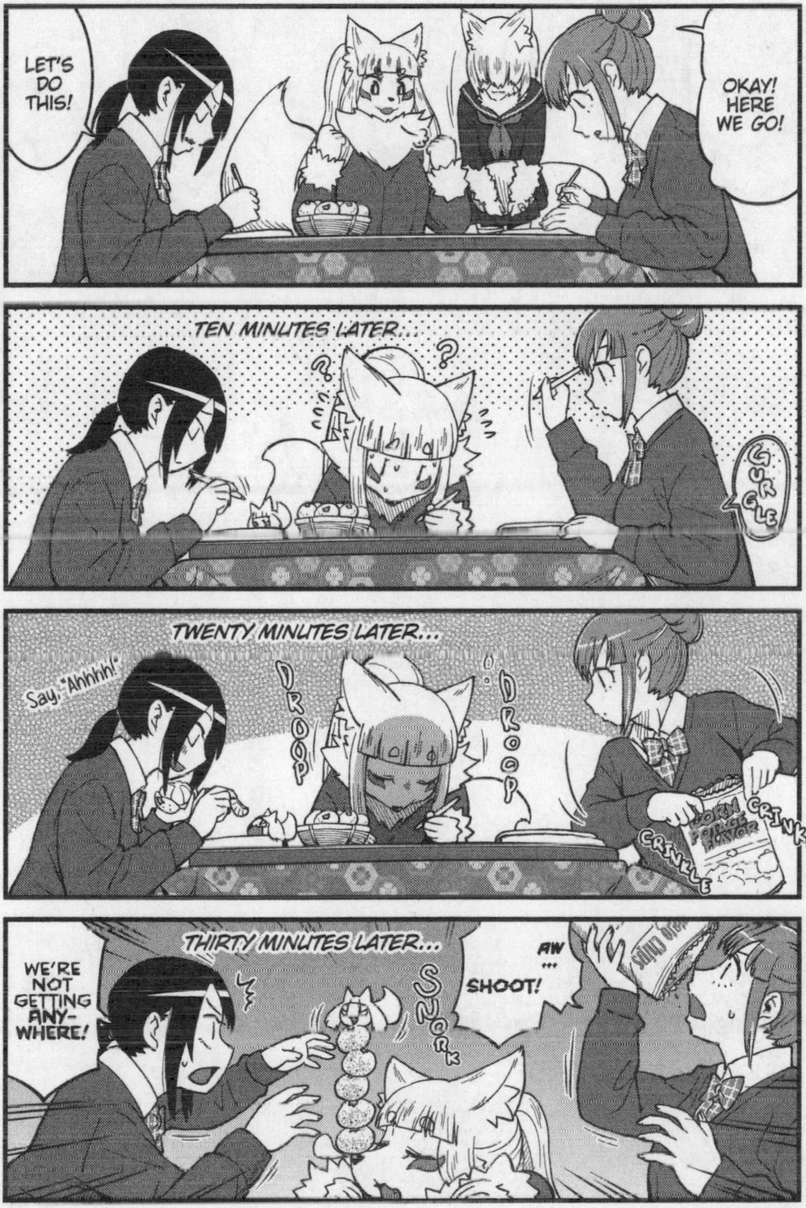
OKAY! HERE WE GO!
LET'S DO THIS!
TEN MINUTES LATER...
GURGLE
TWENTY MINUTES LATER...
CRINKLE
CRINKLE
DROOP
DROOP
Say, "Ahhhh!"
THIRTY MINUTES LATER...
AW... SHOOT!
SNORK
WE'RE NOT GETTING ANY-WHERE!

Three heads aren't always better than one.

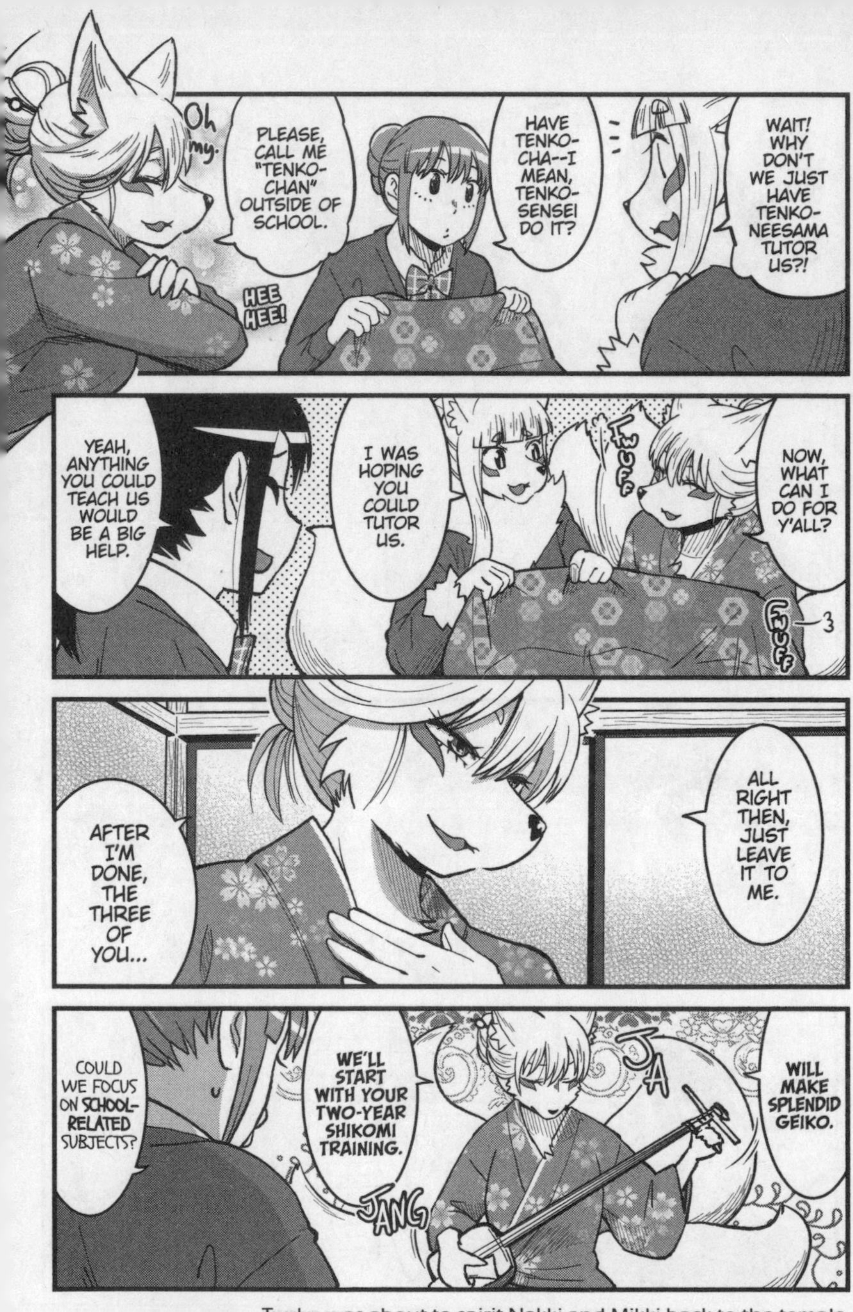
WAIT! WHY DON'T WE JUST HAVE TENKO-NEESAMA TUTOR US?!
HAVE TENKO-CHA--I MEAN, TENKO-SENSEI DO IT?
PLEASE, CALL ME "TENKO-CHAN" OUTSIDE OF SCHOOL.
HEE HEE!
Oh my.
NOW, WHAT CAN I DO FOR Y'ALL?
FWUFF
I WAS HOPING YOU COULD TUTOR US.
YEAH, ANYTHING YOU COULD TEACH US WOULD BE A BIG HELP.
FWUFF
ALL RIGHT THEN, JUST LEAVE IT TO ME.
AFTER I'M DONE, THE THREE OF YOU...
WILL MAKE SPLENDID GEIKO.
JA
WE'LL START WITH YOUR TWO-YEAR SHIKOMI TRAINING.
JANG
COULD WE FOCUS ON SCHOOL-RELATED SUBJECTS?

GEISHA CALLED *GEIKO* IN KYOTO. WHEN MAIKO COMPLETE THEIR TRAINING, KNOWN AS SHIKOMI TRAINING, THEY GRADUATE AND BECOME GEIKO, OR GEISHA.

Tenko was about to spirit Nakki and Mikki back to the temple.

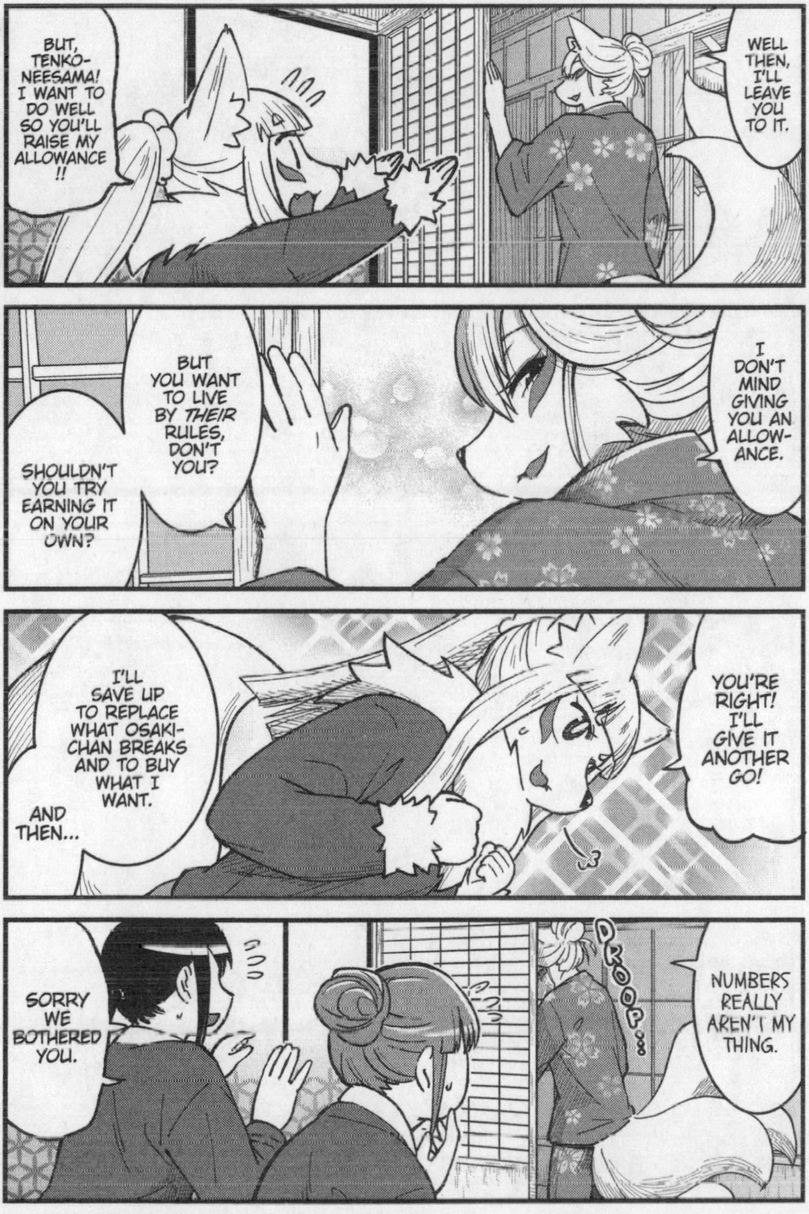
WELL THEN, I'LL LEAVE YOU TO IT.
BUT, TENKO-NEESAMA! I WANT TO DO WELL SO YOU'LL RAISE MY ALLOWANCE!!
I DON'T MIND GIVING YOU AN ALLOW-ANCE.
BUT YOU WANT TO LIVE BY *THEIR* RULES, DON'T YOU?
SHOULDN'T YOU TRY EARNING IT ON YOUR OWN?
YOU'RE RIGHT! I'LL GIVE IT ANOTHER GO!
I'LL SAVE UP TO REPLACE WHAT OSAKI-CHAN BREAKS AND TO BUY WHAT I WANT.
AND THEN...
NUMBERS REALLY AREN'T MY THING.
DROOP...
SORRY WE BOTHERED YOU.

RULES IN ORDER FOR TAMAMO TO REMAIN IN THE HUMAN WORLD, HER STATUS AS A DIVINE MESSENGER MUST BE KEPT SECRET. COMPLETELY SECRET.

Tenko's just pretending to be a teacher, anyway.

STUDYING! IT'S FUN TO STUDY THE HUMAN WORLD AND MODERN SOCIETY AND ALL SORTS OF OTHER THINGS! BUT I ALWAYS GET SO SLEEPY WHEN I STUDY...ZZZ

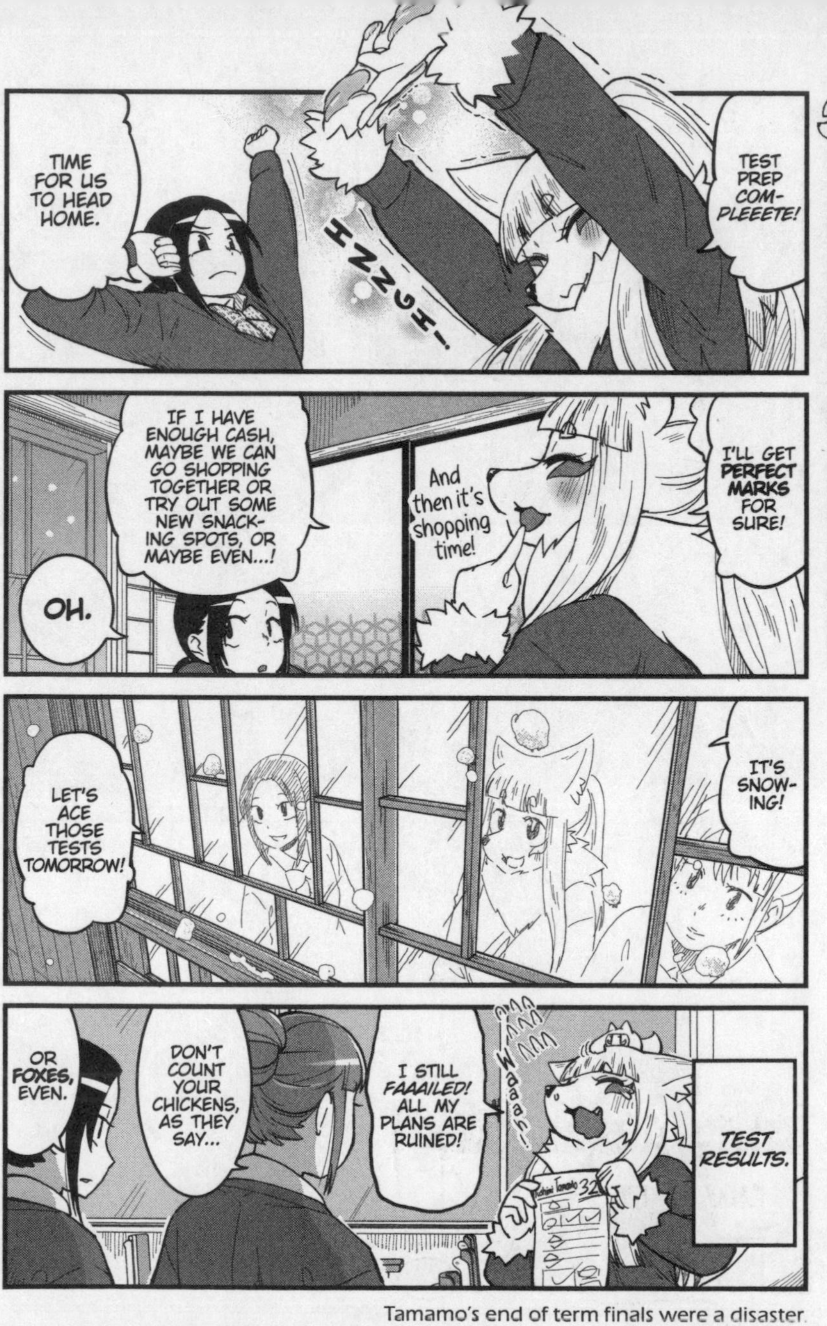
TEST PREP COM-PLEEEETE!
HNNNGH!
TIME FOR US TO HEAD HOME.
I'LL GET PERFECT MARKS FOR SURE!
And then it's shopping time!
IF I HAVE ENOUGH CASH, MAYBE WE CAN GO SHOPPING TOGETHER OR TRY OUT SOME NEW SNACK-ING SPOTS, OR MAYBE EVEN...!
OH.
IT'S SNOW-ING!
LET'S ACE THOSE TESTS TOMORROW!
TEST RESULTS.
Waaah...
I STILL FAAAILED! ALL MY PLANS ARE RUINED!
DON'T COUNT YOUR CHICKENS, AS THEY SAY...
OR FOXES, EVEN.

Tamamo's end of term finals were a disaster.

Tamamo-chan's a FOX!

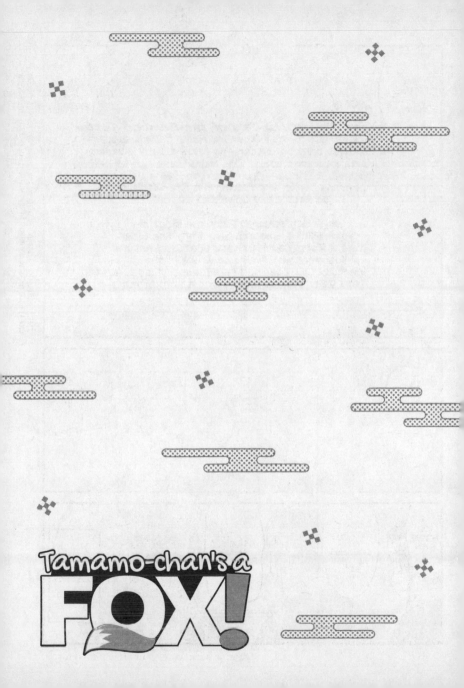

* P. 6, side caption: *The Tale of the Bamboo Cutter* *
A Japanese folktale from the Heian period about
a childless bamboo cutter who finds a baby sleeping
inside a bamboo stalk. This baby turns out to be
Kaguya, a princess from the moon. She devises
impossible tasks, like finding the Fire-Rat's robe,
to keep away unwanted suitors.

* P. 10, panel 1: Pliny the Elder *
Gaius Plinius Secundus, or Pliny the Elder,
was a Roman author, naturalist, and natural
philosopher who lived and wrote in the first
century CE. The line Miura-sensei quotes is
from Pliny's *Natural History*, a sort of early
encyclopedia.

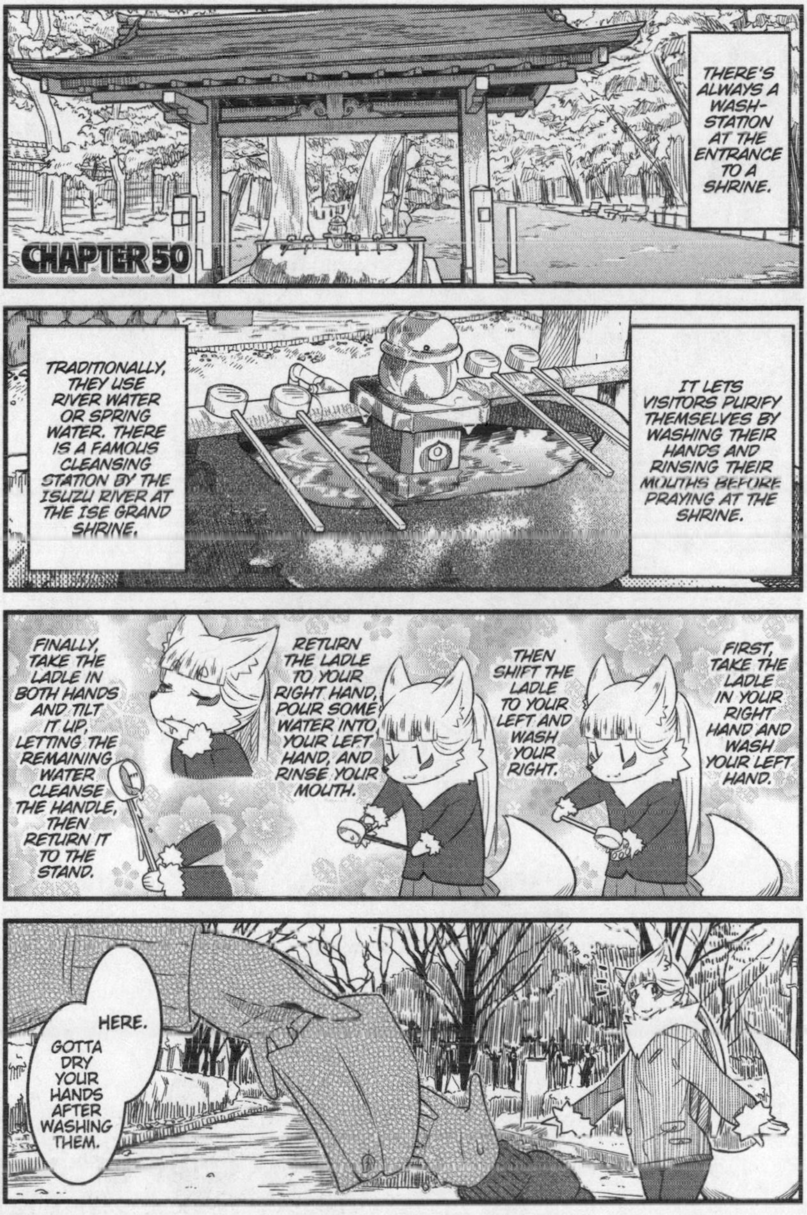
THERE'S ALWAYS A WASH-STATION AT THE ENTRANCE TO A SHRINE.
CHAPTER 50
IT LETS VISITORS PURIFY THEMSELVES BY WASHING THEIR HANDS AND RINSING THEIR MOUTHS BEFORE PRAYING AT THE SHRINE.
TRADITIONALLY, THEY USE RIVER WATER OR SPRING WATER. THERE IS A FAMOUS CLEANSING STATION BY THE ISUZU RIVER AT THE ISE GRAND SHRINE.
FIRST, TAKE THE LADLE IN YOUR RIGHT HAND AND WASH YOUR LEFT HAND.
THEN SHIFT THE LADLE TO YOUR LEFT AND WASH YOUR RIGHT.
RETURN THE LADLE TO YOUR RIGHT HAND, POUR SOME WATER INTO YOUR LEFT HAND, AND RINSE YOUR MOUTH.
FINALLY, TAKE THE LADLE IN BOTH HANDS AND TILT IT UP, LETTING THE REMAINING WATER CLEANSE THE HANDLE, THEN RETURN IT TO THE STAND.
HERE.
GOTTA DRY YOUR HANDS AFTER WASHING THEM.

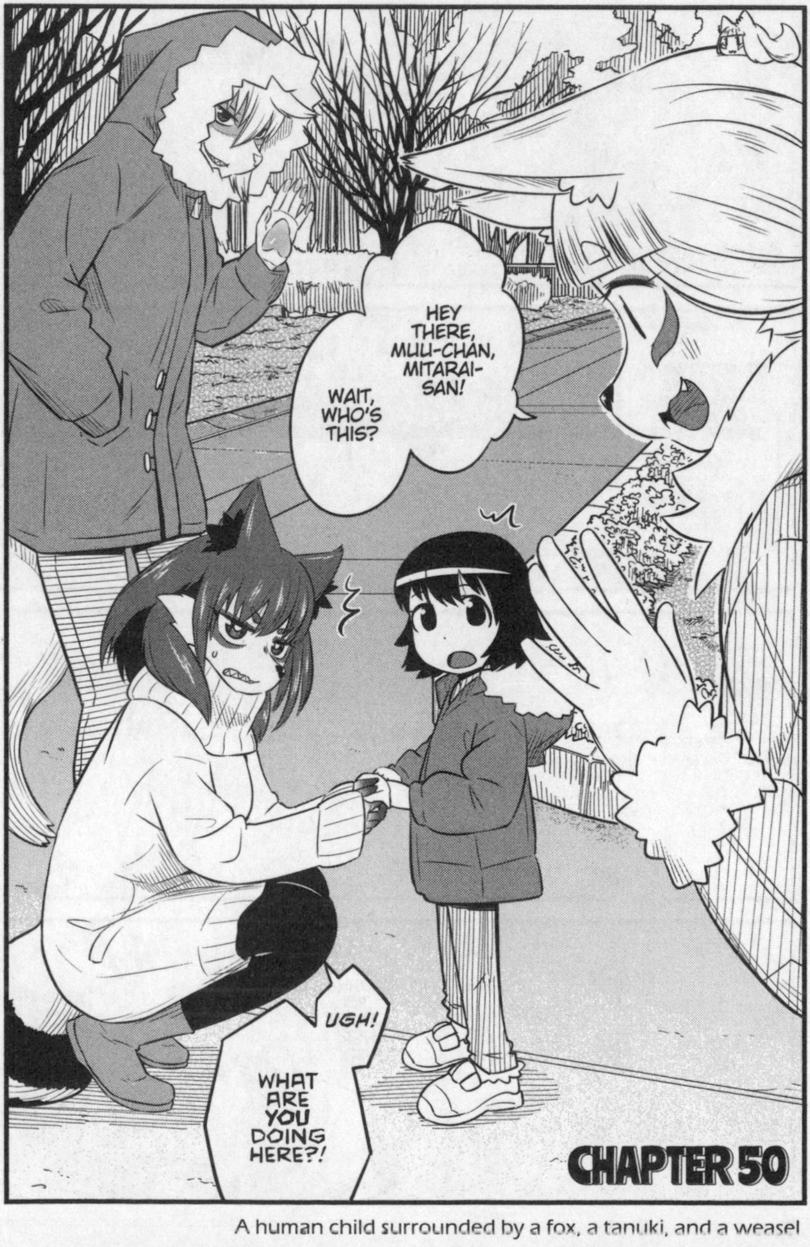
HEY THERE, MUU-CHAN, MITARAI-SAN!
WAIT, WHO'S THIS?
UGH!
WHAT ARE YOU DOING HERE?!
CHAPTER 50

A human child surrounded by a fox, a tanuki, and a weasel

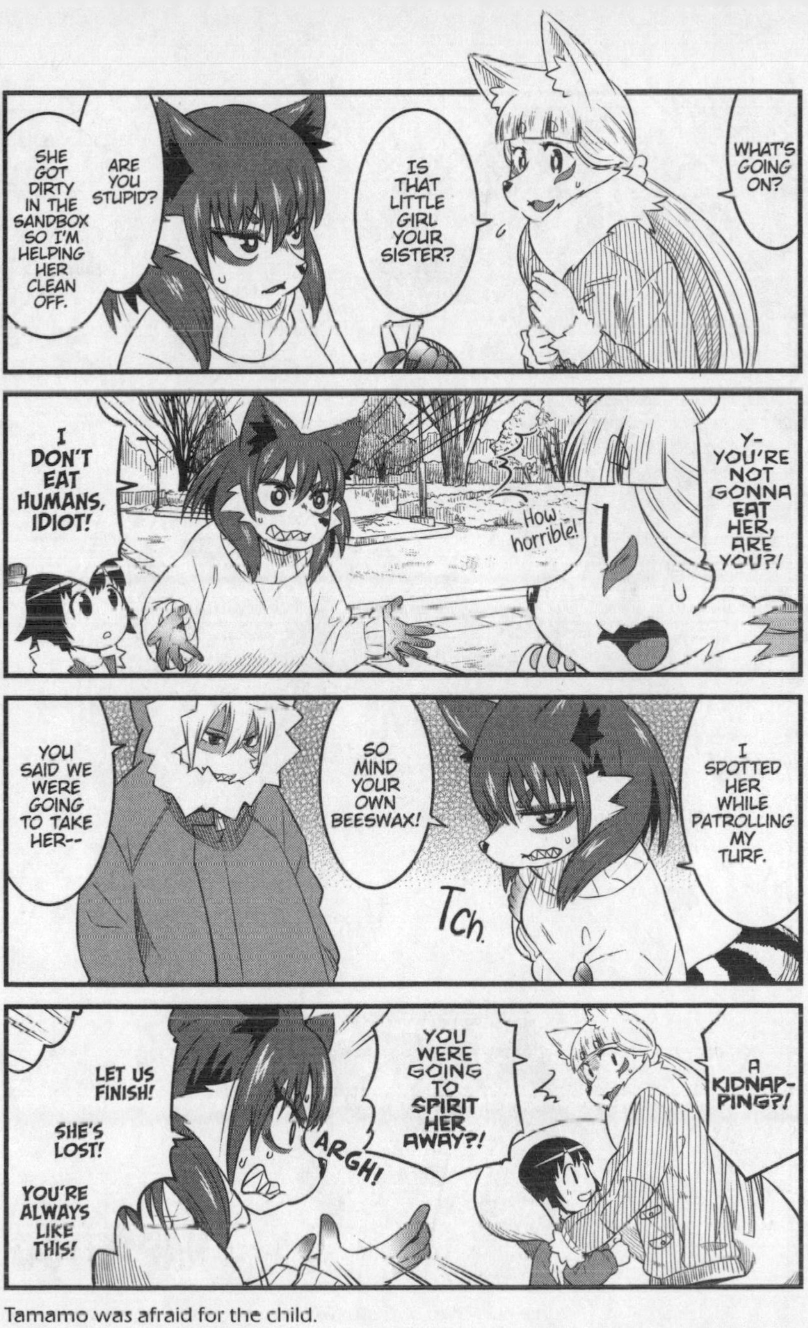
WHAT'S GOING ON?
IS THAT LITTLE GIRL YOUR SISTER?
ARE YOU STUPID?
SHE GOT DIRTY IN THE SANDBOX SO I'M HELPING HER CLEAN OFF.
Y-YOU'RE NOT GONNA EAT HER, ARE YOU?!
How horrible!
I DON'T EAT HUMANS, IDIOT!
I SPOTTED HER WHILE PATROLLING MY TURF.
SO MIND YOUR OWN BEESWAX!
Tch.
YOU SAID WE WERE GOING TO TAKE HER--
A KIDNAPPING?!
YOU WERE GOING TO SPIRIT HER AWAY?!
ARGH!
LET US FINISH!
SHE'S LOST!
YOU'RE ALWAYS LIKE THIS!

SPIRITED AWAY WHEN PEOPLE VANISH WITHOUT A TRACE IT'S SOMETIMES SAID THAT THEY WERE SPIRITED AWAY BY THE GODS OR OTHER MYSTICAL BEINGS. IT'S SOMETIMES ALSO SAID THAT THEY WERE "TAKEN BY THE TENGU."

Tamamo was afraid for the child.

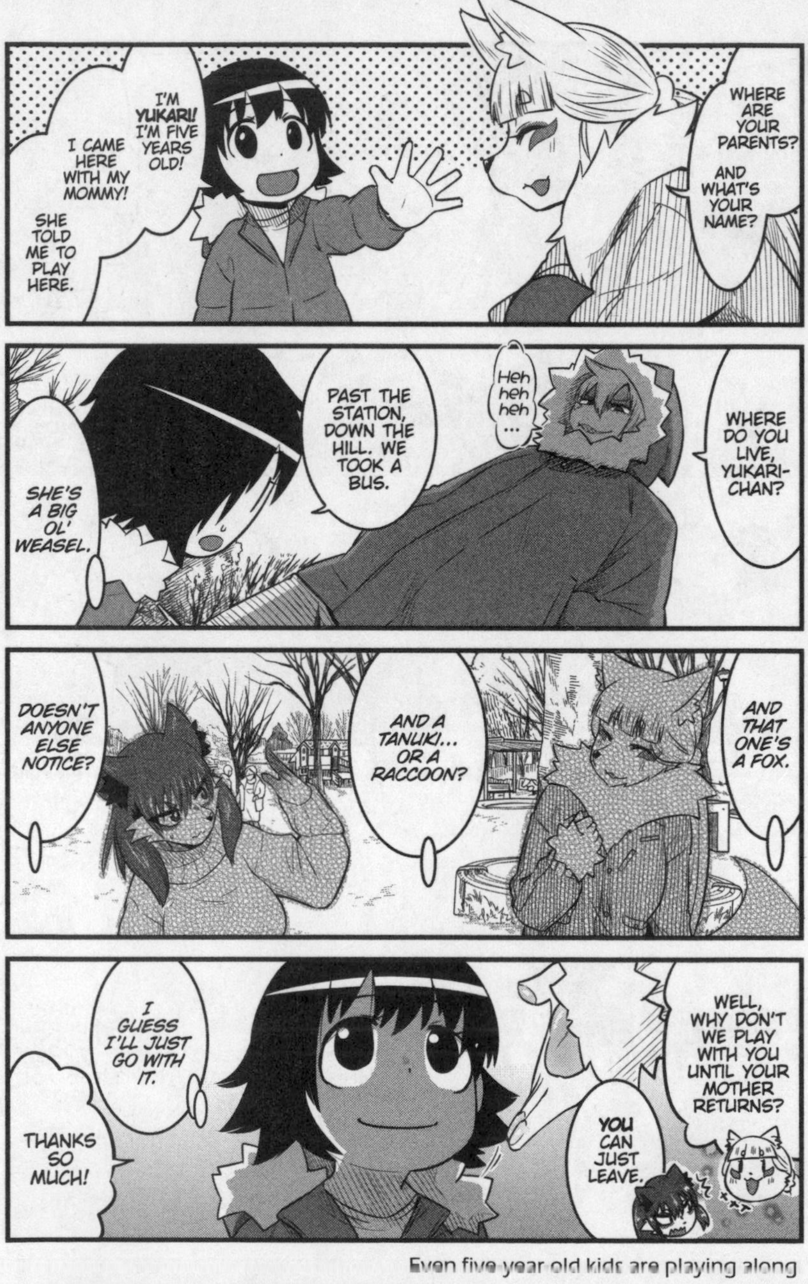
WHERE ARE YOUR PARENTS?
AND WHAT'S YOUR NAME?
I'M **YUKARI!** I'M FIVE YEARS OLD!
I CAME HERE WITH MY MOMMY!
SHE TOLD ME TO PLAY HERE.
WHERE DO YOU LIVE, YUKARI-CHAN?
Heh heh heh ...
PAST THE STATION, DOWN THE HILL. WE TOOK A BUS.
SHE'S A BIG OL' WEASEL.
AND THAT ONE'S A FOX.
AND A TANUKI... OR A RACCOON?
DOESN'T ANYONE ELSE NOTICE?
WELL, WHY DON'T WE PLAY WITH YOU UNTIL YOUR MOTHER RETURNS?
YOU CAN JUST LEAVE.
I GUESS I'LL JUST GO WITH IT.
THANKS SO MUCH!

YUKARI THE WORD *YUKARI* MEANS TIES OR RELATIONSHIPS THAT BRING PEOPLE OR THINGS TOGETHER. IT'S BELIEVED THAT IN OCTOBER THE GODS GATHER IN IZUMO TO DISCUSS HOW TO BIND PEOPLE'S FORTUNES TO ONE ANOTHER.

Even five year old kids are playing along

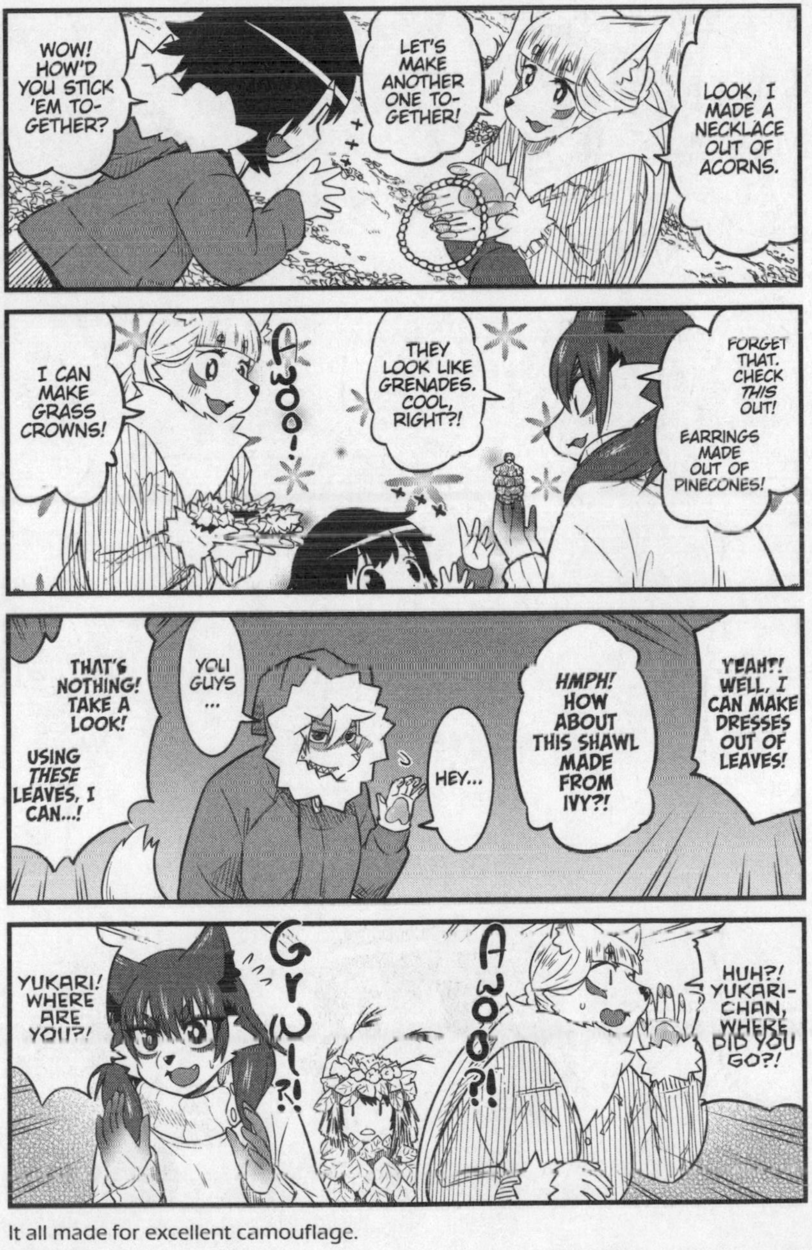
LOOK, I MADE A NECKLACE OUT OF ACORNS.
LET'S MAKE ANOTHER ONE TO-GETHER!
WOW! HOW'D YOU STICK 'EM TO-GETHER?
FORGET THAT. CHECK *THIS* OUT!
EARRINGS MADE OUT OF PINECONES!
THEY LOOK LIKE GRENADES. COOL, RIGHT?!
AWOO!
I CAN MAKE GRASS CROWNS!
YEAH?! WELL, *I* CAN MAKE DRESSES OUT OF LEAVES!
HMPH! HOW ABOUT THIS SHAWL MADE FROM IVY?!
HEY...
YOU GUYS ...
THAT'S NOTHING! TAKE A LOOK!
USING *THESE* LEAVES, I CAN...!
HUH?! YUKARI-CHAN, WHERE DID YOU GO?!
AWOO?!
GRWL?!
YUKARI! WHERE ARE YOU?!

CAMOUFLAGE THE USE OF IRREGULAR PATTERNS TO BLEND IN WITH YOUR SURROUNDINGS AND DECEIVE YOUR OPPONENT. AN ANIMAL'S WHITE BELLY IS A TYPE OF CAMOUFLAGE.

It all made for excellent camouflage.

COTTON CANDY A TREAT MADE BY HEATING SUGAR AND SPINNING IT INTO LONG STRANDS THAT GET WOUND AROUND A STICK. TAMAMO'S WINTER NECK FLUFF IS SOFTER THAN COTTON CANDY.

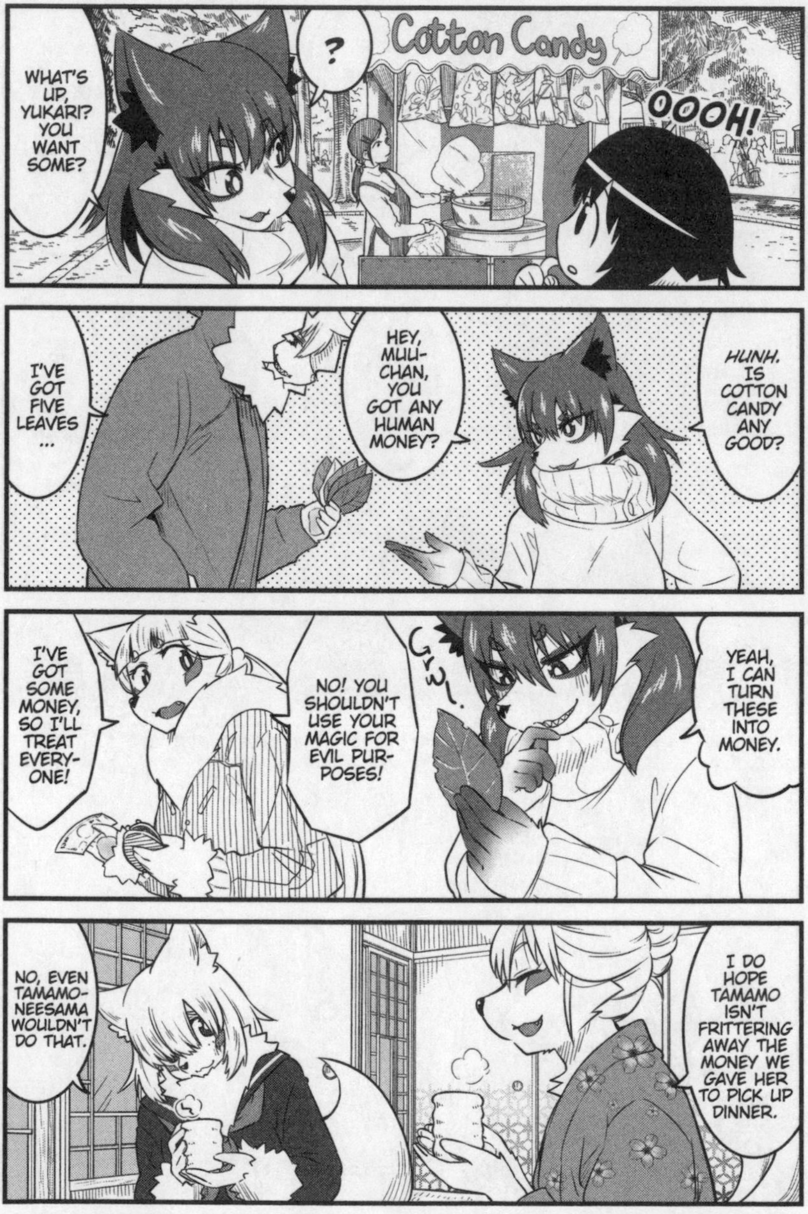
Cotton Candy
OOOH!
?
WHAT'S UP, YUKARI? YOU WANT SOME?
HUNH. IS COTTON CANDY ANY GOOD?
HEY, MUU-CHAN, YOU GOT ANY HUMAN MONEY?
I'VE GOT FIVE LEAVES ...
YEAH, I CAN TURN THESE INTO MONEY.
NO! YOU SHOULDN'T USE YOUR MAGIC FOR EVIL PURPOSES!
I'VE GOT SOME MONEY, SO I'LL TREAT EVERYONE!
I DO HOPE TAMAMO ISN'T FRITTERING AWAY THE MONEY WE GAVE HER TO PICK UP DINNER.
NO, EVEN TAMAMO-NEESAMA WOULDN'T DO THAT.

Tenko's fear was right on the money.

LOST CHILD A CHILD WHO'S BECOME SEPARATED FROM THEIR PARENTS OR WHO HAS LOST THEIR WAY AND DOESN'T KNOW WHERE THEY ARE.

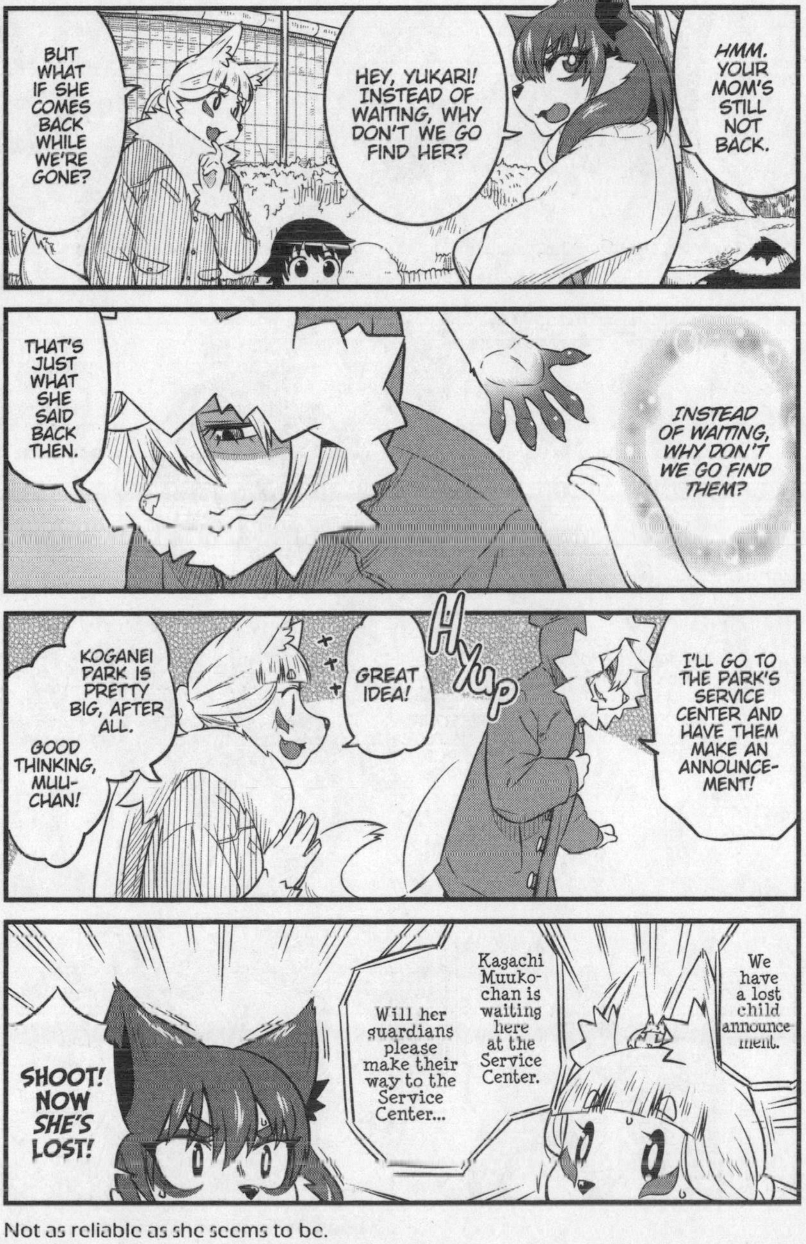
HMM. YOUR MOM'S STILL NOT BACK.
HEY, YUKARI! INSTEAD OF WAITING, WHY DON'T WE GO FIND HER?
BUT WHAT IF SHE COMES BACK WHILE WE'RE GONE?
INSTEAD OF WAITING, WHY DON'T WE GO FIND THEM?
THAT'S JUST WHAT SHE SAID BACK THEN.
I'LL GO TO THE PARK'S SERVICE CENTER AND HAVE THEM MAKE AN ANNOUNCEMENT!
HYUP
GREAT IDEA!
KOGANEI PARK IS PRETTY BIG, AFTER ALL.
GOOD THINKING, MUU-CHAN!
We have a lost child announcement.
Kagachi Muuko-chan is waiting here at the Service Center.
Will her guardians please make their way to the Service Center...
SHOOT! NOW SHE'S LOST!

Not as reliable as she seems to be.

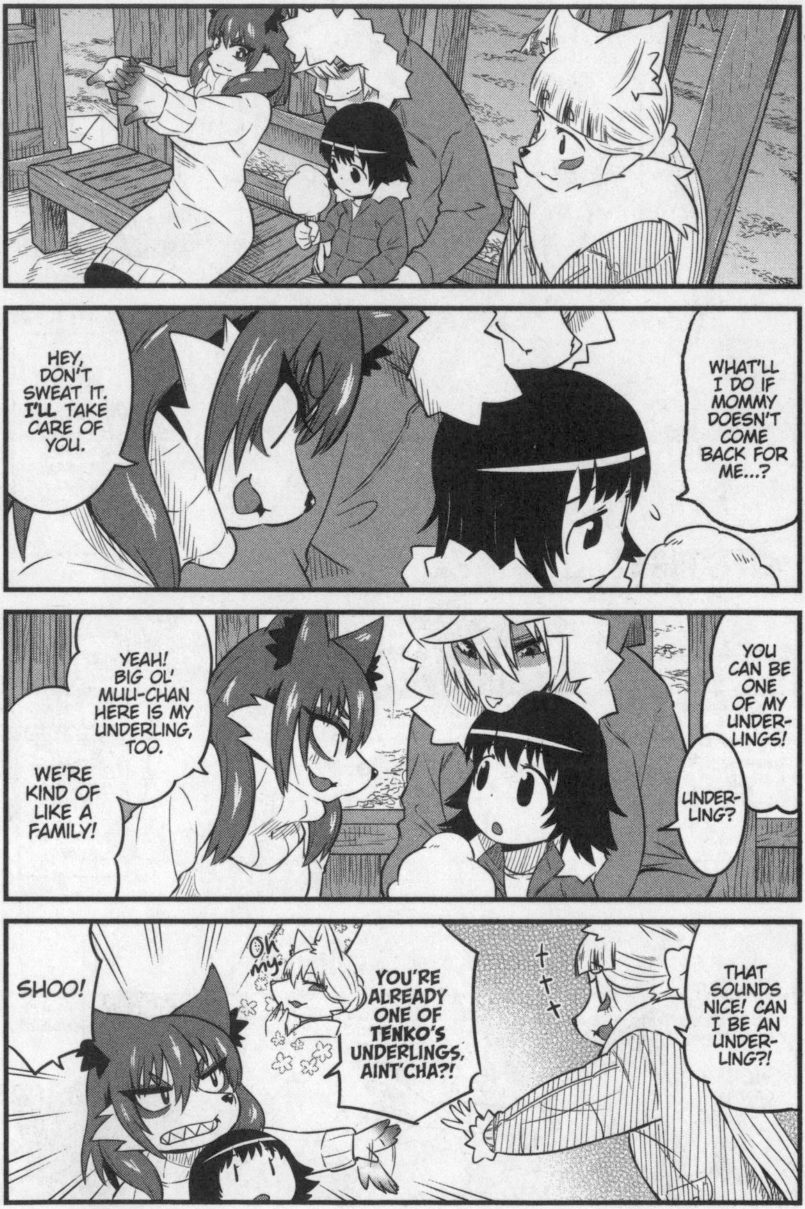
WHAT'LL I DO IF MOMMY DOESN'T COME BACK FOR ME...?
HEY, DON'T SWEAT IT. **I'LL** TAKE CARE OF YOU.
YOU CAN BE ONE OF MY UNDERLINGS!
UNDERLING?
YEAH! BIG OL' MUU-CHAN HERE IS MY UNDERLING, TOO.
WE'RE KIND OF LIKE A FAMILY!
THAT SOUNDS NICE! CAN I BE AN UNDERLING?!
YOU'RE ALREADY ONE OF TENKO'S UNDERLINGS, AINT'CHA?!
Oh my.
SHOO!

ME TOO! IF IT MEANS WE'RE FRIENDS, I'LL BE A BOSS OR AN UNDERLING OR WHATEVER! BUT MITARAI-SAN WON'T LET ME BE HER UNDERLING FOR SOME REASON.

It's a good thing Tenko wasn't here for this.

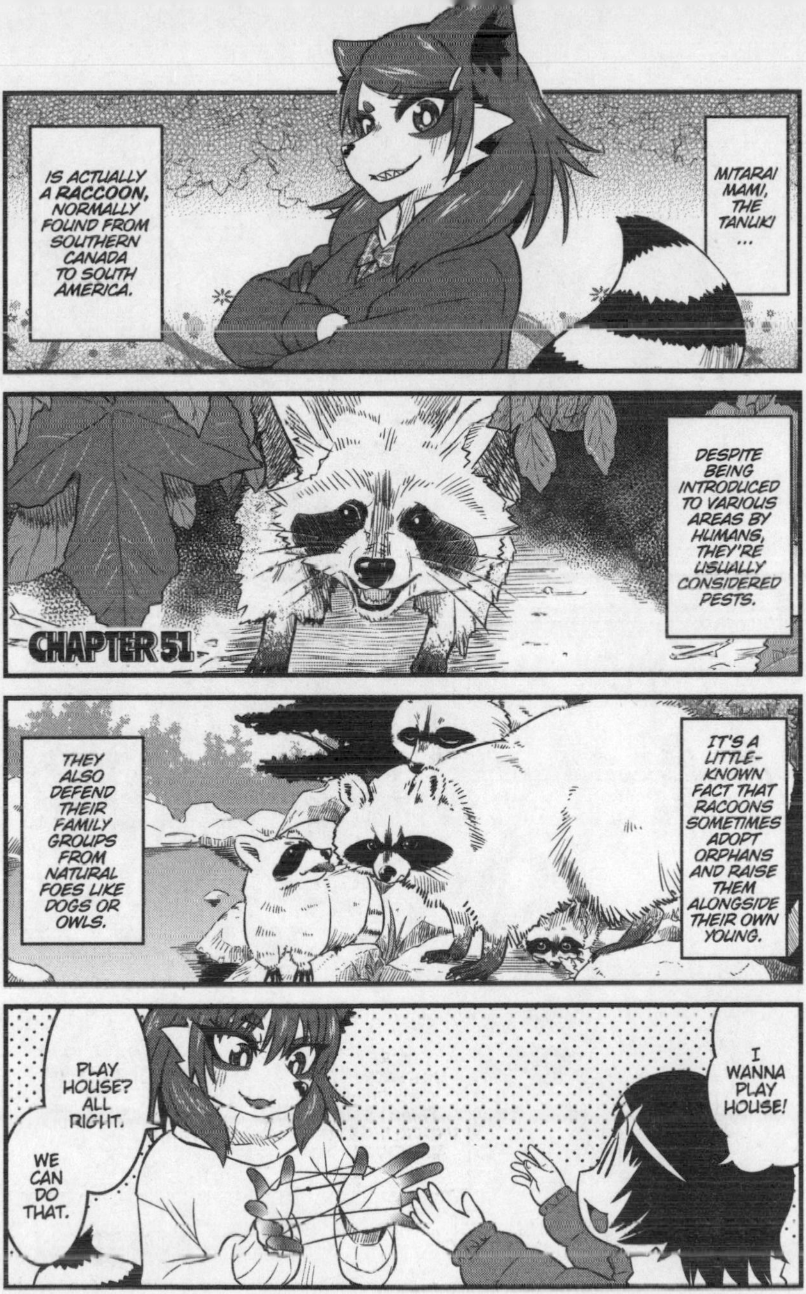
MITARAI MAMI, THE TANUKI ...
IS ACTUALLY A RACCOON, NORMALLY FOUND FROM SOUTHERN CANADA TO SOUTH AMERICA.
DESPITE BEING INTRODUCED TO VARIOUS AREAS BY HUMANS, THEY'RE USUALLY CONSIDERED PESTS.
CHAPTER 51
IT'S A LITTLE-KNOWN FACT THAT RACOONS SOMETIMES ADOPT ORPHANS AND RAISE THEM ALONGSIDE THEIR OWN YOUNG.
THEY ALSO DEFEND THEIR FAMILY GROUPS FROM NATURAL FOES LIKE DOGS OR OWLS.
I WANNA PLAY HOUSE!
PLAY HOUSE? ALL RIGHT.
WE CAN DO THAT.

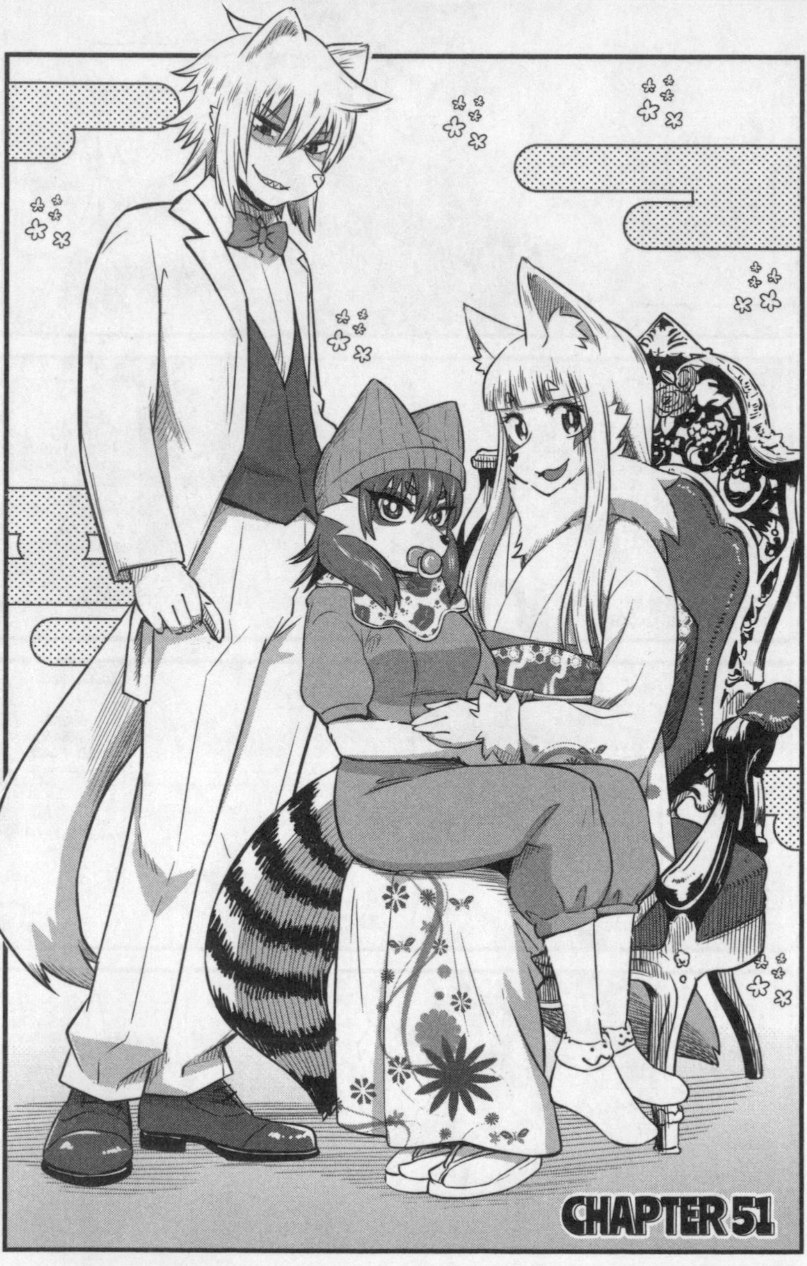
CHAPTER 51

PLAYING HOUSE CALLED "PLAYING MAMA" IN JAPANESE, WHICH STEMS FROM A WORD FOR "FOOD." IT'S A GAME WHERE CHILDREN PRETEND THEY'RE RUNNING A HOUSEHOLD. CLASSIC HEIAN-PERIOD TEXTS HAVE DESCRIPTIONS OF DOLLS USED FOR SUCH GAMES.

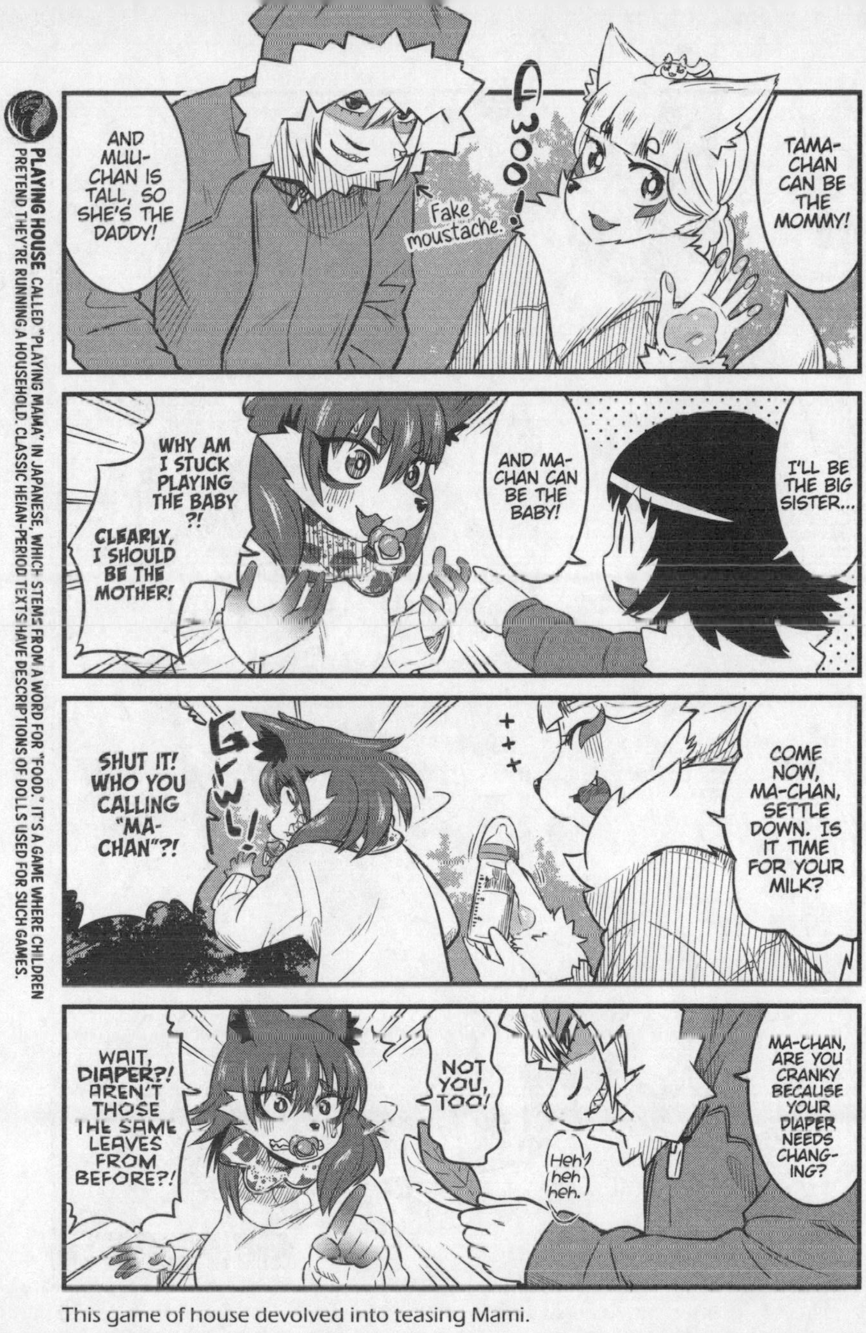
TAMA-CHAN CAN BE THE MOMMY!
Fake moustache.
AND MUU-CHAN IS TALL, SO SHE'S THE DADDY!
I'LL BE THE BIG SISTER...
AND MA-CHAN CAN BE THE BABY!
WHY AM I STUCK PLAYING THE BABY?!
CLEARLY, I SHOULD BE THE MOTHER!
COME NOW, MA-CHAN, SETTLE DOWN. IS IT TIME FOR YOUR MILK?
+++
SHUT IT! WHO YOU CALLING "MA-CHAN"?!
MA-CHAN, ARE YOU CRANKY BECAUSE YOUR DIAPER NEEDS CHANGING?
Heh heh heh.
NOT YOU, TOO!
WAIT, DIAPER?! AREN'T THOSE THE SAME LEAVES FROM BEFORE?!

This game of house devolved into teasing Mami.

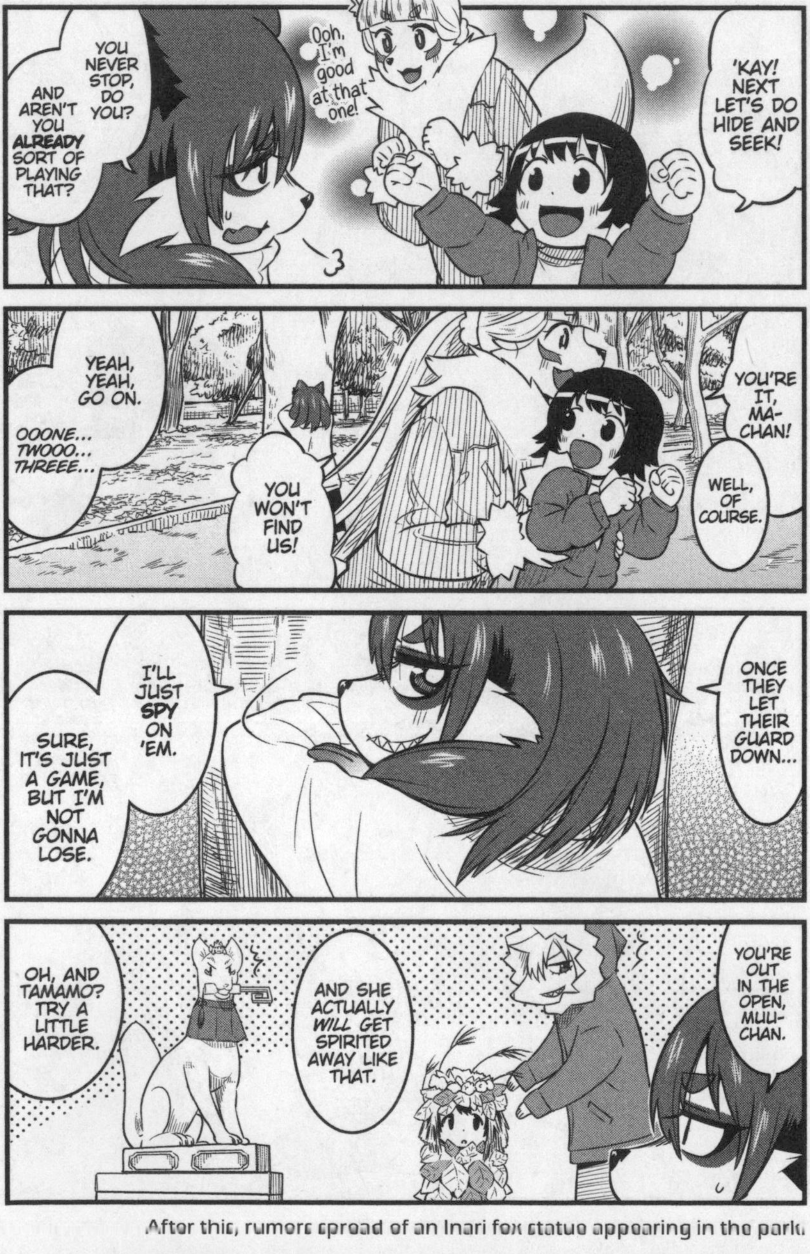
'KAY! NEXT LET'S DO HIDE AND SEEK!
Ooh, I'm good at that one!
YOU NEVER STOP, DO YOU?
AND AREN'T YOU ALREADY SORT OF PLAYING THAT?
YOU'RE IT, MA-CHAN!
WELL, OF COURSE.
YOU WON'T FIND US!
YEAH, YEAH, GO ON.
OOONE... TWOOO... THREEE...
ONCE THEY LET THEIR GUARD DOWN...
I'LL JUST SPY ON 'EM.
SURE, IT'S JUST A GAME, BUT I'M NOT GONNA LOSE.
YOU'RE OUT IN THE OPEN, MUU-CHAN.
AND SHE ACTUALLY WILL GET SPIRITED AWAY LIKE THAT.
OH, AND TAMAMO? TRY A LITTLE HARDER.

HIDE AND SEEK THIS CLASSIC CHILDREN'S GAME HAS ALL SORTS OF VARIATIONS. IT'S SAID TO HAVE BEEN PLAYED AS FAR BACK AS THE HEIAN PERIOD AND DRAWS ITS ROOTS FROM THE ANCIENT CHINESE GAME OF *ZHUOMICANG*.

After this, rumors spread of an Inari fox statue appearing in the park.

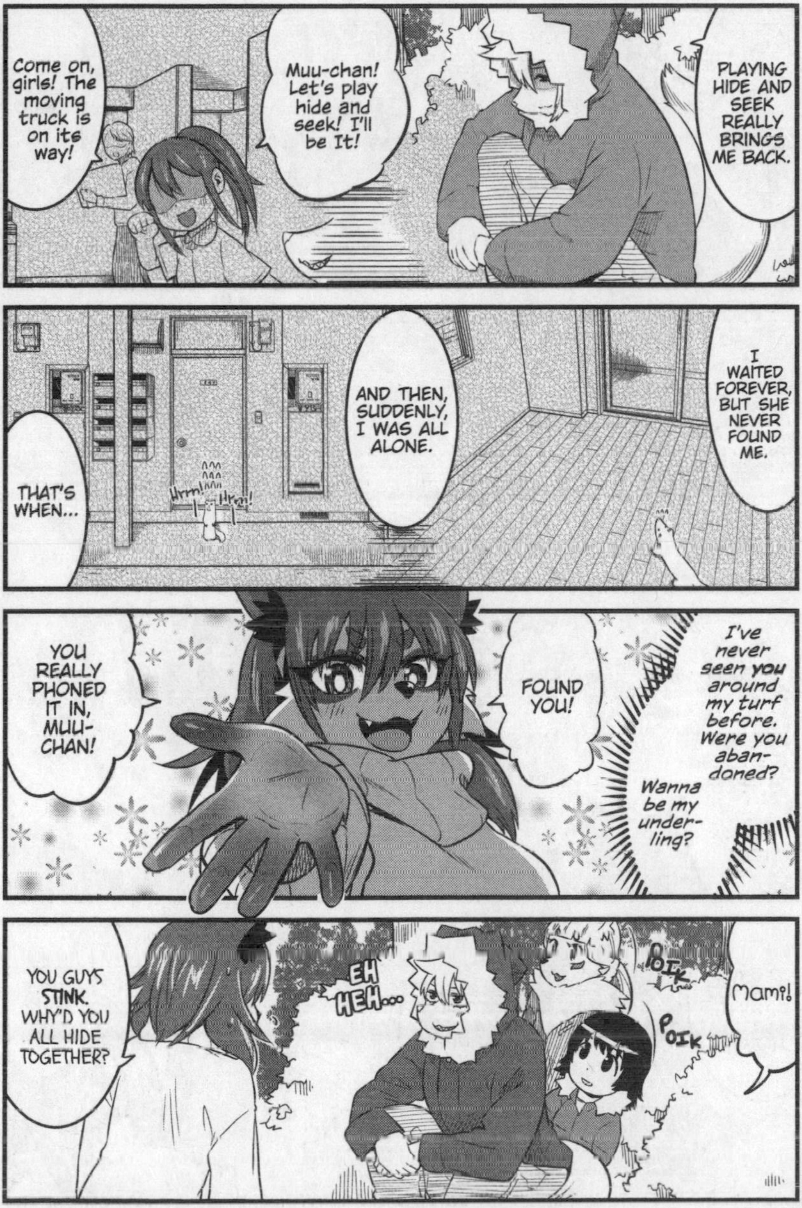
PLAYING HIDE AND SEEK REALLY BRINGS ME BACK.
Muu-chan! Let's play hide and seek! I'll be It!
Come on, girls! The moving truck is on its way!
I WAITED FOREVER, BUT SHE NEVER FOUND ME.
AND THEN, SUDDENLY, I WAS ALL ALONE.
Hrrn! Hrrn!
THAT'S WHEN...
I've never seen you around my turf before. Were you abandoned?
Wanna be my underling?
FOUND YOU!
YOU REALLY PHONED IT IN, MUU-CHAN!
Mami!
POIK
POIK
EH HEH...
YOU GUYS STINK. WHY'D YOU ALL HIDE TOGETHER?

After Mami found Muuko that day, they moved in together.

UNDERLING SIMILAR TO THE SLANG TERM "HENCHMAN," IT DENOTES SOMEONE IN SERVICE TO SOMEONE ELSE. MAMI HAS DECLARED HERSELF THE BOSS OF THE AREA WHERE TAMAMO LIVES.

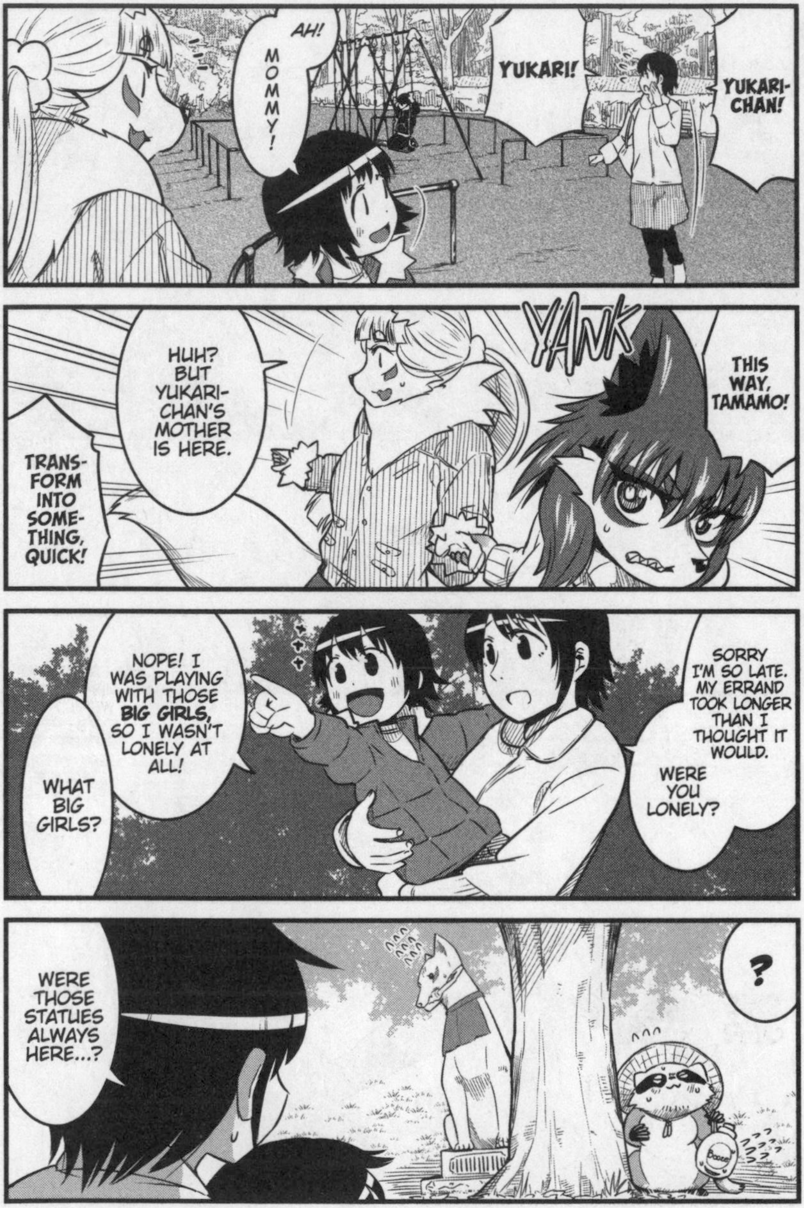
YUKARI-CHAN!
YUKARI!
AH! MOMMY!
THIS WAY, TAMAMO!
YANK
HUH? BUT YUKARI-CHAN'S MOTHER IS HERE.
TRANSFORM INTO SOMETHING, QUICK!
SORRY I'M SO LATE. MY ERRAND TOOK LONGER THAN I THOUGHT IT WOULD.
WERE YOU LONELY?
NOPE! I WAS PLAYING WITH THOSE BIG GIRLS, SO I WASN'T LONELY AT ALL!
WHAT BIG GIRLS?
?
WERE THOSE STATUES ALWAYS HERE...?
Booze

Mysterious statues spotted in local park.

SHIGARAKI WARE A TYPE OF POTTERY PRIMARILY MADE IN KOKA IN SHIGA PREFECTURE. IT'S BEST KNOWN FOR THE TANUKI STATUES THAT ARE PLACED OUTSIDE SHOPS AS GOOD LUCK CHARMS. FIGURES OF RACCOONS ARE MUCH RARER.

MA-CHAN I GUESS I'M CALLING MITARAI-SAN "MA-CHAN" NOW! AND SHE'S JUST USING MY NAME, SO WE'RE CLEARLY FRIENDS!

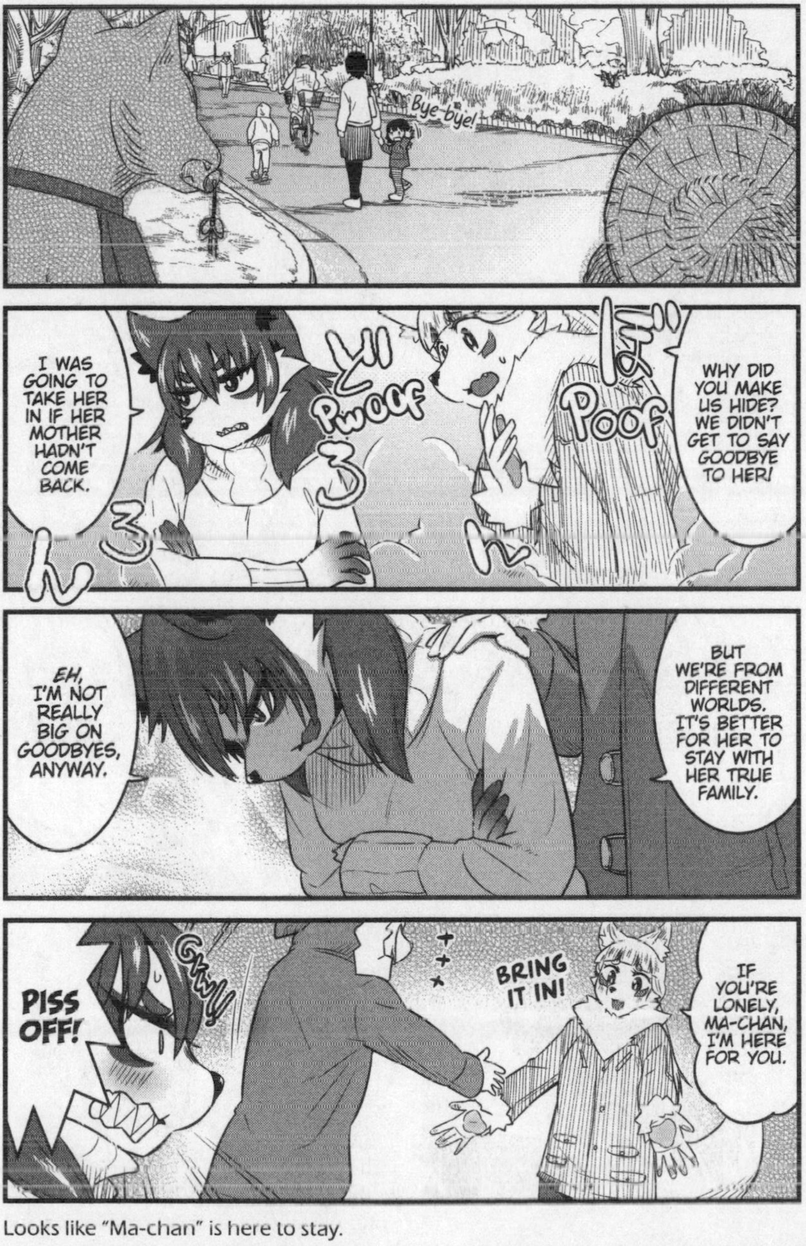
Bye-bye!
WHY DID YOU MAKE US HIDE? WE DIDN'T GET TO SAY GOODBYE TO HER!
Poof
Pwoof
I WAS GOING TO TAKE HER IN IF HER MOTHER HADN'T COME BACK.
BUT WE'RE FROM DIFFERENT WORLDS. IT'S BETTER FOR HER TO STAY WITH HER TRUE FAMILY.
EH, I'M NOT REALLY BIG ON GOODBYES, ANYWAY.
IF YOU'RE LONELY, MA-CHAN, I'M HERE FOR YOU.
BRING IT IN!
Grwl
PISS OFF!

Looks like "Ma-chan" is here to stay.

COTTON CANDY 2 COTTON CANDY MELTS IN WATER.

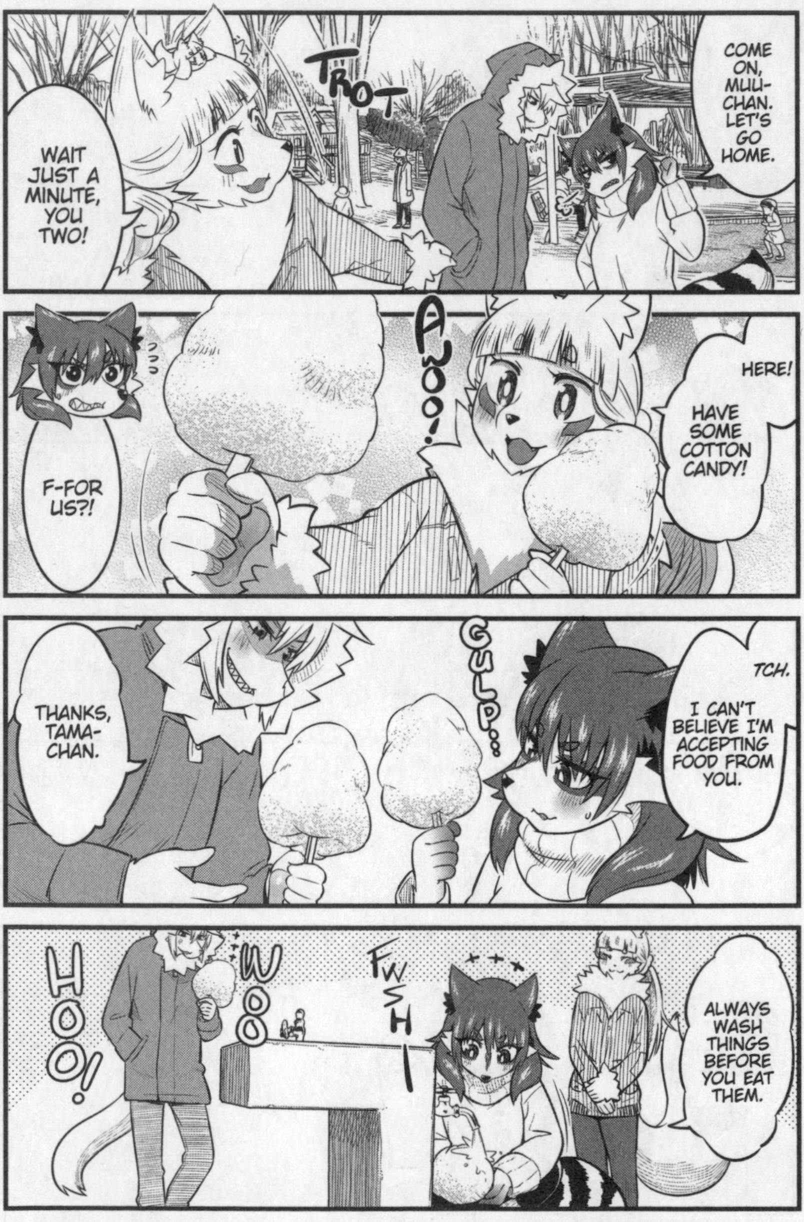
COME ON, MUU-CHAN. LET'S GO HOME.
TROT
WAIT JUST A MINUTE, YOU TWO!
HERE!
HAVE SOME COTTON CANDY!
AWOO!
F-FOR US?!
TCH.
I CAN'T BELIEVE I'M ACCEPTING FOOD FROM YOU.
GULP...
THANKS, TAMA-CHAN.
ALWAYS WASH THINGS BEFORE YOU EAT THEM.
FWSH
WOO
HOO!

This only led to tears.

Tamamo-chan's a FOX!

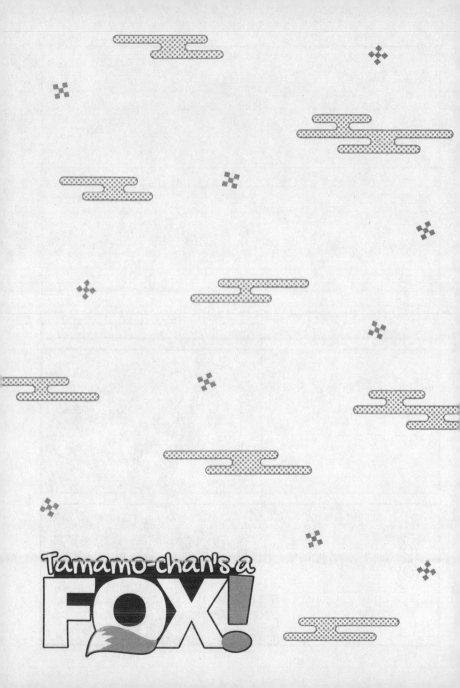

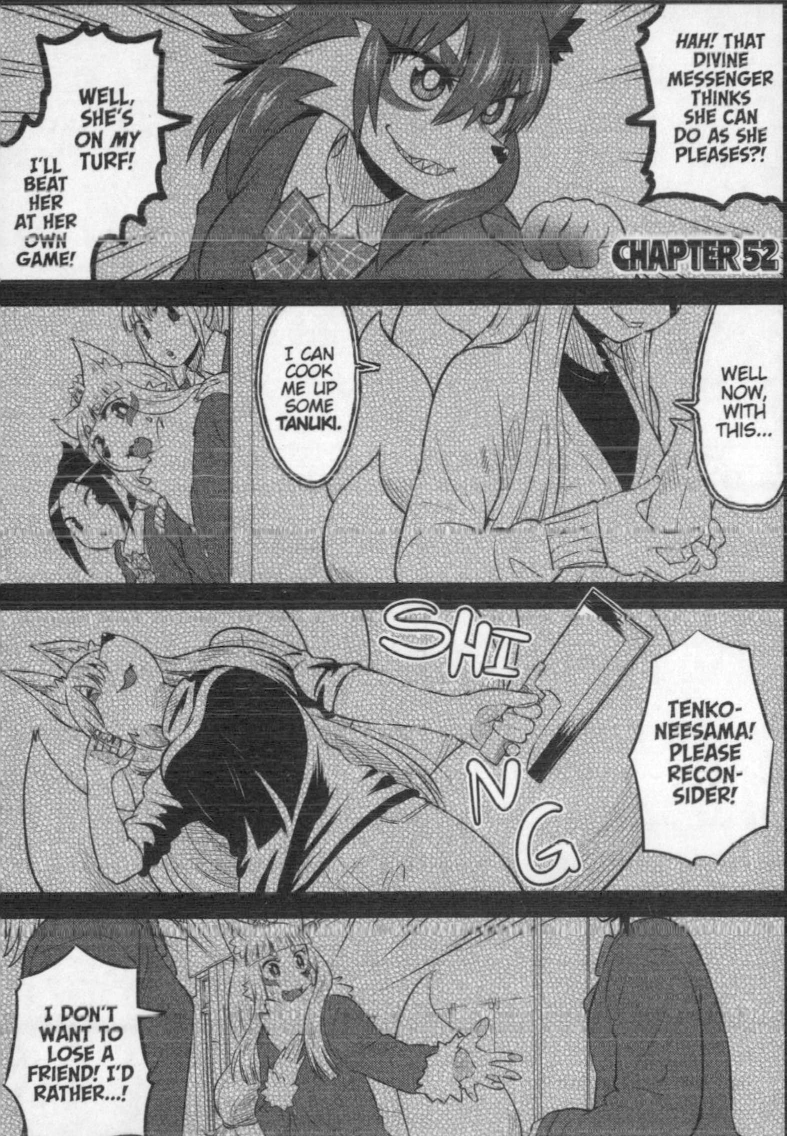
HAH! THAT DIVINE MESSENGER THINKS SHE CAN DO AS SHE PLEASES?!
WELL, SHE'S ON MY TURF!
I'LL BEAT HER AT HER OWN GAME!
CHAPTER 52
WELL NOW, WITH THIS...
I CAN COOK ME UP SOME TANUKI.
TENKO-NEESAMA! PLEASE RECONSIDER!
SHING
I DON'T WANT TO LOSE A FRIEND! I'D RATHER...!

CHAPTER 52

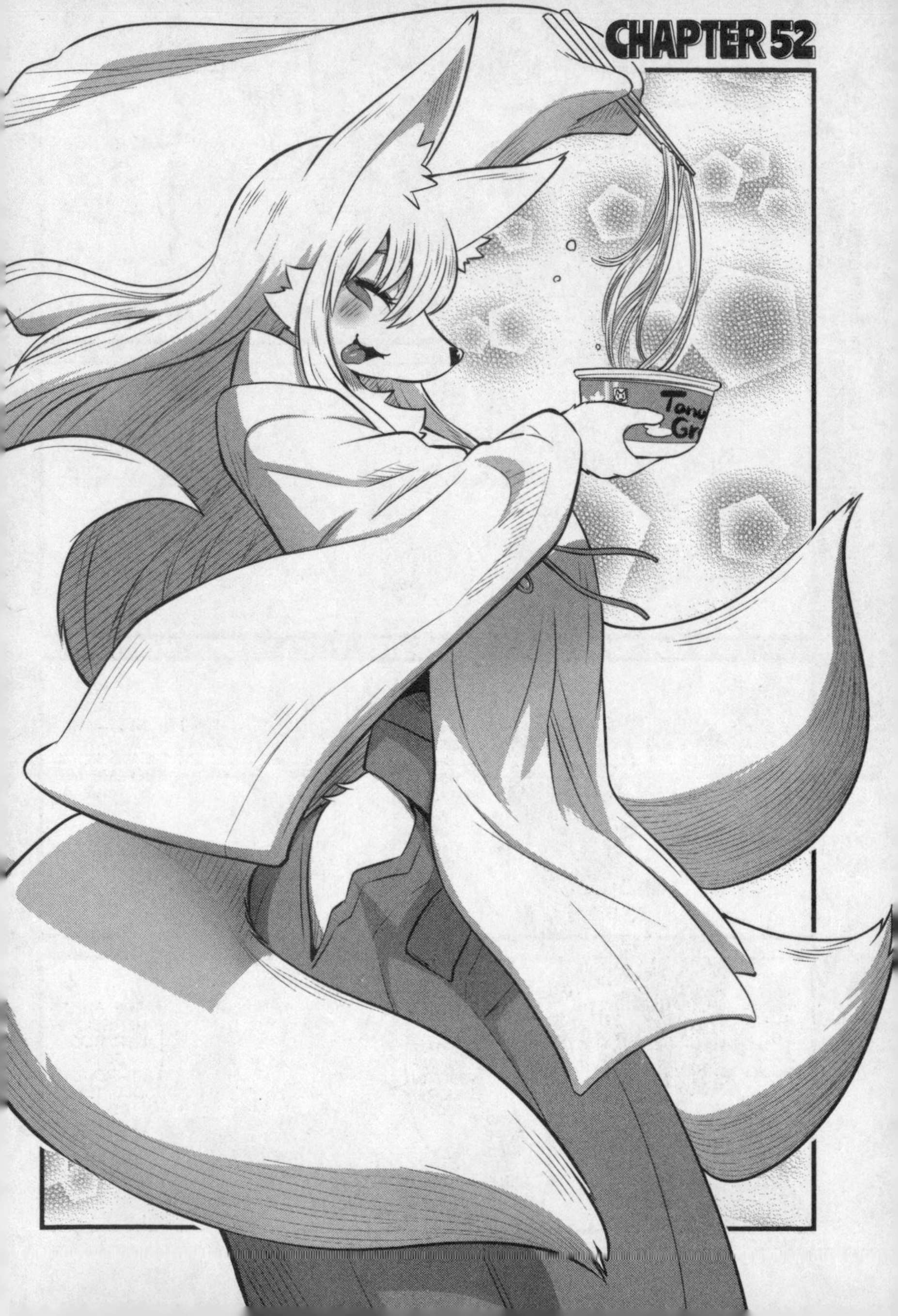

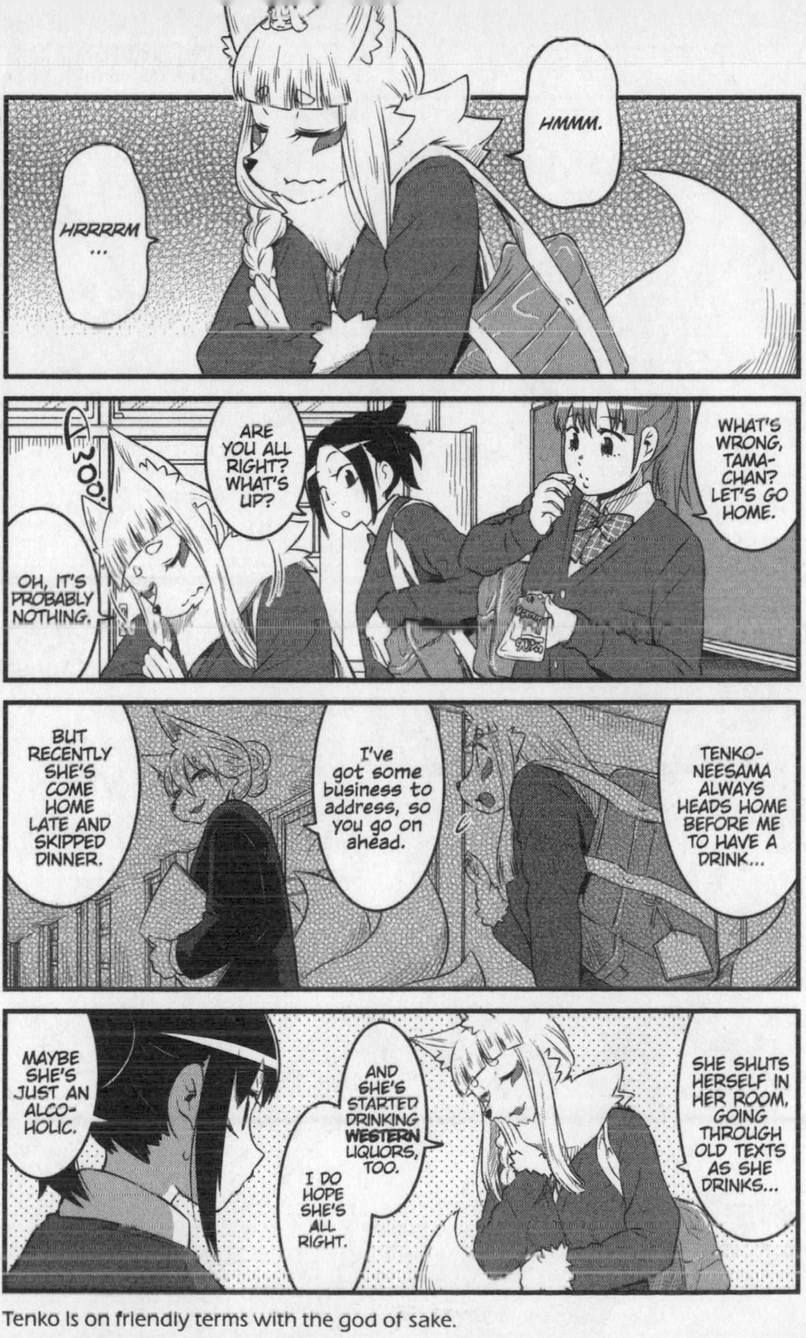
HMMM.
HRRRRM ...
WHAT'S WRONG, TAMA-CHAN? LET'S GO HOME.
ARE YOU ALL RIGHT? WHAT'S UP?
OH, IT'S PROBABLY NOTHING.
TENKO-NEESAMA ALWAYS HEADS HOME BEFORE ME TO HAVE A DRINK...
I've got some business to address, so you go on ahead.
BUT RECENTLY SHE'S COME HOME LATE AND SKIPPED DINNER.
SHE SHUTS HERSELF IN HER ROOM, GOING THROUGH OLD TEXTS AS SHE DRINKS...
AND SHE'S STARTED DRINKING WESTERN LIQUORS, TOO.
I DO HOPE SHE'S ALL RIGHT.
MAYBE SHE'S JUST AN ALCO-HOLIC.

TIPPLER AN OLD-TIMEY WORD FOR SOMEONE WHO LIKES ALCOHOL AND DRINKS A BIT TOO MUCH OF IT. TENKO-NEE'S DRINKING COULD LEAVE EVEN THE YAMATO-NO-OROCHI SERPENT AGHAST.

Tenko is on friendly terms with the god of sake.

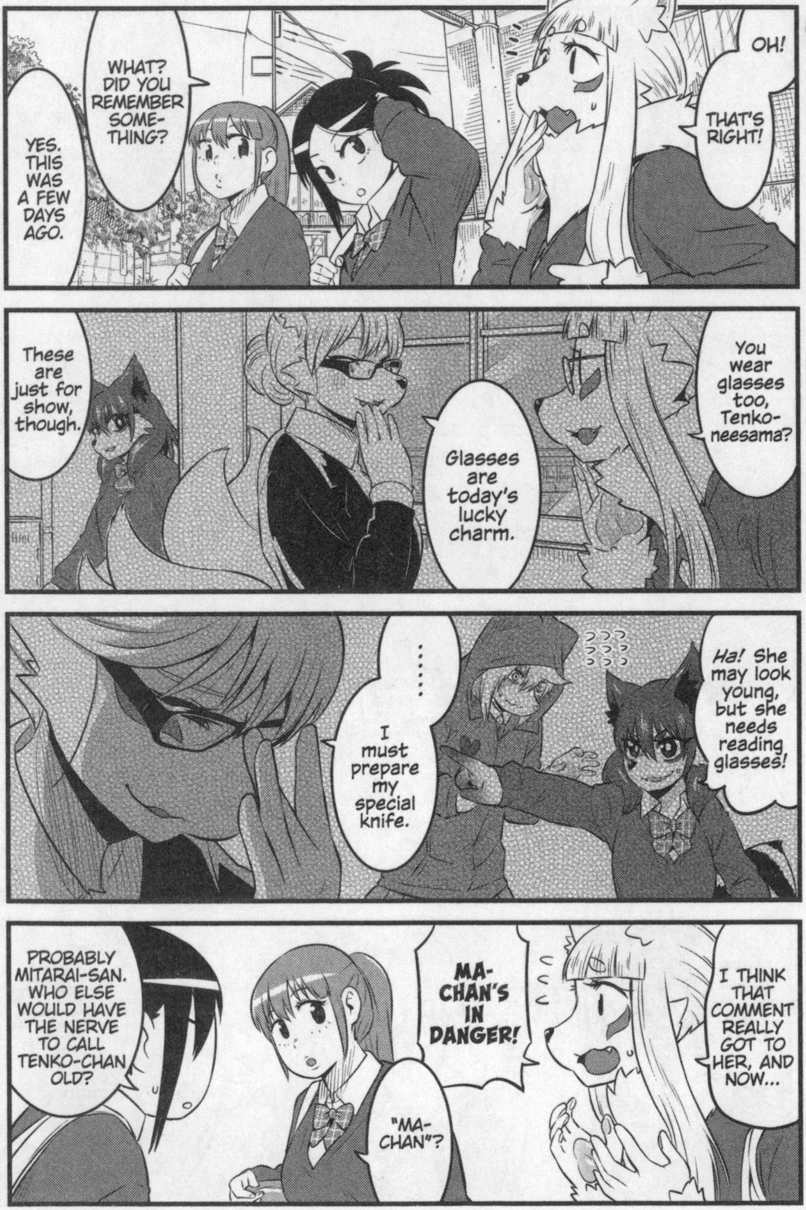
OH!
THAT'S RIGHT!
WHAT? DID YOU REMEMBER SOME-THING?
YES. THIS WAS A FEW DAYS AGO.
You wear glasses too, Tenko-neesama?
Glasses are today's lucky charm.
These are just for show, though.
Ha! She may look young, but she needs reading glasses!
......
I must prepare my special knife.
I THINK THAT COMMENT REALLY GOT TO HER, AND NOW...
MA-CHAN's IN DANGER!
"MA-CHAN"?
PROBABLY MITARAI-SAN. WHO ELSE WOULD HAVE THE NERVE TO CALL TENKO-CHAN OLD?

LUCKY CHARMS ITEMS SAID TO BRING GOOD FORTUNE, SUCH AS DARUMA FIGURES, BECKONING CATS, FESTIVAL MEN, AND MORE. SOME DATE BACK TO ANCIENT JAPAN WHILE OTHERS WERE IMPORTED FROM INDIA, CHINA, OR OTHER PLACES.

Mami knew the risks but couldn't pass up such a golden opportunity.

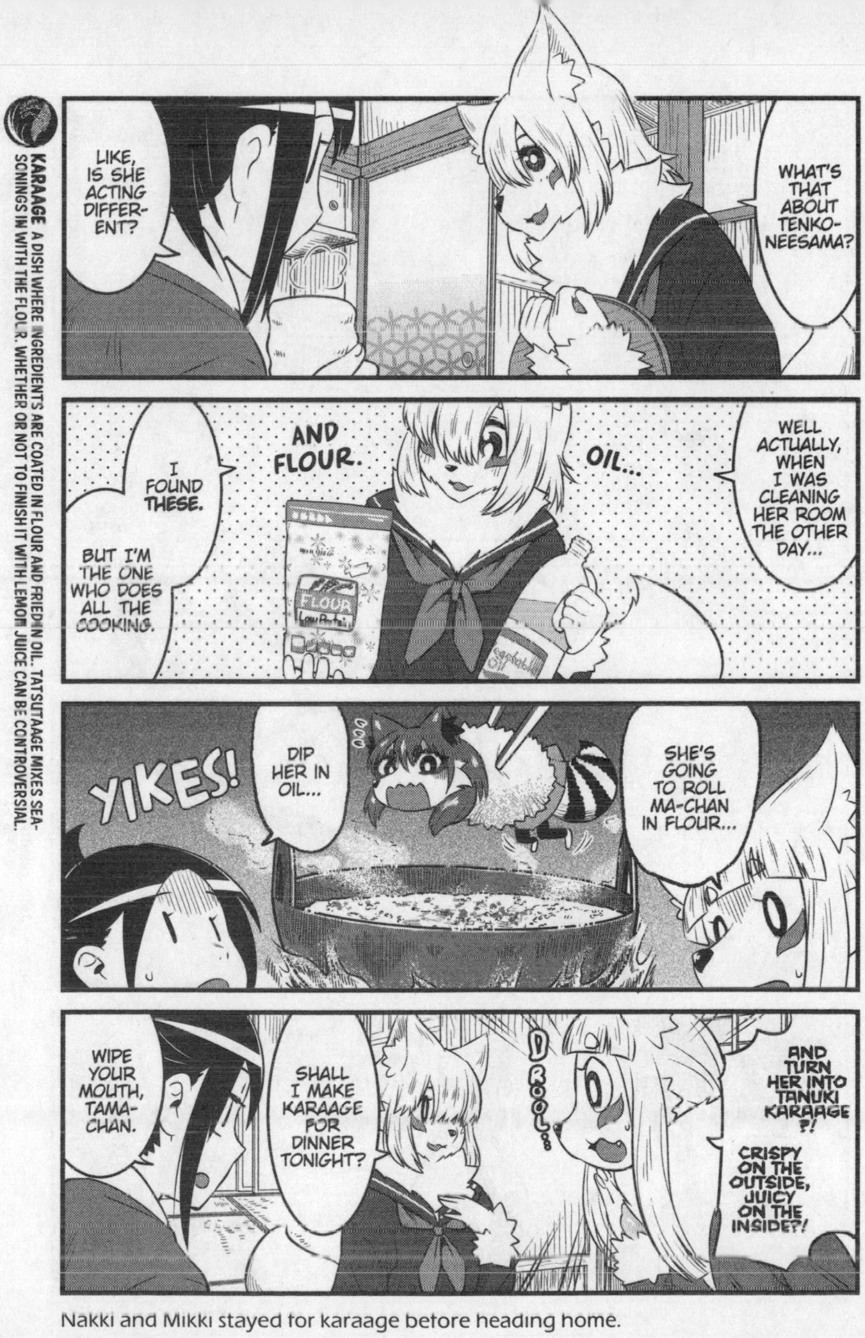
WHAT'S THAT ABOUT TENKO-NEESAMA?
LIKE, IS SHE ACTING DIFFERENT?
WELL ACTUALLY, WHEN I WAS CLEANING HER ROOM THE OTHER DAY...
OIL...
AND FLOUR.
I FOUND THESE.
BUT I'M THE ONE WHO DOES ALL THE COOKING.
FLOUR
SHE'S GOING TO ROLL MA-CHAN IN FLOUR...
DIP HER IN OIL...
YIKES!
AND TURN HER INTO TANUKI KARAAGE?!
CRISPY ON THE OUTSIDE, JUICY ON THE INSIDE?!
DROOL...
SHALL I MAKE KARAAGE FOR DINNER TONIGHT?
WIPE YOUR MOUTH, TAMA-CHAN.

Nakki and Mikki stayed for karaage before heading home.

KARAAGE A DISH WHERE INGREDIENTS ARE COATED IN FLOUR AND FRIED IN OIL. TATSUTAAGE MIXES SEASONINGS IN WITH THE FLOUR. WHETHER OR NOT TO FINISH IT WITH LEMON JUICE CAN BE CONTROVERSIAL.

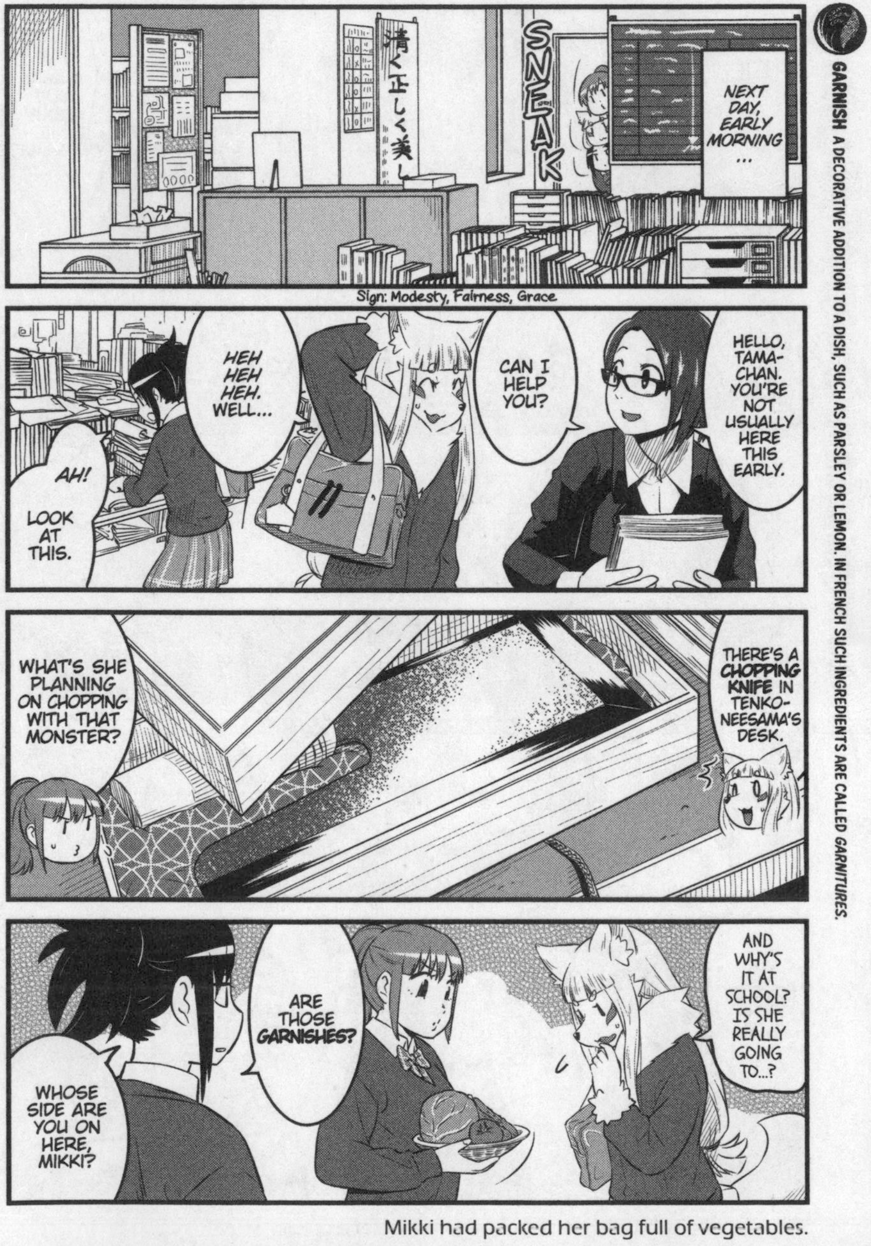

NEXT DAY, EARLY MORNING ...
SNEAK
清く正しく美し
Sign: Modesty, Fairness, Grace
HELLO, TAMA-CHAN. YOU'RE NOT USUALLY HERE THIS EARLY.
CAN I HELP YOU?
HEH HEH HEH. WELL...
AH!
LOOK AT THIS.
THERE'S A **CHOPPING KNIFE** IN TENKO-NEESAMA'S DESK.
WHAT'S SHE PLANNING ON CHOPPING WITH THAT MONSTER?
AND WHY'S IT AT SCHOOL? IS SHE REALLY GOING TO...?
ARE THOSE **GARNISHES?**
WHOSE SIDE ARE YOU ON HERE, MIKKI?

GARNISH A DECORATIVE ADDITION TO A DISH, SUCH AS PARSLEY OR LEMON. IN FRENCH SUCH INGREDIENTS ARE CALLED *GARNITURES*.

Mikki had packed her bag full of vegetables.

BRUSH WITH DEATH: A PHRASE USED WHEN ONE BARELY AVOIDS A DANGEROUS SITUATION OR CRISIS. BUT WHEN YOU'VE ANGERED TENKO, NO NUMBER OF LIVES WILL BE ENOUGH TO SAVE YOU.

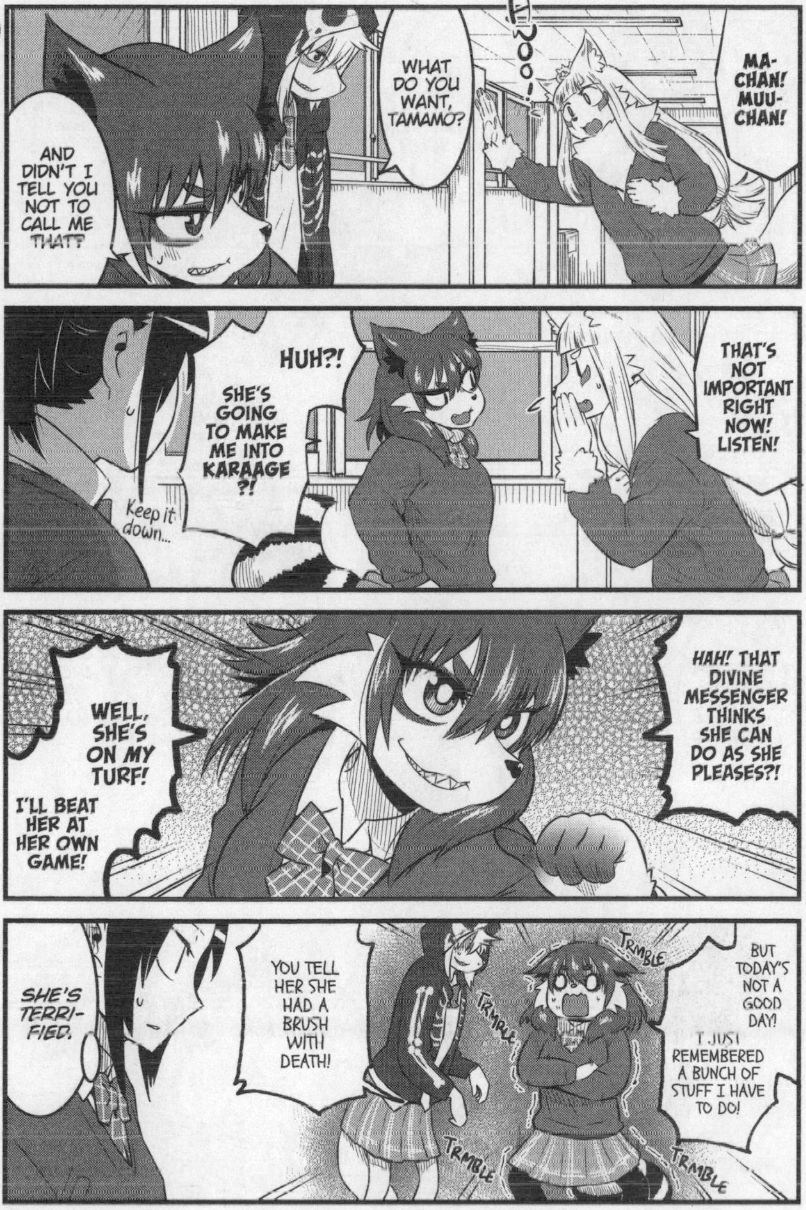
MA-CHAN! MUU-CHAN!
WHAT DO YOU WANT, TAMAMO?
AND DIDN'T I TELL YOU NOT TO CALL ME THAT?
THAT'S NOT IMPORTANT RIGHT NOW! LISTEN!
HUH?!
SHE'S GOING TO MAKE ME INTO KARAAGE?!
Keep it down...
HAH! THAT DIVINE MESSENGER THINKS SHE CAN DO AS SHE PLEASES?!
WELL, SHE'S ON MY TURF!
I'LL BEAT HER AT HER OWN GAME!
BUT TODAY'S NOT A GOOD DAY!
I JUST REMEMBERED A BUNCH OF STUFF I HAVE TO DO!
TRMBLE
TRMBLE
TRMBLE
TRMBLE
YOU TELL HER SHE HAD A BRUSH WITH DEATH!
SHE'S TERRI-FIED.

She may put up a bold front, but Mami's a bit of a wuss.

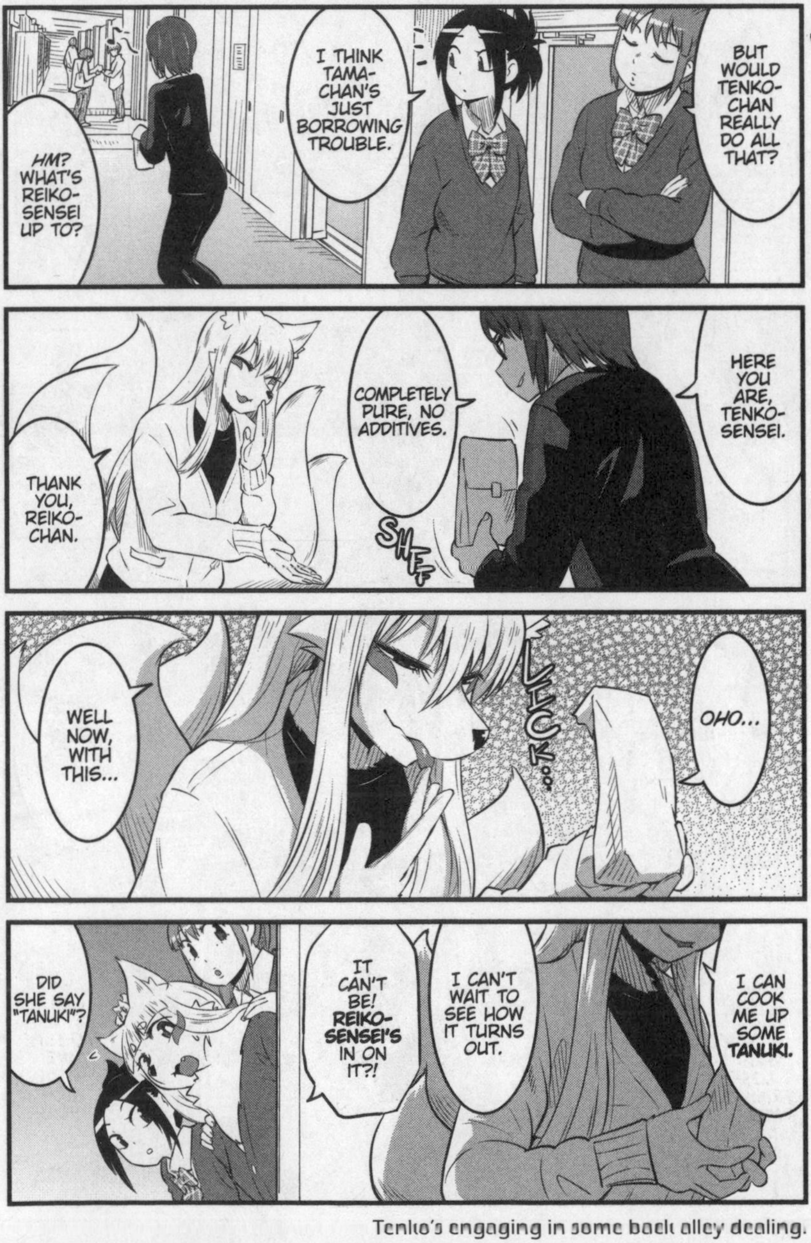
BUT WOULD TENKO-CHAN REALLY DO ALL THAT?
I THINK TAMA-CHAN'S JUST BORROWING TROUBLE.
HM? WHAT'S REIKO-SENSEI UP TO?
HERE YOU ARE, TENKO-SENSEI.
COMPLETELY PURE, NO ADDITIVES.
SHFF
THANK YOU, REIKO-CHAN.
OHO...
LICK...
WELL NOW, WITH THIS...
I CAN COOK ME UP SOME TANUKI.
I CAN'T WAIT TO SEE HOW IT TURNS OUT.
IT CAN'T BE! REIKO-SENSEI'S IN ON IT?!
DID SHE SAY "TANUKI"?

OTHER FORMS TENKO-NEESAMA CAME OVER FROM THE CONTINENT WITH OKAMI-SAMA BEFORE THE FAITHS WERE UNIFIED. EVEN I'M AMAZED AT HOW MANY DIFFERENT NAMES SHE HAS.

Tenko's engaging in some back alley dealing.

CHAPTER 53

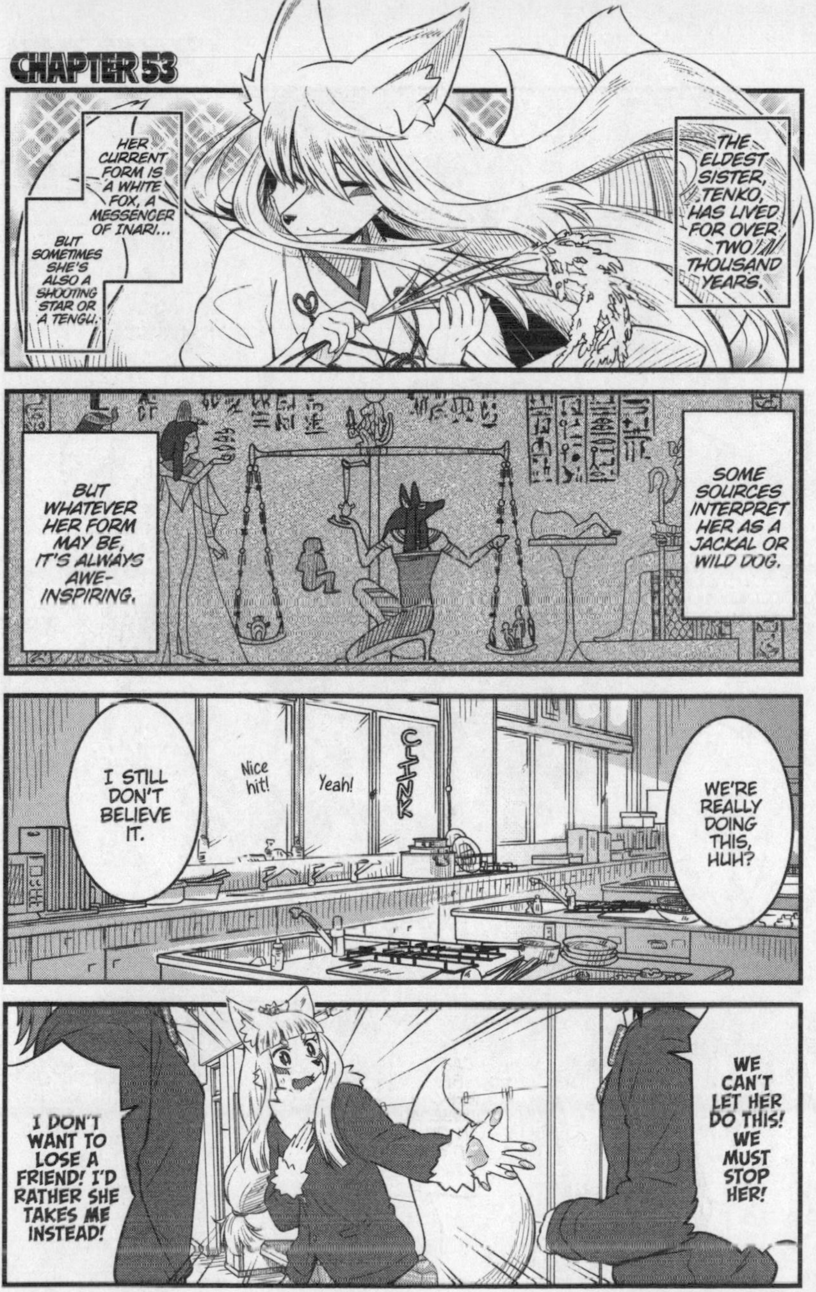

THE ELDEST SISTER, TENKO, HAS LIVED FOR OVER TWO THOUSAND YEARS.
HER CURRENT FORM IS A WHITE FOX, A MESSENGER OF INARI...
BUT SOMETIMES SHE'S ALSO A SHOOTING STAR OR A TENGU.
SOME SOURCES INTERPRET HER AS A JACKAL OR WILD DOG.
BUT WHATEVER HER FORM MAY BE, IT'S ALWAYS AWE-INSPIRING.
WE'RE REALLY DOING THIS, HUH?
CLINK
Yeah!
Nice hit!
I STILL DON'T BELIEVE IT.
WE CAN'T LET HER DO THIS! WE MUST STOP HER!
I DON'T WANT TO LOSE A FRIEND! I'D RATHER SHE TAKES ME INSTEAD!

CHAPTER 53

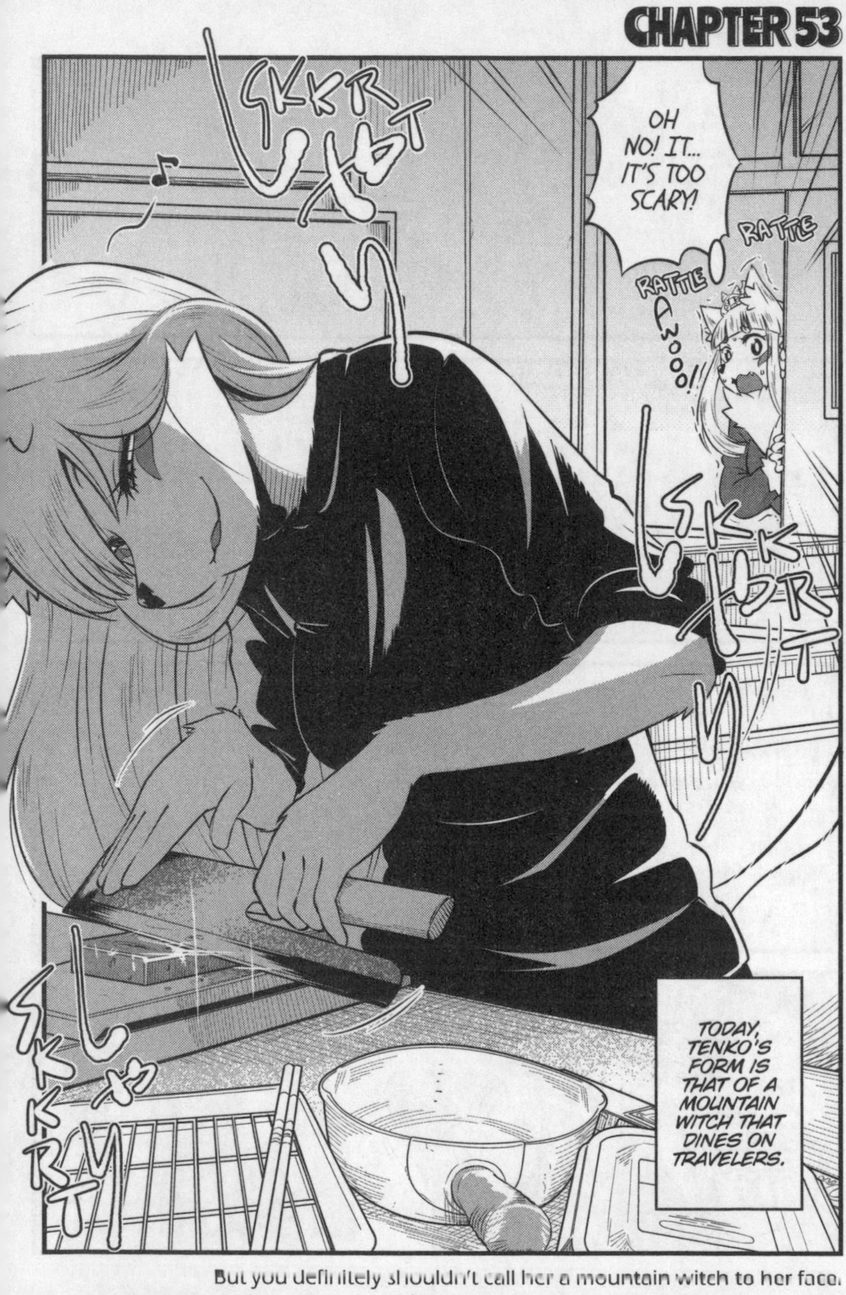
OH NO! IT... IT'S TOO SCARY!
RATTLE
RATTLE
AWOOO!
SKKR SKT
SKKR SKT
TODAY, TENKO'S FORM IS THAT OF A MOUNTAIN WITCH THAT DINES ON TRAVELERS.
SKKRT
SKKR

But you definitely shouldn't call her a mountain witch to her face.

TERROR! PEOPLE WHO SMILE ALL THE TIME ARE THE WORST TO MAKE ANGRY. TO APPEASE TENKO-NEESAMA I'LL HAVE TO MAKE OFFERINGS OF SAKE FOR THREE DAYS AND THREE NIGHTS.

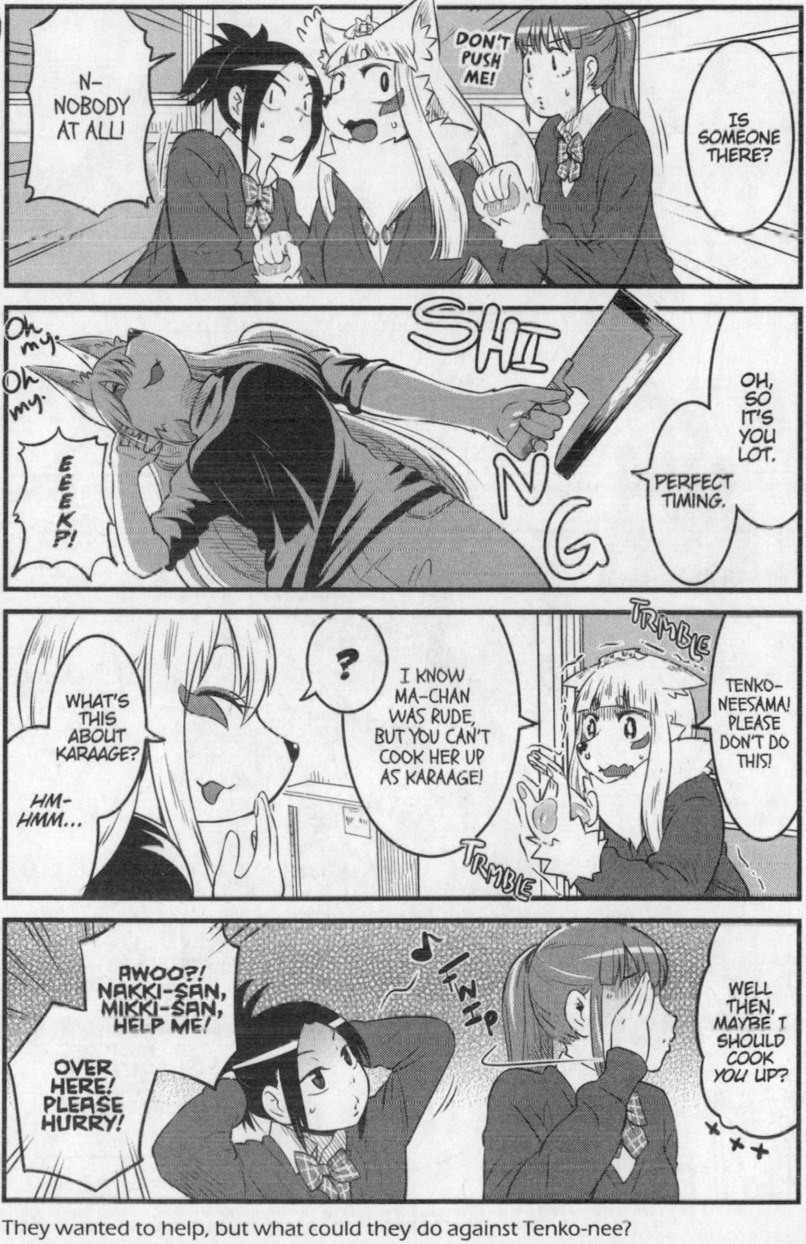

IS SOMEONE THERE?
DON'T PUSH ME!
N- NOBODY AT ALL!
OH, SO IT'S YOU LOT.
PERFECT TIMING.
SHIING
Oh my. Oh my.
EEEEK?!
TENKO-NEESAMA! PLEASE DON'T DO THIS!
TRMBLE
I KNOW MA-CHAN WAS RUDE, BUT YOU CAN'T COOK HER UP AS KARAAGE!
?
WHAT'S THIS ABOUT KARAAGE?
HM-HMM...
TRMBLE
WELL THEN, MAYBE I SHOULD COOK YOU UP?
FWIP
AWOO?! NAKKI-SAN, MIKKI-SAN, HELP ME!
OVER HERE! PLEASE HURRY!

They wanted to help, but what could they do against Tenko-nee?

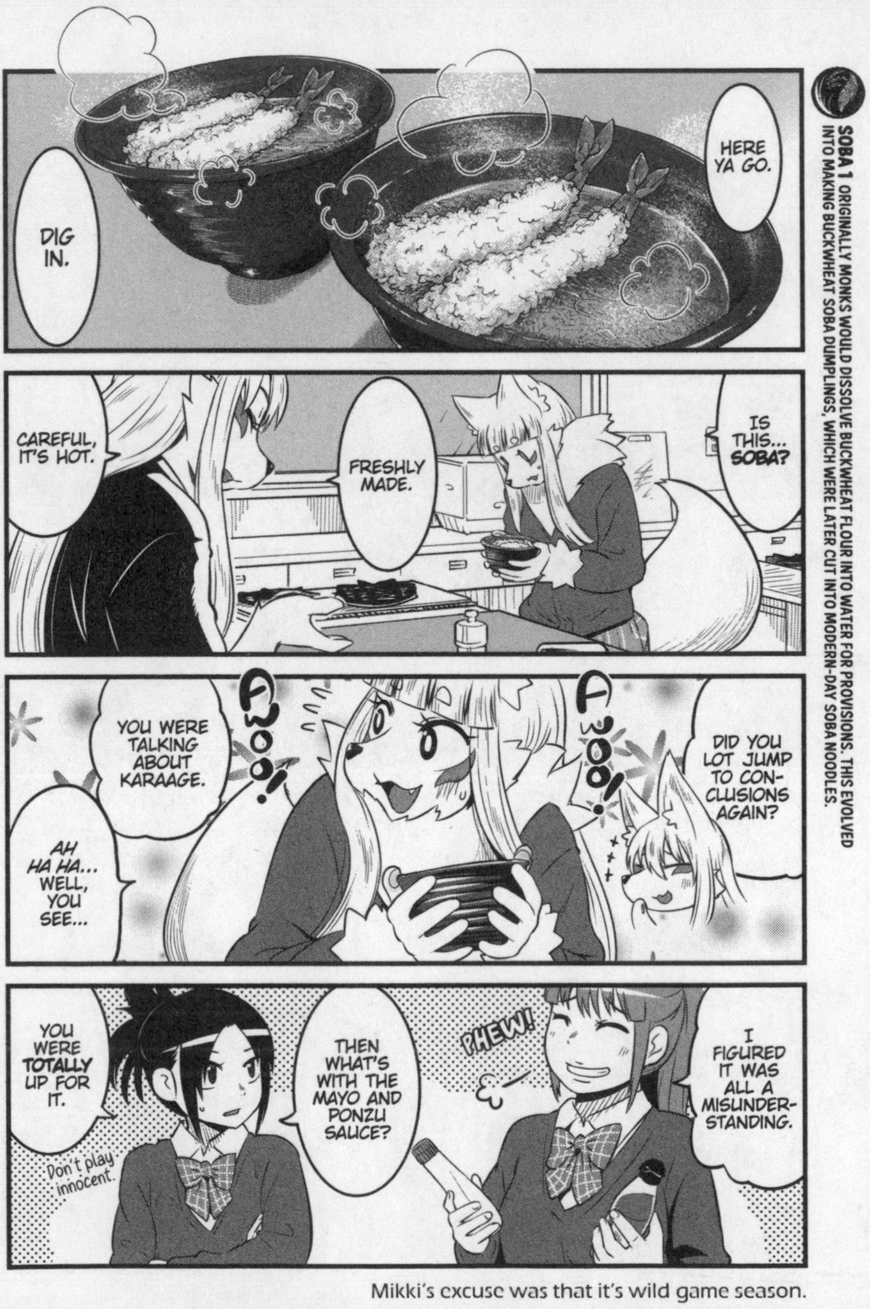
HERE YA GO.
DIG IN.
IS THIS... SOBA?
FRESHLY MADE.
CAREFUL, IT'S HOT.
DID YOU LOT JUMP TO CON-CLUSIONS AGAIN?
AWOO!
AWOO!
YOU WERE TALKING ABOUT KARAAGE.
AH HA HA... WELL, YOU SEE...
I FIGURED IT WAS ALL A MISUNDER-STANDING.
PHEW!
THEN WHAT'S WITH THE MAYO AND PONZU SAUCE?
YOU WERE TOTALLY UP FOR IT.
Don't play innocent.

Mikki's excuse was that it's wild game season.

SOBA 1 ORIGINALLY MONKS WOULD DISSOLVE BUCKWHEAT FLOUR INTO WATER FOR PROVISIONS. THIS EVOLVED INTO MAKING BUCKWHEAT SOBA DUMPLINGS, WHICH WERE LATER CUT INTO MODERN-DAY SOBA NOODLES.

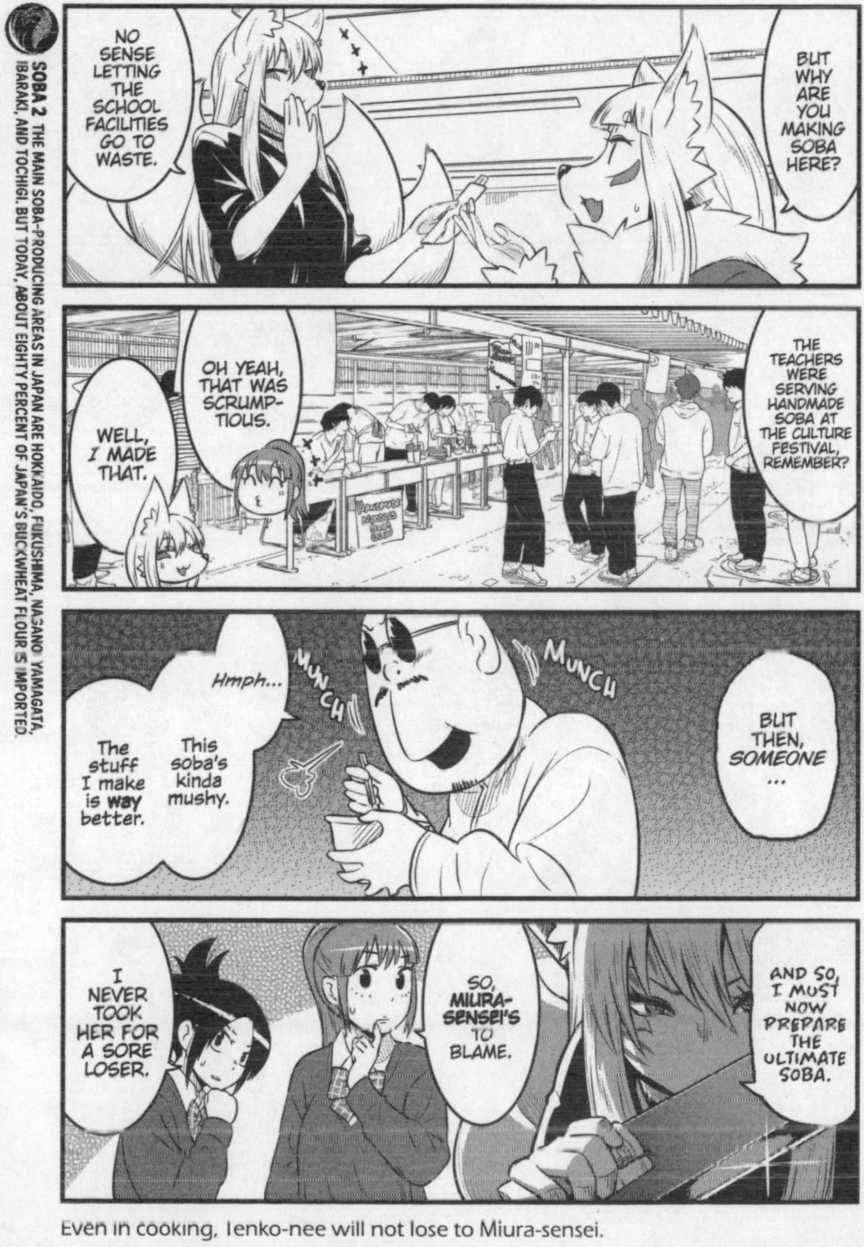
BUT WHY ARE YOU MAKING SOBA HERE?
NO SENSE LETTING THE SCHOOL FACILITIES GO TO WASTE.
THE TEACHERS WERE SERVING HANDMADE SOBA AT THE CULTURE FESTIVAL, REMEMBER?
OH YEAH, THAT WAS SCRUMPTIOUS.
WELL, *I* MADE THAT.
BUT THEN, *SOMEONE* ...
MUNCH
MUNCH
Hmph...
This soba's kinda mushy.
The stuff I make is **way** better.
AND SO, I MUST NOW PREPARE THE ULTIMATE SOBA.
SO, MIURA-SENSEI'S TO BLAME.
I NEVER TOOK HER FOR A SORE LOSER.

SOBA 2 THE MAIN SOBA-PRODUCING AREAS IN JAPAN ARE HOKKAIDO, FUKUSHIMA, NAGANO, YAMAGATA, IBARAKI, AND TOCHIGI. BUT TODAY, ABOUT EIGHTY PERCENT OF JAPAN'S BUCKWHEAT FLOUR IS IMPORTED.

Even in cooking, Tenko-nee will not lose to Miura-sensei.

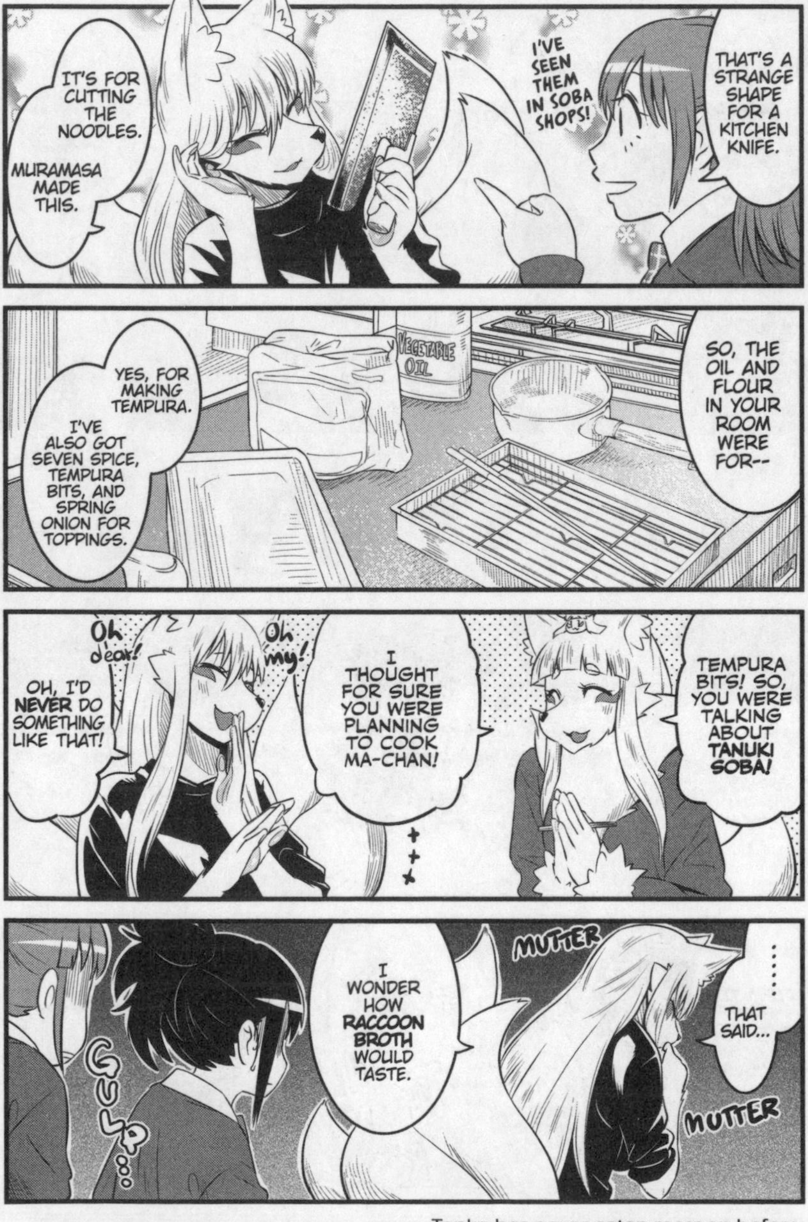
THAT'S A STRANGE SHAPE FOR A KITCHEN KNIFE.
I'VE SEEN THEM IN SOBA SHOPS!
IT'S FOR CUTTING THE NOODLES.
MURAMASA MADE THIS.
SO, THE OIL AND FLOUR IN YOUR ROOM WERE FOR--
VEGETABLE OIL
YES, FOR MAKING TEMPURA.
I'VE ALSO GOT SEVEN SPICE, TEMPURA BITS, AND SPRING ONION FOR TOPPINGS.
TEMPURA BITS! SO, YOU WERE TALKING ABOUT TANUKI SOBA!
I THOUGHT FOR SURE YOU WERE PLANNING TO COOK MA-CHAN!
Oh my!
Oh dear!
OH, I'D NEVER DO SOMETHING LIKE THAT!
......
THAT SAID...
MUTTER
MUTTER
I WONDER HOW RACCOON BROTH WOULD TASTE.
GULP...

MURAMASA ONE OF THE WORLD'S MOST FAMOUS SWORDSMITHS, HE LIVED IN KUWANA, ISE PROVINCE, IN THE EARLY MUROMACHI PERIOD. MANY OF HIS BLADES ARE KNOWN AS YOTO, OR "WICKED KATANA." THIS KNIFE IS ONE OF TENKO-NEE'S PERSONAL TREASURES.

Tenko has never eaten raccoon before.

TEMPURA A JAPANESE DISH WHERE INGREDIENTS ARE COATED WITH A FLOUR BATTER THEN DEEP FRIED. IT CAME TO NAGASAKI AROUND THE SAME TIME GUNS WERE INTRODUCED TO JAPAN, AND THE NAME IS SAID TO COME FROM THE PORTUGUESE LANGUAGE.

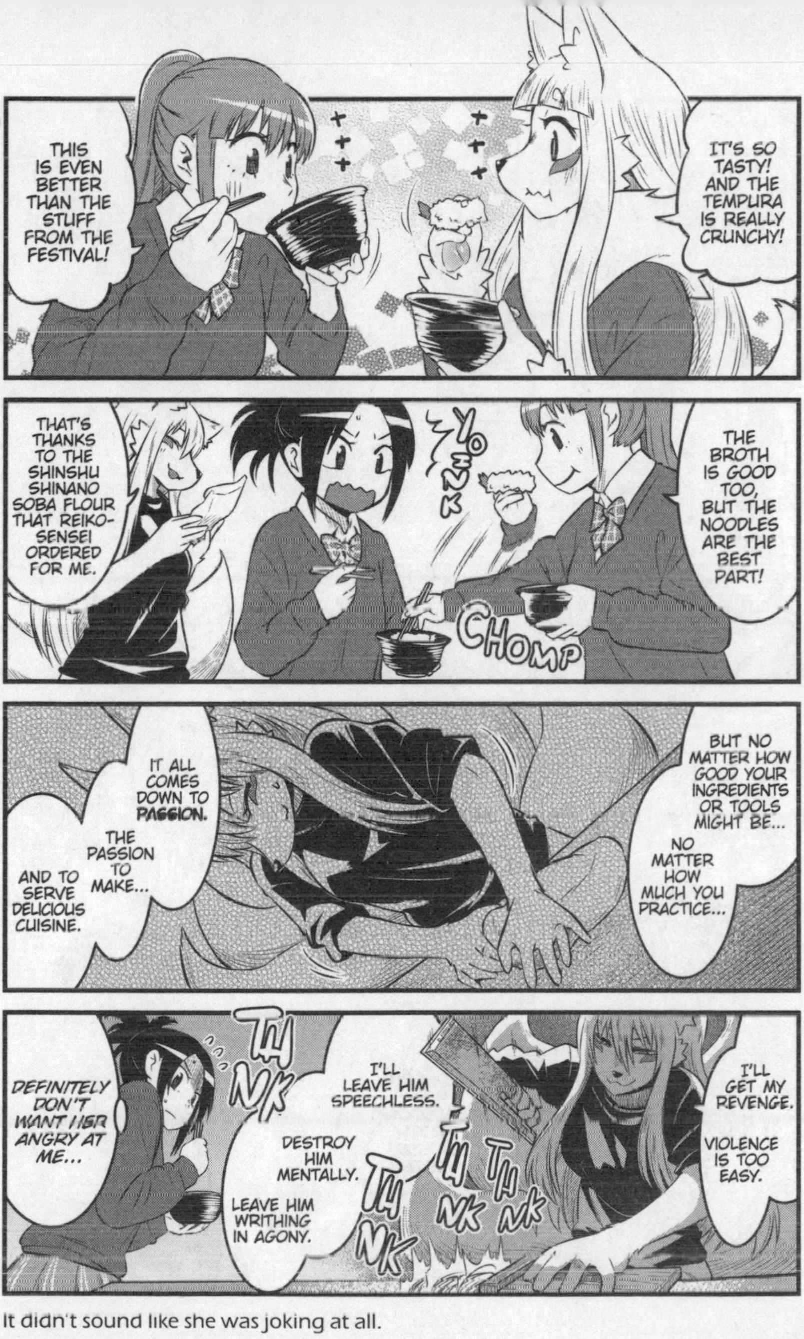
IT'S SO TASTY! AND THE TEMPURA IS REALLY CRUNCHY!
THIS IS EVEN BETTER THAN THE STUFF FROM THE FESTIVAL!
THE BROTH IS GOOD TOO, BUT THE NOODLES ARE THE BEST PART!
YOINK
THAT'S THANKS TO THE SHINSHU SHINANO SOBA FLOUR THAT REIKO-SENSEI ORDERED FOR ME.
CHOMP
BUT NO MATTER HOW GOOD YOUR INGREDIENTS OR TOOLS MIGHT BE...
NO MATTER HOW MUCH YOU PRACTICE...
IT ALL COMES DOWN TO PASSION.
THE PASSION TO MAKE...
AND TO SERVE DELICIOUS CUISINE.
I'LL GET MY REVENGE.
VIOLENCE IS TOO EASY.
I'LL LEAVE HIM SPEECHLESS.
DESTROY HIM MENTALLY.
LEAVE HIM WRITHING IN AGONY.
THUNK
THUNK
THUNK
THUNK
DEFINITELY DON'T WANT HER ANGRY AT ME...
It didn't sound like she was joking at all.

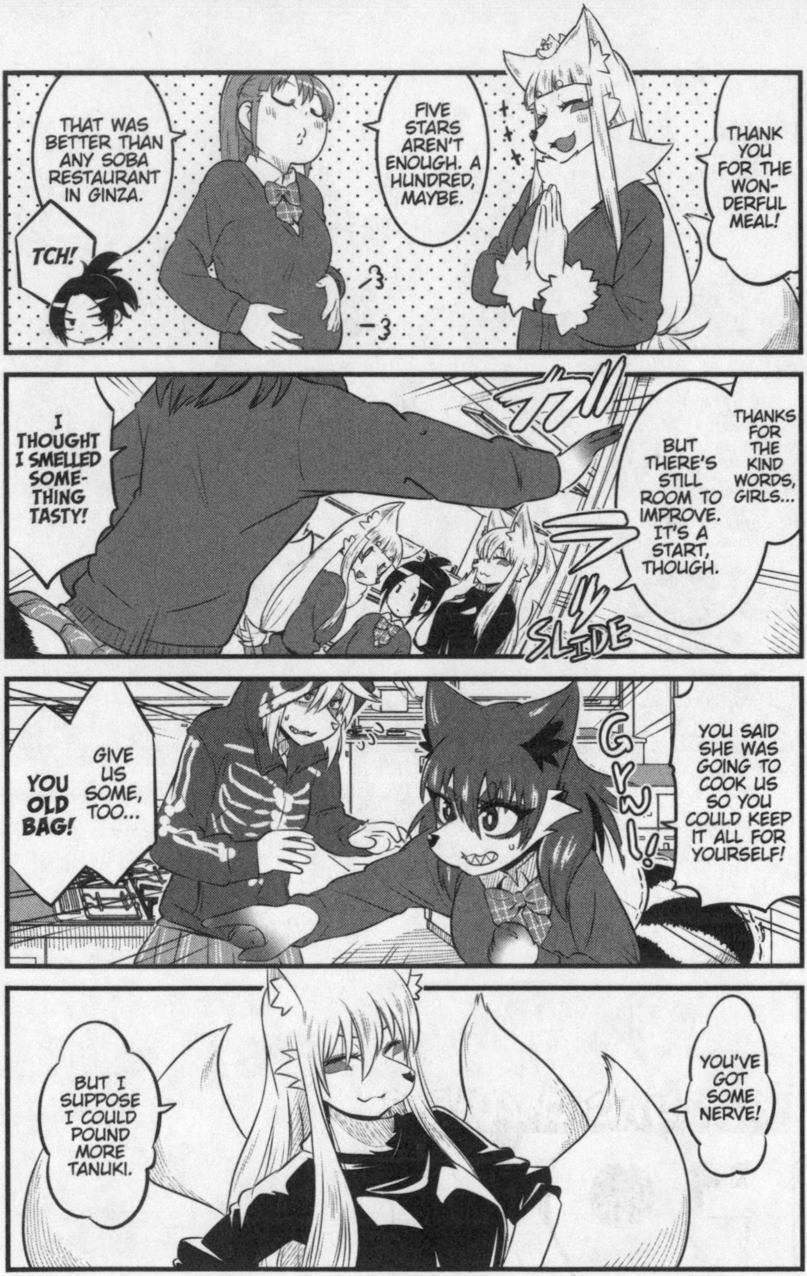
THANK YOU FOR THE WON-DERFUL MEAL!
FIVE STARS AREN'T ENOUGH. A HUNDRED, MAYBE.
THAT WAS BETTER THAN ANY SOBA RESTAURANT IN GINZA.
TCH!
THANKS FOR THE KIND WORDS, GIRLS...
BUT THERE'S STILL ROOM TO IMPROVE. IT'S A START, THOUGH.
SLIDE
I THOUGHT I SMELLED SOME-THING TASTY!
YOU SAID SHE WAS GOING TO COOK US SO YOU COULD KEEP IT ALL FOR YOURSELF!
GYWL!
GIVE US SOME, TOO...
YOU OLD BAG!
YOU'VE GOT SOME NERVE!
BUT I SUPPOSE I COULD POUND MORE TANUKI.

After trying it, Mami couldn't find any faults with Tenko-nee's soba.

OLD BAG THAT WAS RISKY! SURE, SHE'S BEEN A DIVINE FOX FOR OVER TWO THOUSAND YEARS BUT... WAIT, JUST HOW OLD IS SHE?

Tamamo-chan's a FOX!

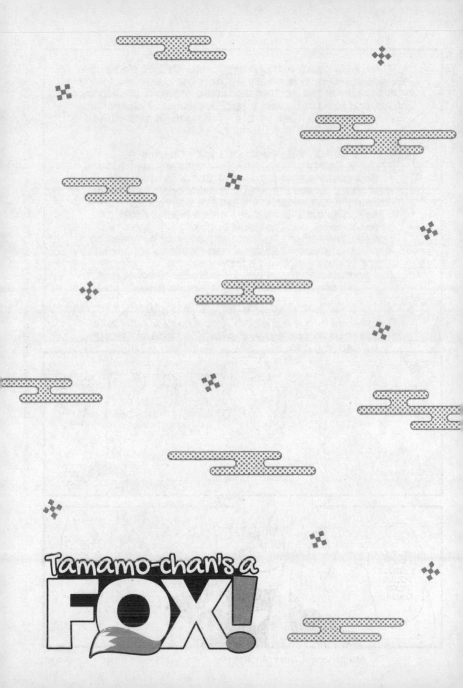

✳ P. 41, side caption: The Yamato-no-Orochi Serpent ✳
Yamato-no-Orochi is a serpent from Japanese mythology
that appears in the earliest Japanese writings. It has eight
heads and eight tails, and a huge appetite for alcohol and
human flesh. It is killed by the storm god Susano-o, who
lulls it to sleep with sake.

✳ P. 42, side caption: Lucky Charms ✳
Daruma figures are round hollow dolls modeled after
Bodhidharma, the founder of Zen Buddhism. It's
customary to make a wish and paint one of its eyes,
then paint the other eye when the wish comes true.
Beckoning cats, sometimes called "lucky cats" or
maneki neko, are Japanese bobtail cat figures with
a raised paw, often displayed in places of business to
attract customers. Festival men refers to an annual
race in Japan in which a limited number of runners
can participate. Those who do become "festival men"
and are considered lucky charms.

✳ p. 52, panel 3: Tanuki Soba ✳
Tanuki soba is not made with actual tanuki, but rather
is soba in dashi broth topped with fried bits of tempura
batter. You can also get tanuki ramen or udon.

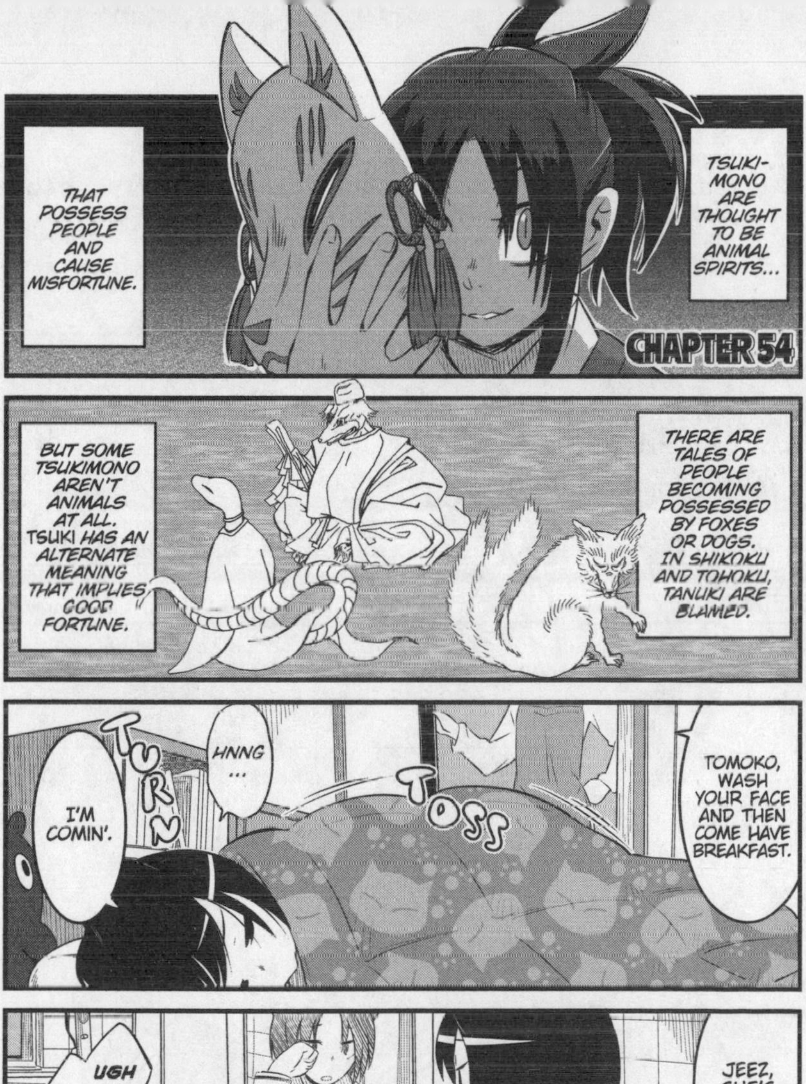
TSUKI-MONO ARE THOUGHT TO BE ANIMAL SPIRITS...
THAT POSSESS PEOPLE AND CAUSE MISFORTUNE.
CHAPTER 54
THERE ARE TALES OF PEOPLE BECOMING POSSESSED BY FOXES OR DOGS. IN SHIKOKU AND TOHOKU, TANUKI ARE BLAMED.
BUT SOME TSUKIMONO AREN'T ANIMALS AT ALL. TSUKI HAS AN ALTERNATE MEANING THAT IMPLIES GOOD FORTUNE.
TOMOKO, WASH YOUR FACE AND THEN COME HAVE BREAKFAST.
TOSS
HNNG ...
TURN
I'M COMIN'.
JEEZ, SHE'S SUCH A NAG.
UGH ... WH-WHAT THE ...?!

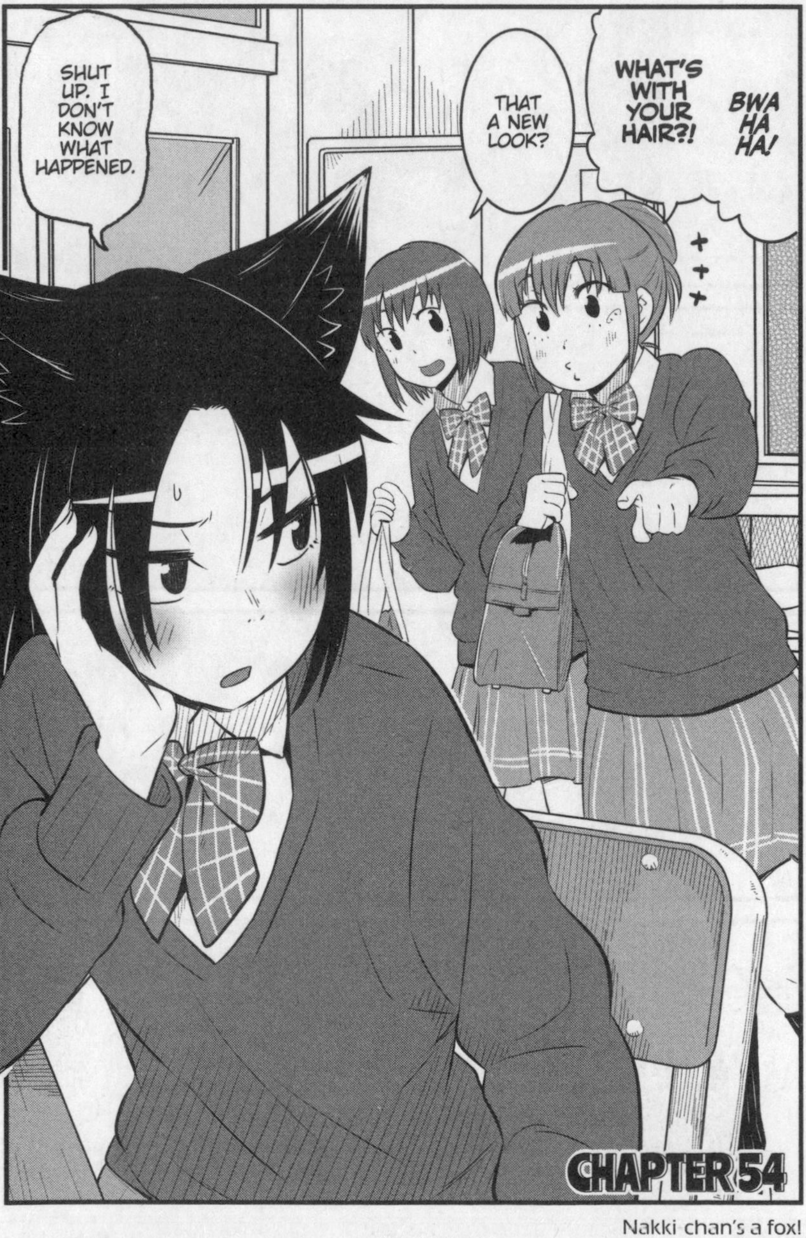
BWA HA HA!
WHAT'S WITH YOUR HAIR?!
THAT A NEW LOOK?
SHUT UP. I DON'T KNOW WHAT HAPPENED.
CHAPTER 54

Nakki-chan's a fox!

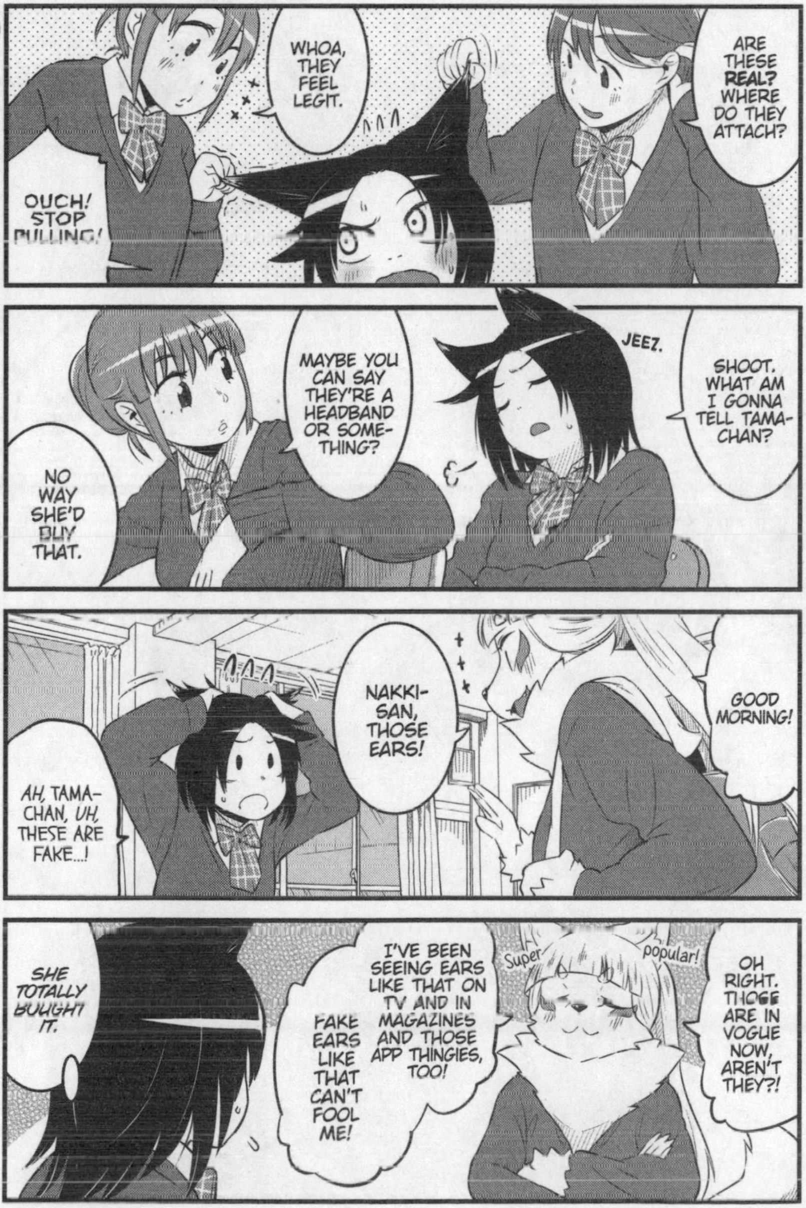
ARE THESE REAL? WHERE DO THEY ATTACH?
WHOA, THEY FEEL LEGIT.
OUCH! STOP PULLING!
SHOOT. WHAT AM I GONNA TELL TAMA-CHAN?
JEEZ.
MAYBE YOU CAN SAY THEY'RE A HEADBAND OR SOME-THING?
NO WAY SHE'D BUY THAT.
GOOD MORNING!
NAKKI-SAN, THOSE EARS!
AH, TAMA-CHAN, UH, THESE ARE FAKE...!
OH RIGHT. THOSE ARE IN VOGUE NOW, AREN'T THEY?!
Super popular!
I'VE BEEN SEEING EARS LIKE THAT ON TV AND IN MAGAZINES AND THOSE APP THINGIES, TOO!
FAKE EARS LIKE THAT CAN'T FOOL ME!
SHE TOTALLY BOUGHT IT.

DECEPTION THE JAPANESE WORD FOR DECEPTION, *GOMAKASU*, HAS AN UNCLEAR ETYMOLOGY, POSSIBLY STEMMING FROM EITHER SESAME (*GOMA*) SWEETS OR THE BUDDHIST RITUAL OF HOMA BLENDED WITH ANOTHER WORD MEANING "CONFUSION." ITS KANJI WERE CHOSEN FOR SOUND RATHER THAN MEANING AND IT'S OFTEN WRITTEN OUT WITH HIRAGANA INSTEAD.

Tamamo's overconfidence stems from her faith in her own disguise.

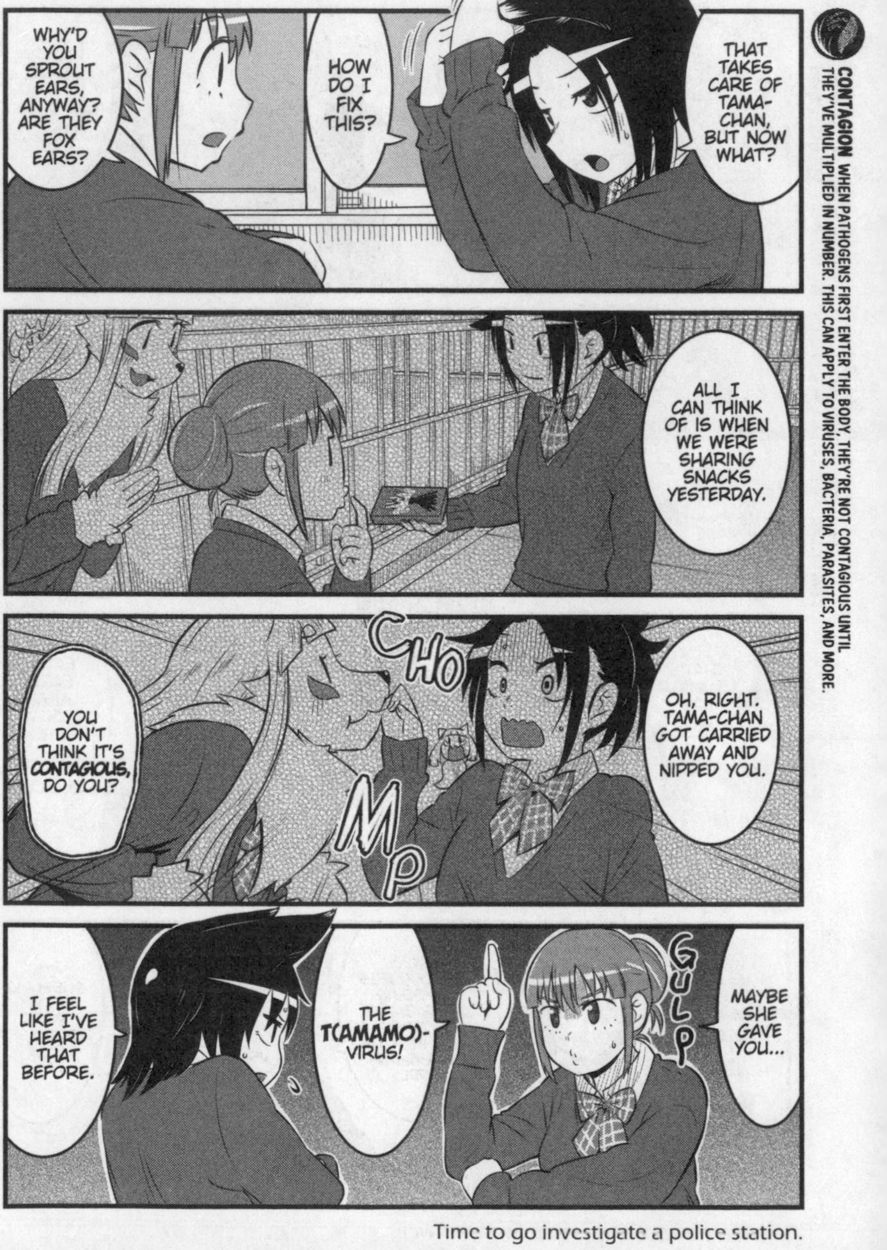
THAT TAKES CARE OF TAMA-CHAN, BUT NOW WHAT?
HOW DO I FIX THIS?
WHY'D YOU SPROUT EARS, ANYWAY? ARE THEY FOX EARS?
ALL I CAN THINK OF IS WHEN WE WERE SHARING SNACKS YESTERDAY.
OH, RIGHT. TAMA-CHAN GOT CARRIED AWAY AND NIPPED YOU.
CHOMP
YOU DON'T THINK IT'S **CONTAGIOUS,** DO YOU?
MAYBE SHE GAVE YOU...
GULP
THE **T(AMAMO)-**VIRUS!
I FEEL LIKE I'VE HEARD THAT BEFORE.

CONTAGION WHEN PATHOGENS FIRST ENTER THE BODY, THEY'RE NOT CONTAGIOUS UNTIL THEY'VE MULTIPLIED IN NUMBER. THIS CAN APPLY TO VIRUSES, BACTERIA, PARASITES, AND MORE.

Time to go investigate a police station.

TAMAMO-MODE FORGETTING HER HOMEWORK AND TEXTBOOKS, OBSESSED WITH BALLS AND FRIED TOFU... NAKKI ALMOST SEEMS LIKE SOMEONE ELSE TODAY.

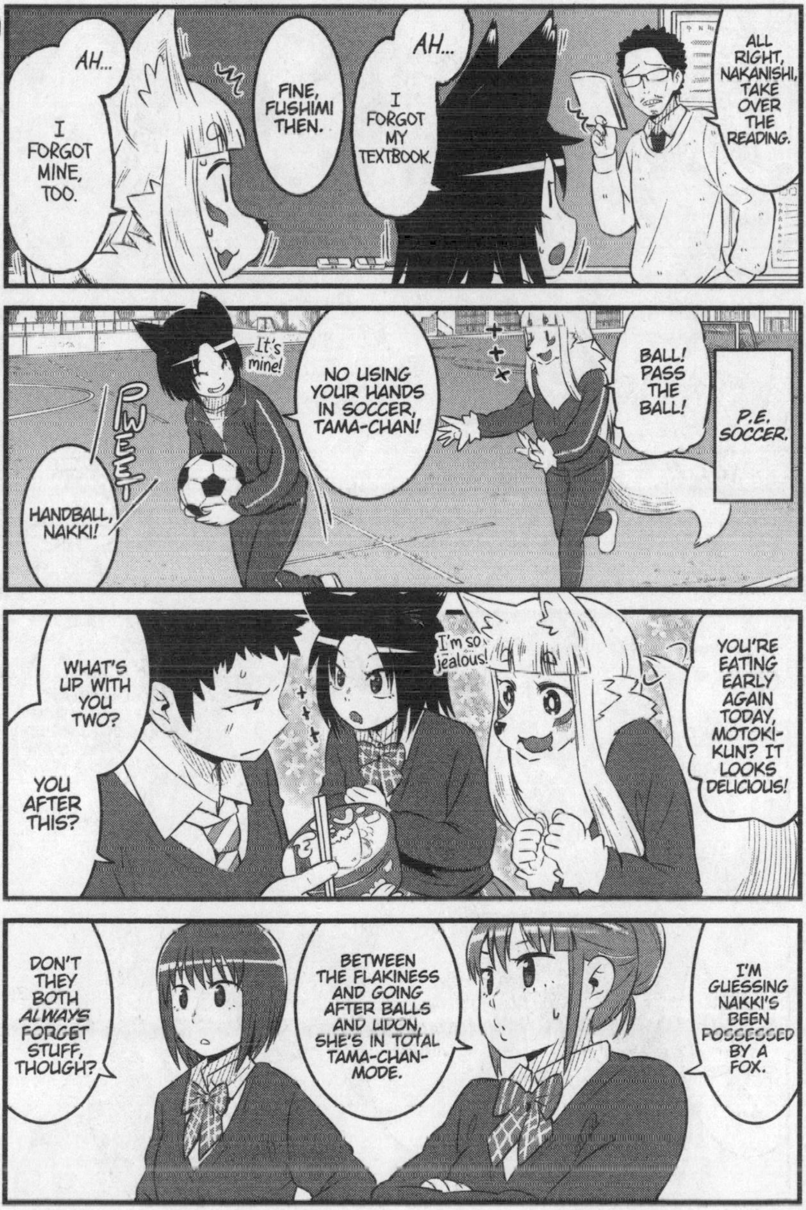
ALL RIGHT, NAKANISHI, TAKE OVER THE READING.
AH...
I FORGOT MY TEXTBOOK.
FINE, FUSHIMI THEN.
AH...
I FORGOT MINE, TOO.
P.E. SOCCER.
BALL! PASS THE BALL!
NO USING YOUR HANDS IN SOCCER, TAMA-CHAN!
It's mine!
PWEET
HANDBALL, NAKKI!
YOU'RE EATING EARLY AGAIN TODAY, MOTOKI-KUN? IT LOOKS DELICIOUS!
I'm so jealous!
WHAT'S UP WITH YOU TWO?
YOU AFTER THIS?
I'M GUESSING NAKKI'S BEEN POSSESSED BY A FOX.
BETWEEN THE FLAKINESS AND GOING AFTER BALLS AND UDON, SHE'S IN TOTAL TAMA-CHAN-MODE.
DON'T THEY BOTH *ALWAYS* FORGET STUFF, THOUGH?

Nakki seemed slightly cuter today as well.

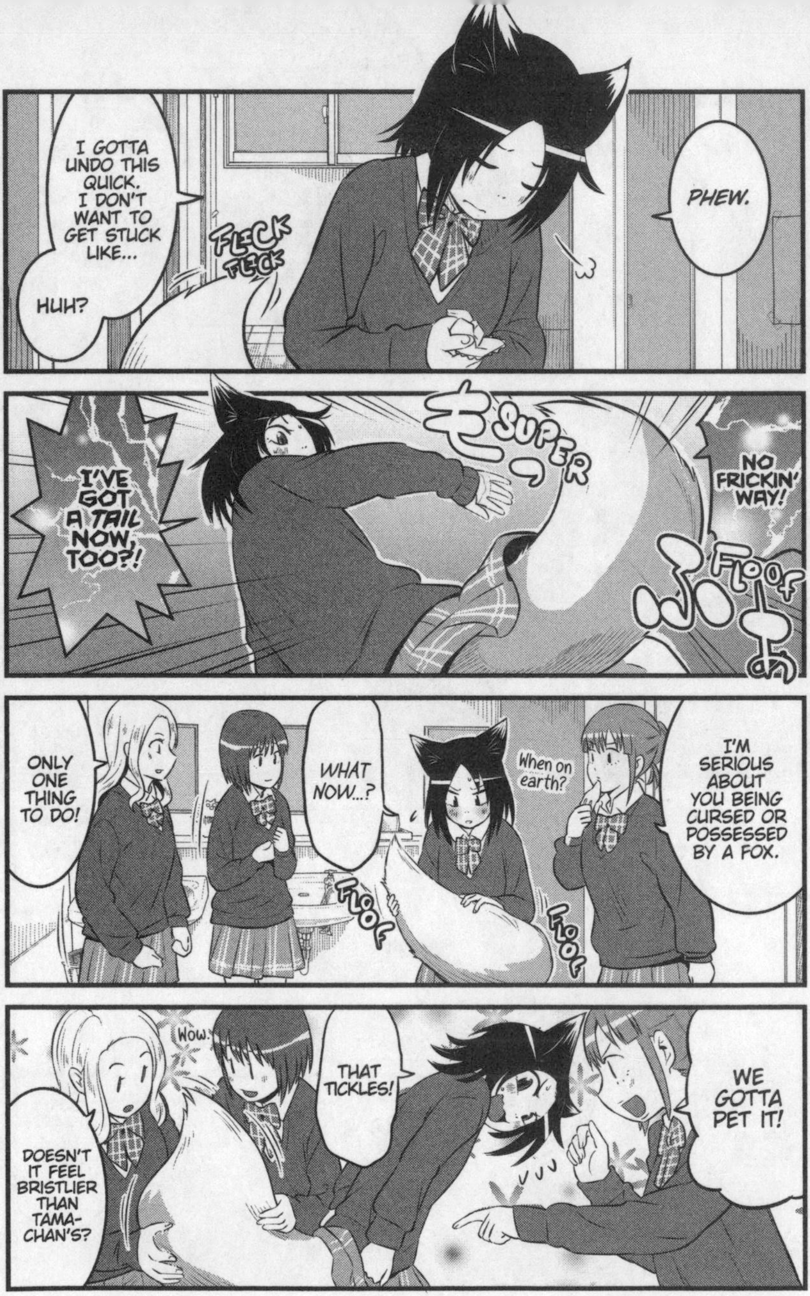
PHEW.
I GOTTA UNDO THIS QUICK. I DON'T WANT TO GET STUCK LIKE...
HUH?
FLICK FLICK
NO FRICKIN' WAY!
SUPER
FLOOF
I'VE GOT A *TAIL* NOW, TOO?!
I'M SERIOUS ABOUT YOU BEING CURSED OR POSSESSED BY A FOX.
When on earth?
FLOOF
FLOOF
WHAT NOW...?
ONLY ONE THING TO DO!
WE GOTTA PET IT!
THAT TICKLES!
Wow.
DOESN'T IT FEEL BRISTLIER THAN TAMA-CHAN'S?

TSUKIMONO TSUKIMONO IN IZUMO INCLUDE THE YAMA-MISAKI AND YABU-ITACHI, IN BIZEN THERE ARE THE INUGAMI AND HIMISAKI, AND IN BICCHU AND BINGO YOU HAVE THE TOBYO. FOX TSUKIMONO INCLUDE OSAKI, OTORA, AND KUDAGITSUNE.

They're all girls, so none of them held back.

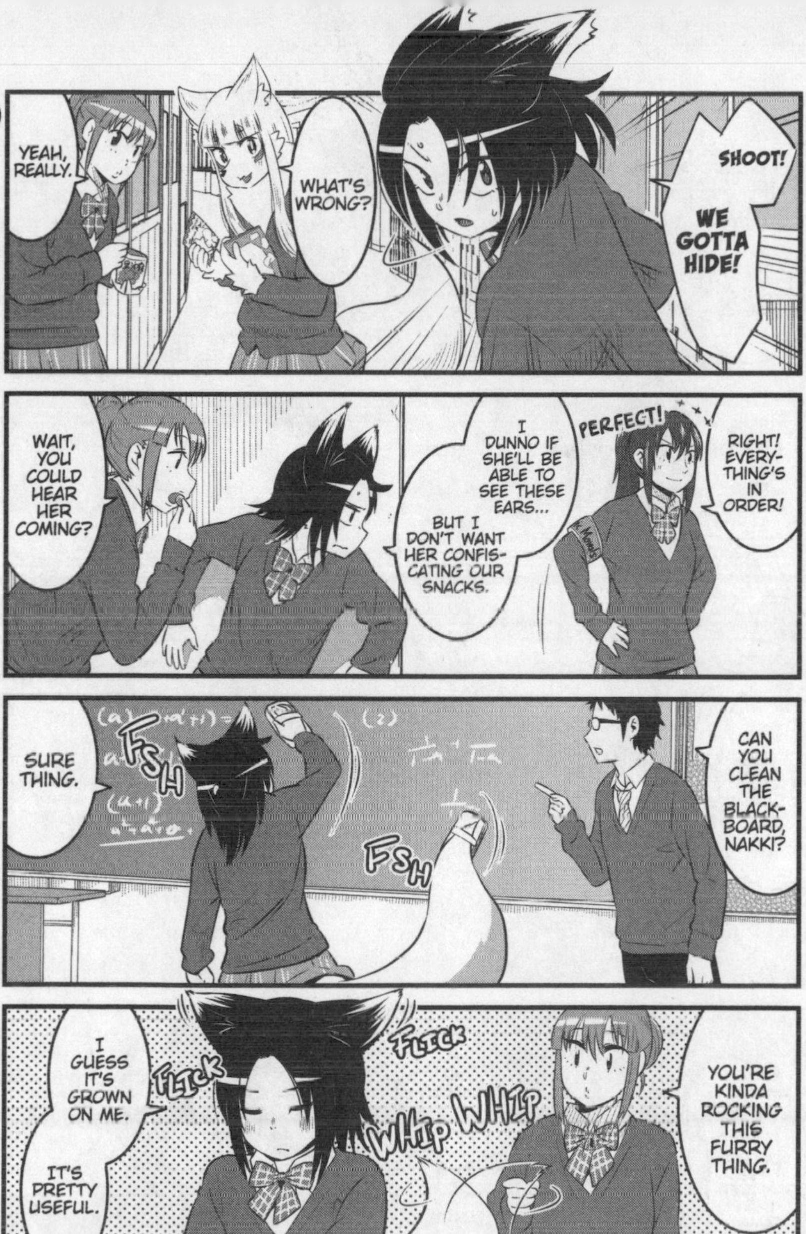
SHOOT!
WE GOTTA HIDE!
WHAT'S WRONG?
YEAH, REALLY.
RIGHT! EVERY-THING'S IN ORDER!
PERFECT!
I DUNNO IF SHE'LL BE ABLE TO SEE THESE EARS...
BUT I DON'T WANT HER CONFIS-CATING OUR SNACKS.
WAIT, YOU COULD HEAR HER COMING?
CAN YOU CLEAN THE BLACK-BOARD, NAKKI?
FSH
FSH
SURE THING.
YOU'RE KINDA ROCKING THIS FURRY THING.
WHIP WHIP
FLICK
FLICK
I GUESS IT'S GROWN ON ME.
IT'S PRETTY USEFUL.

She adapts quickly.

FOX POSSESSION TALES OF FOX POSSESSION COME FROM ALL OVER JAPAN AND ACCOUNTS CAN BE FOUND IN THE COLLECTION OF ANCIENT STORIES WRITTEN IN THE LATE HEIAN PERIOD. AN ALTERED STATE OF MOOD AND MIND ARE SAID TO OCCUR WHEN ONE IS POSSESSED BY A FOX SPIRIT.

POPULAR? THOSE FAKE EARS SURE HAVE MADE NAKKI POPULAR WITH THE BOYS! SHOULD I TRY SOME WITH MY HUMAN DISGUISE?

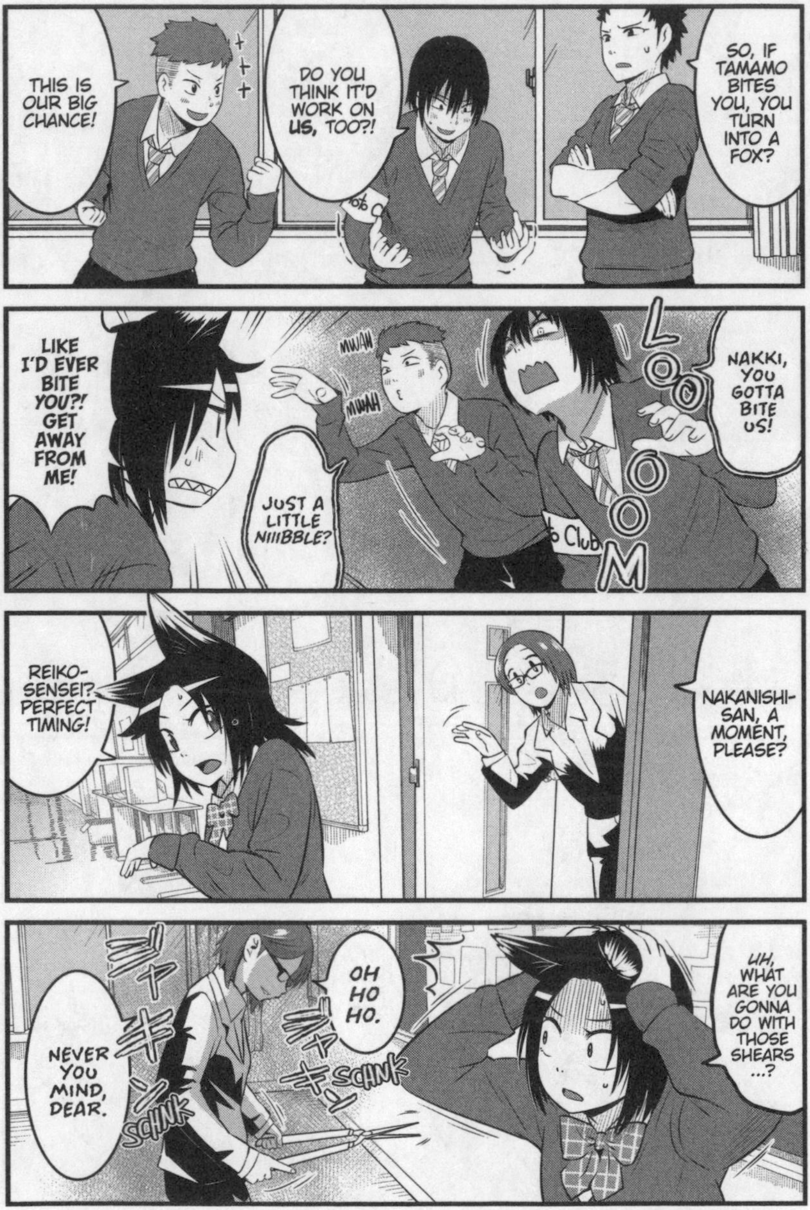
SO, IF TAMAMO BITES YOU, YOU TURN INTO A FOX?
DO YOU THINK IT'D WORK ON US, TOO?!
THIS IS OUR BIG CHANCE!
NAKKI, YOU GOTTA BITE US!
LOOOOOOOM
MWAH
MWAH
JUST A LITTLE NIIIBBLE?
LIKE I'D EVER BITE YOU?! GET AWAY FROM ME!
NAKANISHI-SAN, A MOMENT, PLEASE?
REIKO-SENSEI!? PERFECT TIMING!
UH, WHAT ARE YOU GONNA DO WITH THOSE SHEARS ...?
OH HO HO.
SCHINK
NEVER YOU MIND, DEAR.
SCHINK

Tales of a "Scissor-Fiend" were added to the school's ghost stories.

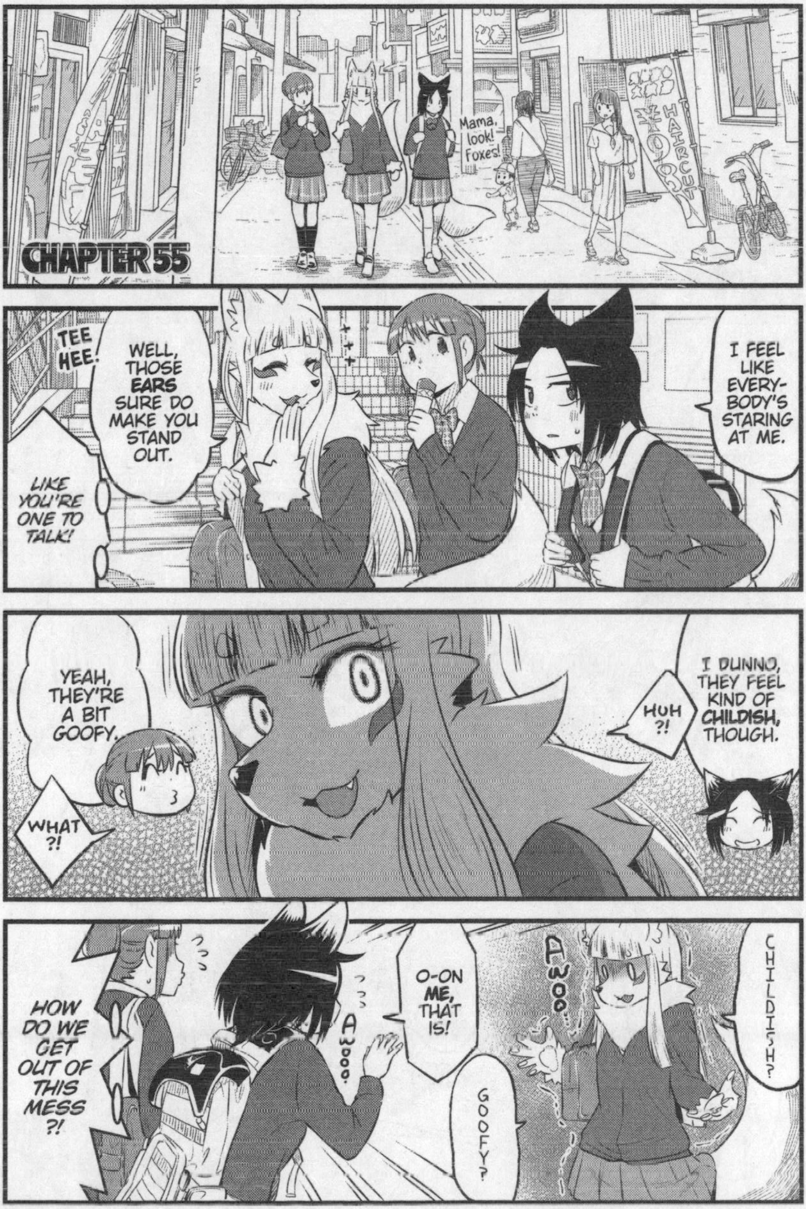
CHAPTER 55
Mama, look! Foxes!
HAIRCUT
I FEEL LIKE EVERYBODY'S STARING AT ME.
WELL, THOSE EARS SURE DO MAKE YOU STAND OUT.
TEE HEE.
LIKE YOU'RE ONE TO TALK!
I DUNNO, THEY FEEL KIND OF CHILDISH, THOUGH.
HUH ?!
YEAH, THEY'RE A BIT GOOFY.
WHAT ?!
CHILDISH?
AWOO...
GOOFY?
O-ON ME, THAT IS!
AWOOO.
HOW DO WE GET OUT OF THIS MESS ?!

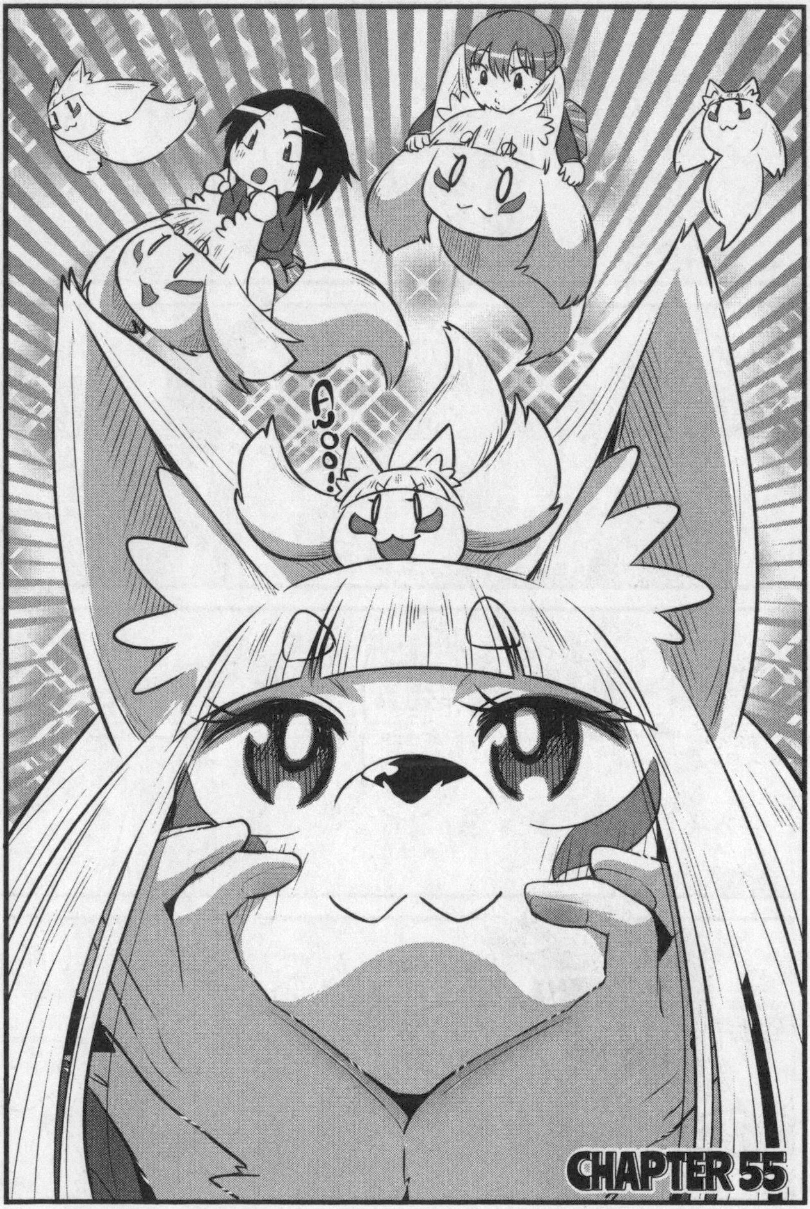
AWOO!
CHAPTER 55

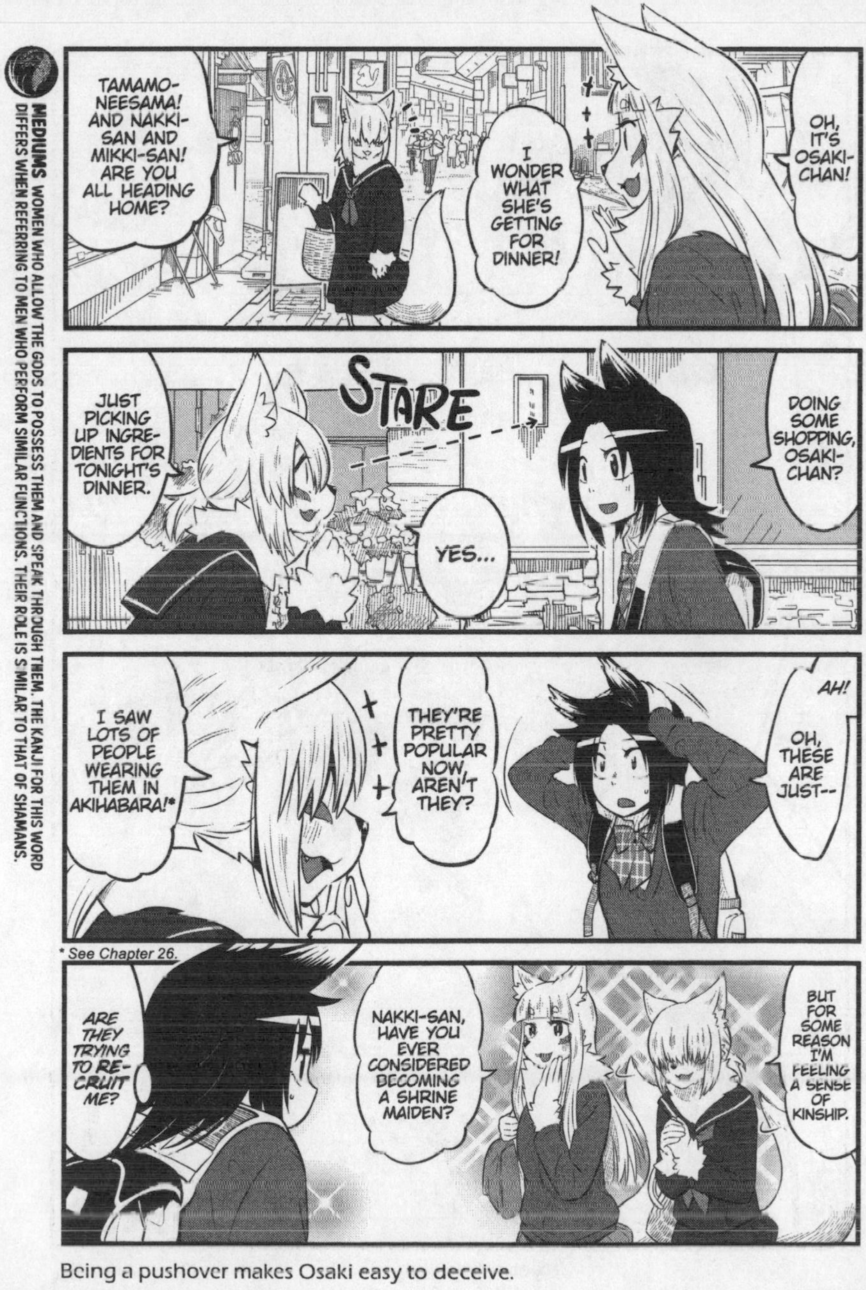
OH, IT'S OSAKI-CHAN!
I WONDER WHAT SHE'S GETTING FOR DINNER!
TAMAMO-NEESAMA! AND NAKKI-SAN AND MIKKI-SAN! ARE YOU ALL HEADING HOME?
DOING SOME SHOPPING, OSAKI-CHAN?
STARE
YES...
JUST PICKING UP INGREDIENTS FOR TONIGHT'S DINNER.
AH!
OH, THESE ARE JUST--
THEY'RE PRETTY POPULAR NOW, AREN'T THEY?
I SAW LOTS OF PEOPLE WEARING THEM IN AKIHABARA!*
BUT FOR SOME REASON I'M FEELING A SENSE OF KINSHIP.
NAKKI-SAN, HAVE YOU EVER CONSIDERED BECOMING A SHRINE MAIDEN?
ARE THEY TRYING TO RE-CRUIT ME?

MEDIUMS WOMEN WHO ALLOW THE GODS TO POSSESS THEM AND SPEAK THROUGH THEM. THE KANJI FOR THIS WORD DIFFERS WHEN REFERRING TO MEN WHO PERFORM SIMILAR FUNCTIONS. THEIR ROLE IS S MILAR TO THAT OF SHAMANS.

** See Chapter 26.*

Being a pushover makes Osaki easy to deceive.

TSUKI (LUCK) AN UNCONTROLLABLE ELEMENT THAT CAN TIP THE BALANCE TOWARDS FORTUNE OR SORROW. COMMONLY USED WHEN REFERRING TO COMPETITIONS.

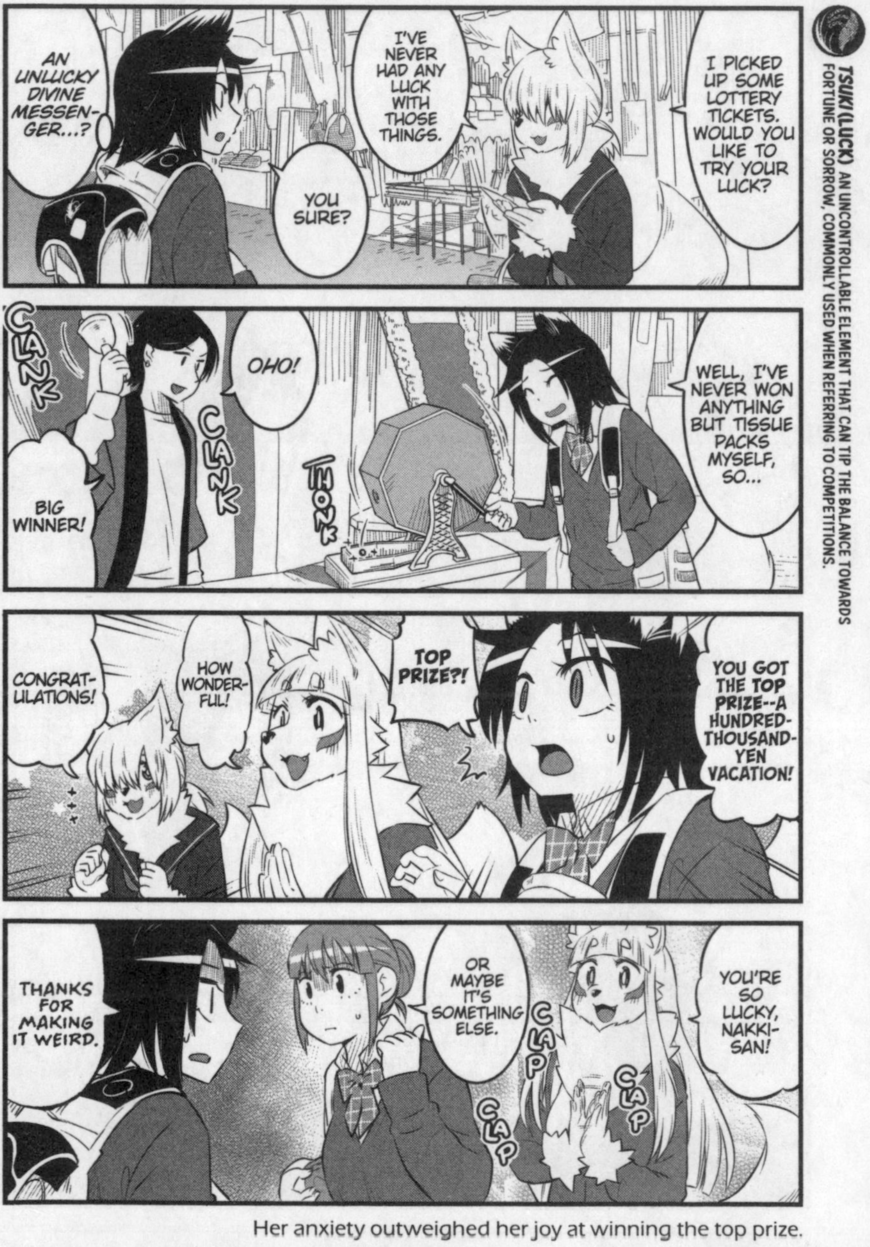
I PICKED UP SOME LOTTERY TICKETS. WOULD YOU LIKE TO TRY YOUR LUCK?
I'VE NEVER HAD ANY LUCK WITH THOSE THINGS.
YOU SURE?
AN UNLUCKY DIVINE MESSENGER...?
WELL, I'VE NEVER WON ANYTHING BUT TISSUE PACKS MYSELF, SO...
THONK
CLANK
OHO!
BIG WINNER!
CLANK
YOU GOT THE TOP PRIZE--A HUNDRED-THOUSAND-YEN VACATION!
TOP PRIZE?!
HOW WONDERFUL!
CONGRATULATIONS!
YOU'RE SO LUCKY, NAKKI-SAN!
CLAP
CLAP
OR MAYBE IT'S SOMETHING ELSE.
CLAP
CLAP
THANKS FOR MAKING IT WEIRD.

Her anxiety outweighed her joy at winning the top prize.

WORLD OF THE GODS IF THE GODS RESIDE IN ALL THINGS, PERHAPS OTHER BEINGS BESIDES THE WHITE FOX MESSENGERS MIGHT BE WANDERING AROUND...

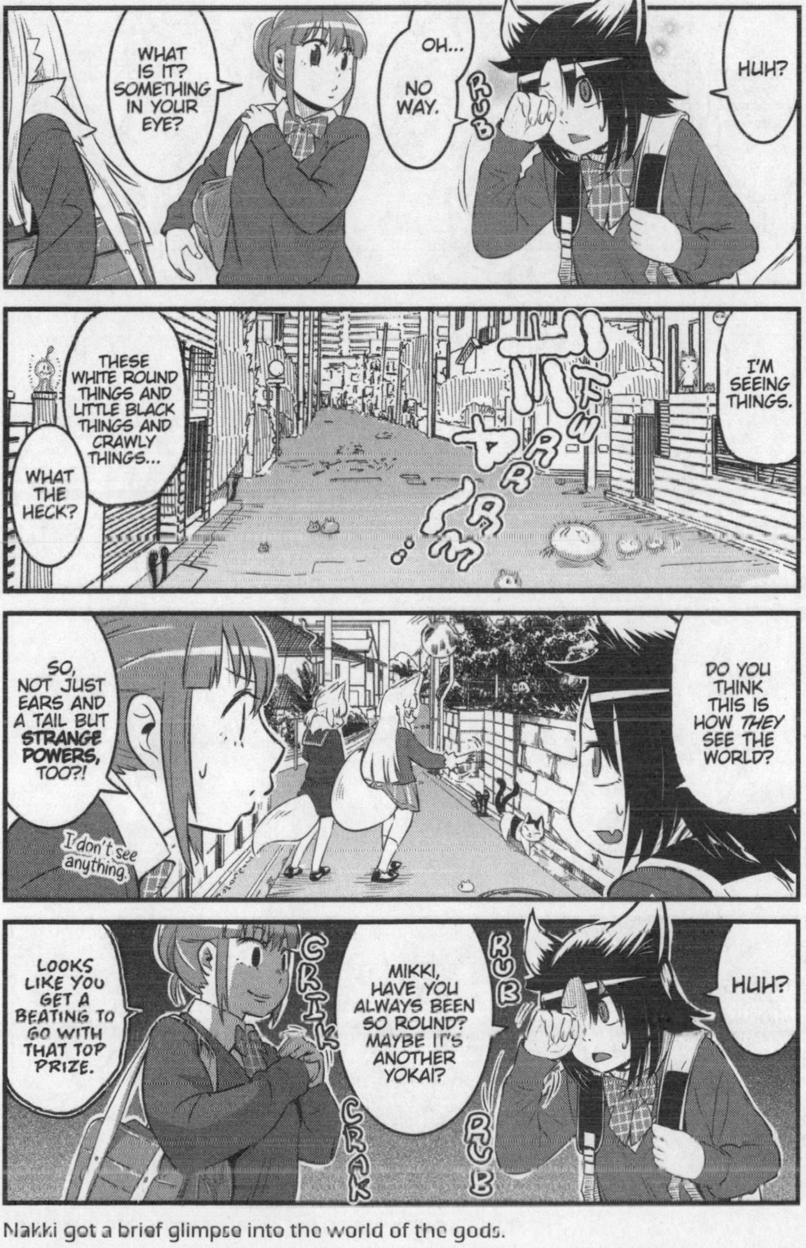
HUH?
OH... NO WAY.
RUB
WHAT IS IT? SOMETHING IN YOUR EYE?
I'M SEEING THINGS.
FWAAAM
THESE WHITE ROUND THINGS AND LITTLE BLACK THINGS AND CRAWLY THINGS...
WHAT THE HECK?
DO YOU THINK THIS IS HOW *THEY* SEE THE WORLD?
SO, NOT JUST EARS AND A TAIL BUT **STRANGE POWERS**, TOO?!
I don't see anything.
HUH?
RUB
RUB
MIKKI, HAVE YOU ALWAYS BEEN SO ROUND? MAYBE IT'S ANOTHER YOKAI?
CRIK
CRAK
LOOKS LIKE YOU GET A BEATING TO GO WITH THAT TOP PRIZE.

Nakki got a brief glimpse into the world of the gods.

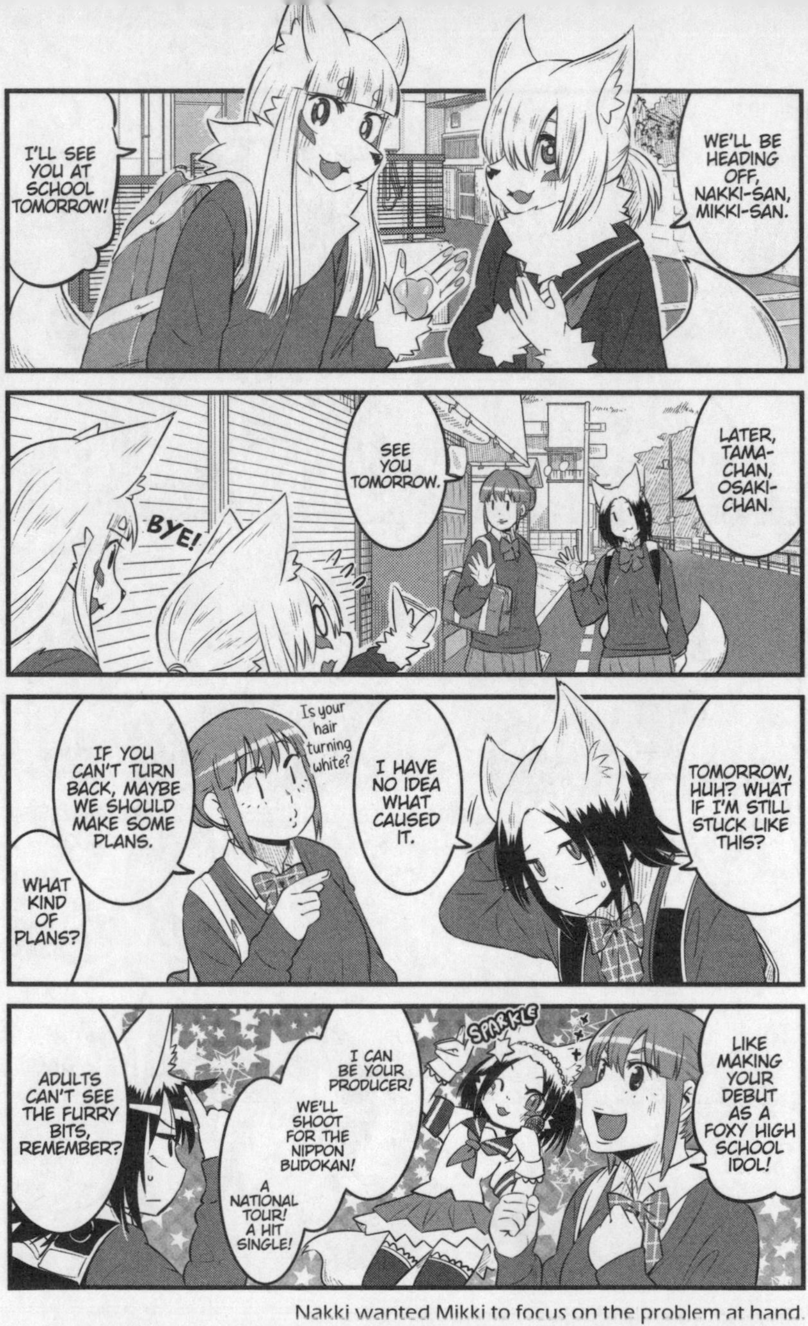
WE'LL BE HEADING OFF, NAKKI-SAN, MIKKI-SAN.
I'LL SEE YOU AT SCHOOL TOMORROW!
LATER, TAMA-CHAN, OSAKI-CHAN.
SEE YOU TOMORROW.
BYE!
TOMORROW, HUH? WHAT IF I'M STILL STUCK LIKE THIS?
I HAVE NO IDEA WHAT CAUSED IT.
Is your hair turning white?
IF YOU CAN'T TURN BACK, MAYBE WE SHOULD MAKE SOME PLANS.
WHAT KIND OF PLANS?
LIKE MAKING YOUR DEBUT AS A FOXY HIGH SCHOOL IDOL!
SPARKLE
I CAN BE YOUR PRODUCER!
WE'LL SHOOT FOR THE NIPPON BUDOKAN!
A NATIONAL TOUR! A HIT SINGLE!
ADULTS CAN'T SEE THE FURRY BITS, REMEMBER?

Nakki wanted Mikki to focus on the problem at hand.

IDOLS IMAGES OR REPRESENTATIONS OF GODS THAT ARE SOMETIMES WORSHIPPED IN THEIR STEAD. AS IDOLS ARE NOT THE ACTUAL GODS, SOME FAITHS FORBID THEIR WORSHIP.

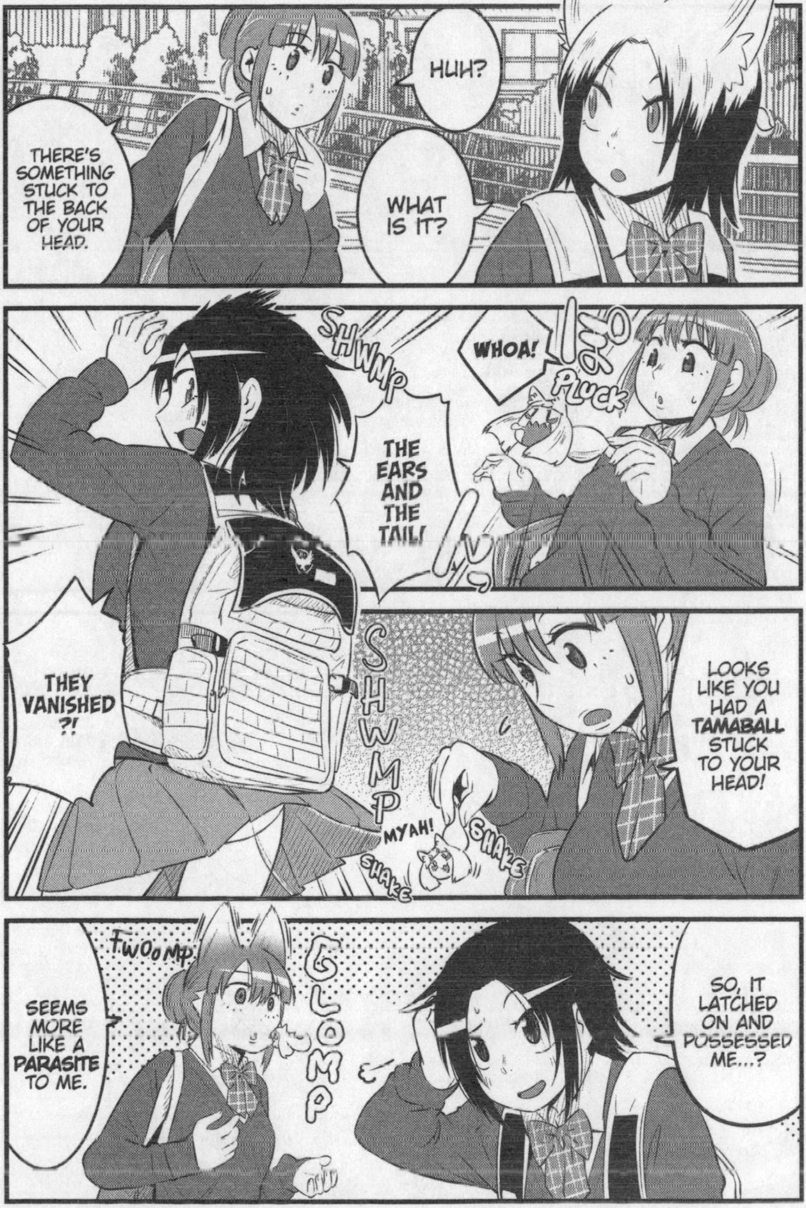
HUH?
WHAT IS IT?
THERE'S SOMETHING STUCK TO THE BACK OF YOUR HEAD.
WHOA!
PLUCK
SHWMP
THE EARS AND THE TAIL!
LOOKS LIKE YOU HAD A TAMABALL STUCK TO YOUR HEAD!
SHWMP
MYAH!
SHAKE
SHAKE
THEY VANISHED?!
SO, IT LATCHED ON AND POSSESSED ME...?
GLOMP
FWOOMP
SEEMS MORE LIKE A PARASITE TO ME.

TSUKIMONO LINEAGE A FOLK BELIEF THAT SOME FAMILIES GAINED THEIR FORTUNES THROUGH SPIRIT POSSESSIONS. IF A FAMILY WAS THOUGHT TO HAVE DONE THIS, THEY'D BE ABHORRED AND SHUNNED BY THE COMMUNITY.

They were just relieved that it wasn't the T-Virus.

OH WELL... OSAKI-CHAN AND I WERE GOING TO SUGGEST THAT NAKKI BECOME A SHRINE MAIDEN, BUT I GUESS THOSE EARS WEREN'T ACTUALLY FOX EARS.

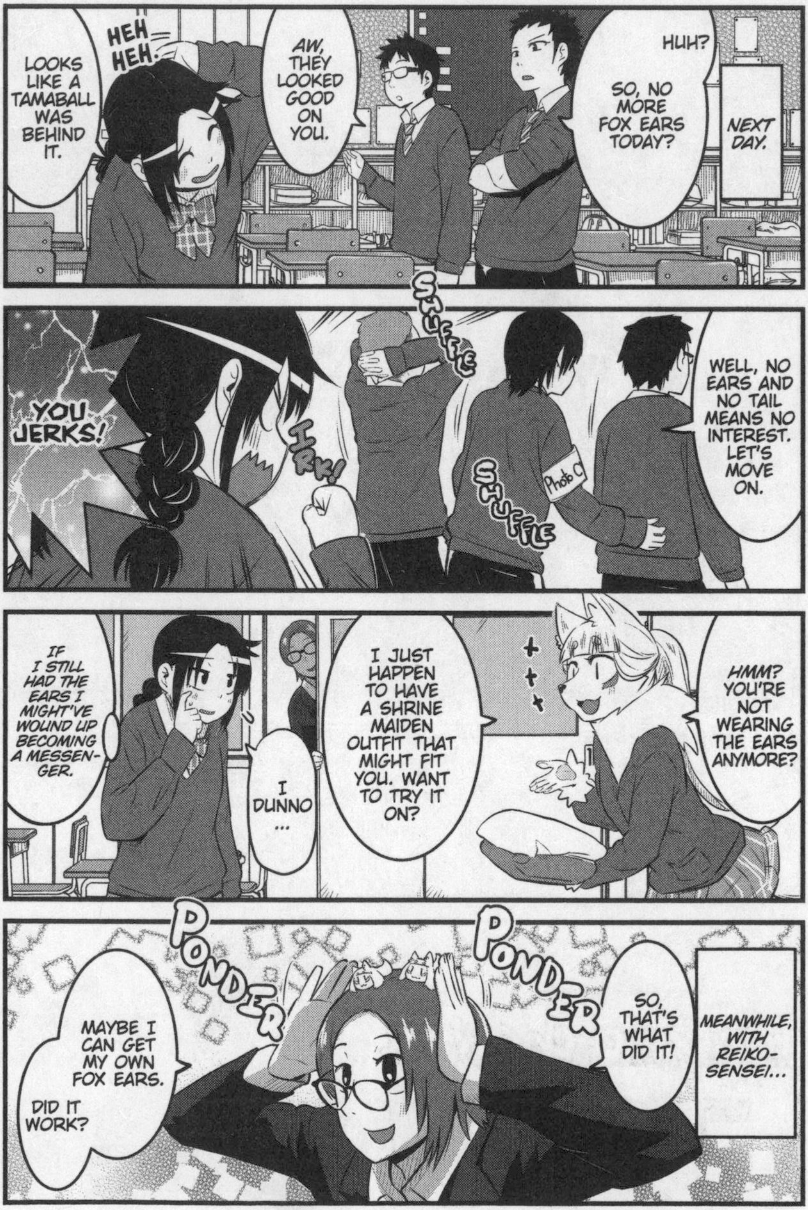
NEXT DAY.
HUH?
SO, NO MORE FOX EARS TODAY?
AW, THEY LOOKED GOOD ON YOU.
HEH HEH.
LOOKS LIKE A TAMABALL WAS BEHIND IT.
WELL, NO EARS AND NO TAIL MEANS NO INTEREST. LET'S MOVE ON.
SHUFFLE
Photo C
SHUFFLE
IRK!
YOU JERKS!
HMM? YOU'RE NOT WEARING THE EARS ANYMORE?
I JUST HAPPEN TO HAVE A SHRINE MAIDEN OUTFIT THAT MIGHT FIT YOU. WANT TO TRY IT ON?
I DUNNO...
IF I STILL HAD THE EARS I MIGHT'VE WOUND UP BECOMING A MESSEN-GER.
MEANWHILE, WITH REIKO-SENSEI...
SO, THAT'S WHAT DID IT!
PONDER
PONDER
MAYBE I CAN GET MY OWN FOX EARS.
DID IT WORK?

She wore the Tamaballs all day but nothing happened.

Tamamo-chan's a FOX!

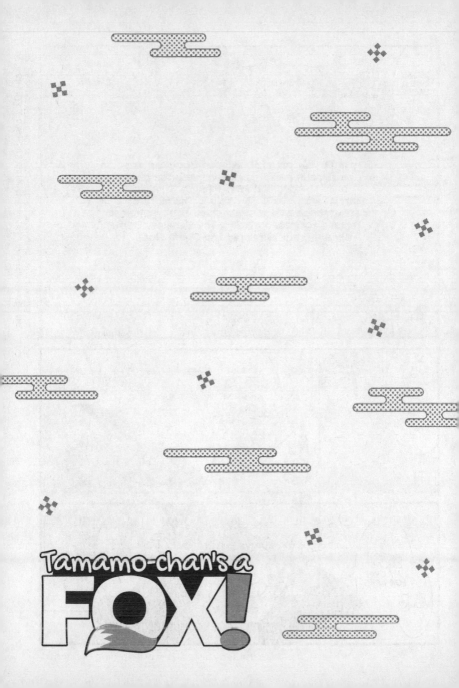

* P. 70, panel 4, Nippon Budokan *
A famous performance venue originally
built to host the 1964 Tokyo Olympic
martial arts event. It has become more of a
performance stage since then, hosting many
famous figures, including The Beatles, Bob
Dylan, Frank Sinatra, and Diana Ross.

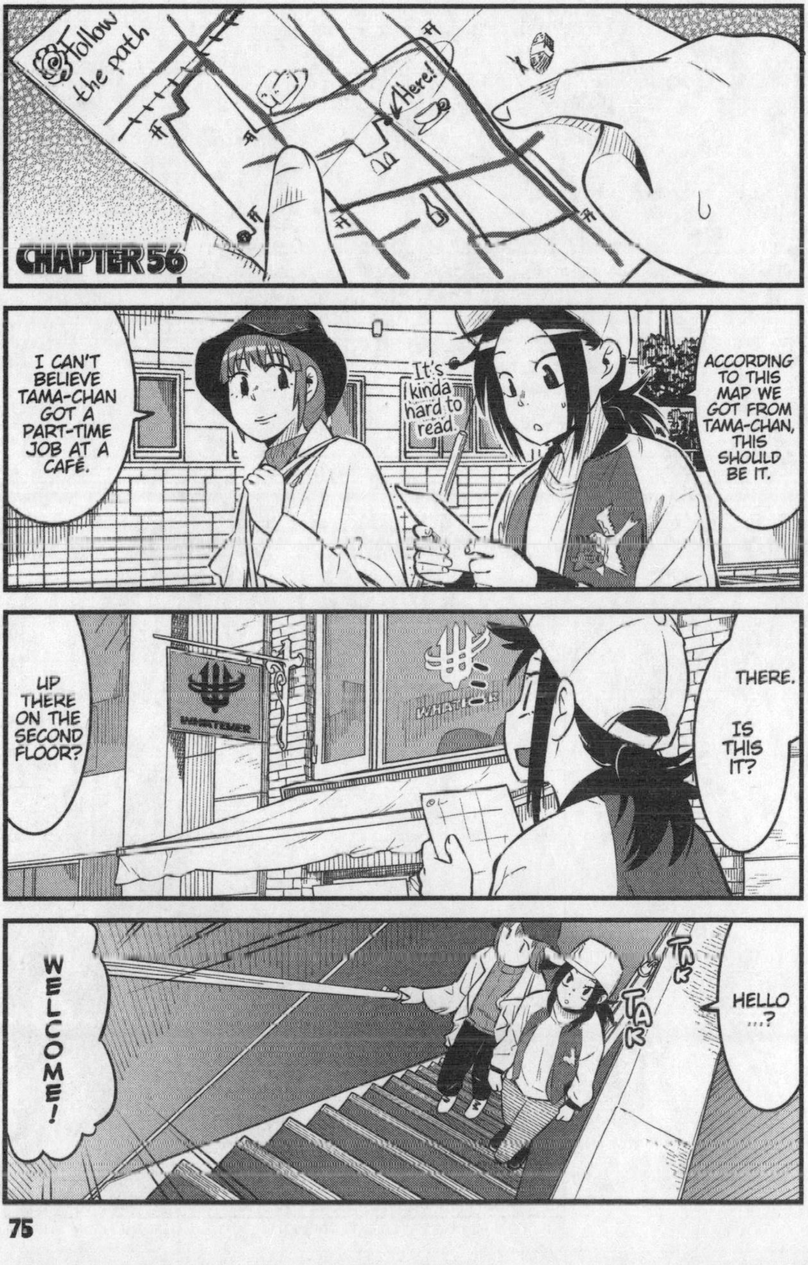
Follow the path
Here!
CHAPTER 56
ACCORDING TO THIS MAP WE GOT FROM TAMA-CHAN, THIS SHOULD BE IT.
It's kinda hard to read.
I CAN'T BELIEVE TAMA-CHAN GOT A PART-TIME JOB AT A CAFÉ.
THERE.
IS THIS IT?
UP THERE ON THE SECOND FLOOR?
HELLO ...?
TAK
TAK
WELCOME!

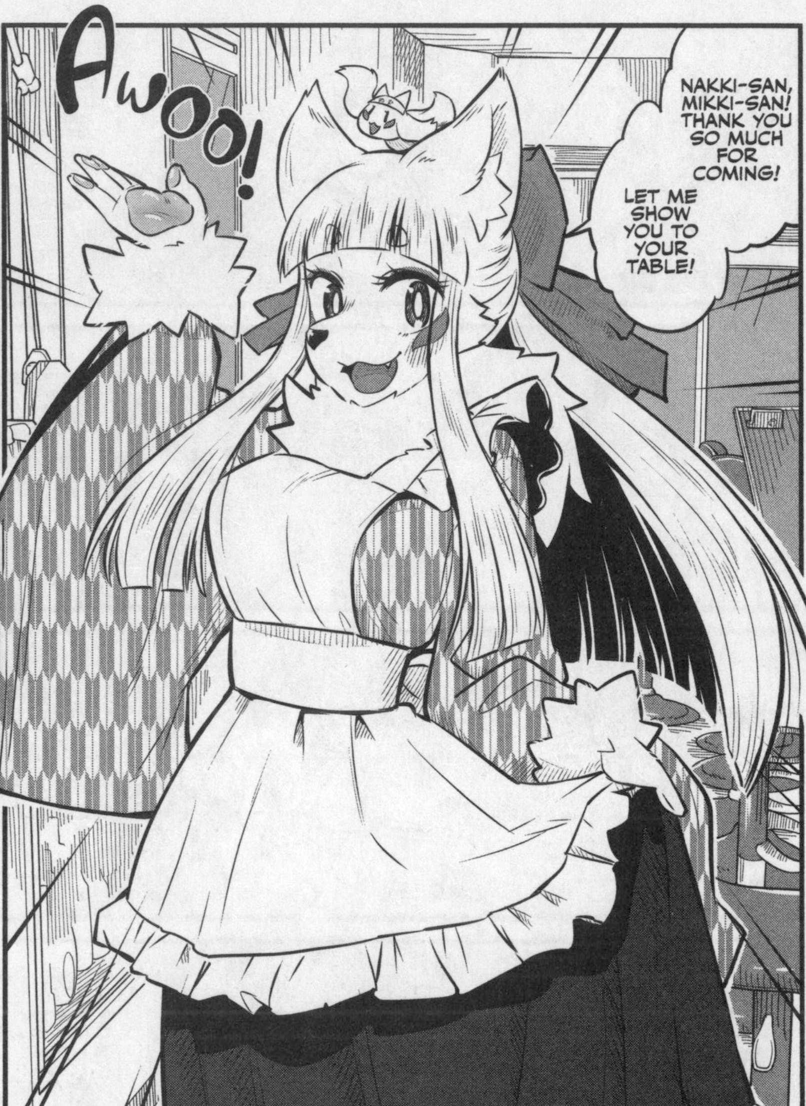
AWOO!
NAKKI-SAN, MIKKI-SAN! THANK YOU SO MUCH FOR COMING!
LET ME SHOW YOU TO YOUR TABLE!
CHAPTER 56

A poster girl straight out of Fushimi Inari Shrine

KISSATEN JAPANESE FOR "CAFÉ." THE FIRST WESTERN-STYLE CAFÉ IN JAPAN WAS A COFFEE SHOP THAT OPENED IN 1888. NOWADAYS THERE ARE CAFÉS WITH ALL SORTS OF THEMES, INCLUDING JAZZ AND MANGA.

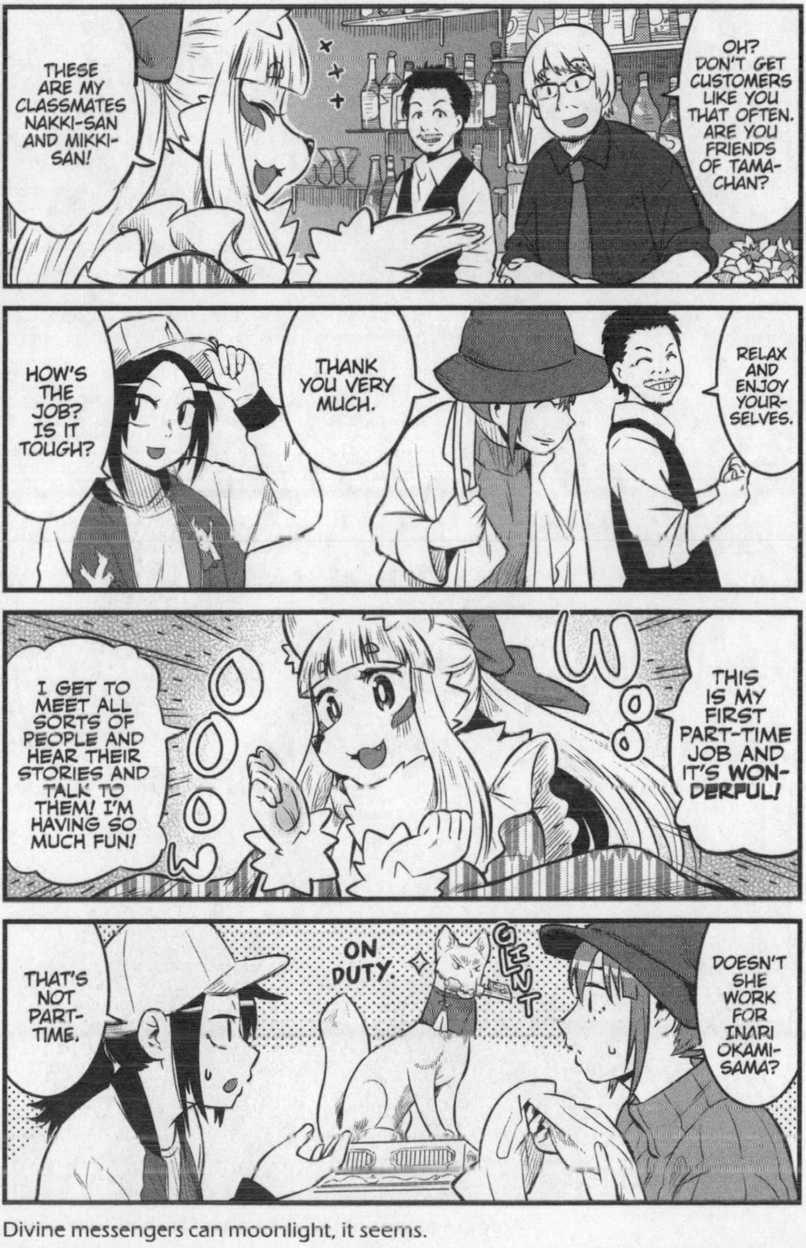
OH? DON'T GET CUSTOMERS LIKE YOU THAT OFTEN. ARE YOU FRIENDS OF TAMA-CHAN?
THESE ARE MY CLASSMATES NAKKI-SAN AND MIKKI-SAN!
RELAX AND ENJOY YOURSELVES.
THANK YOU VERY MUCH.
HOW'S THE JOB? IS IT TOUGH?
THIS IS MY FIRST PART-TIME JOB AND IT'S **WONDERFUL!**
Woo
OOOW
I GET TO MEET ALL SORTS OF PEOPLE AND HEAR THEIR STORIES AND TALK TO THEM! I'M HAVING SO MUCH FUN!
DOESN'T SHE WORK FOR INARI OKAMI-SAMA?
GLINT
ON DUTY.
THAT'S NOT PART-TIME.

Divine messengers can moonlight, it seems.

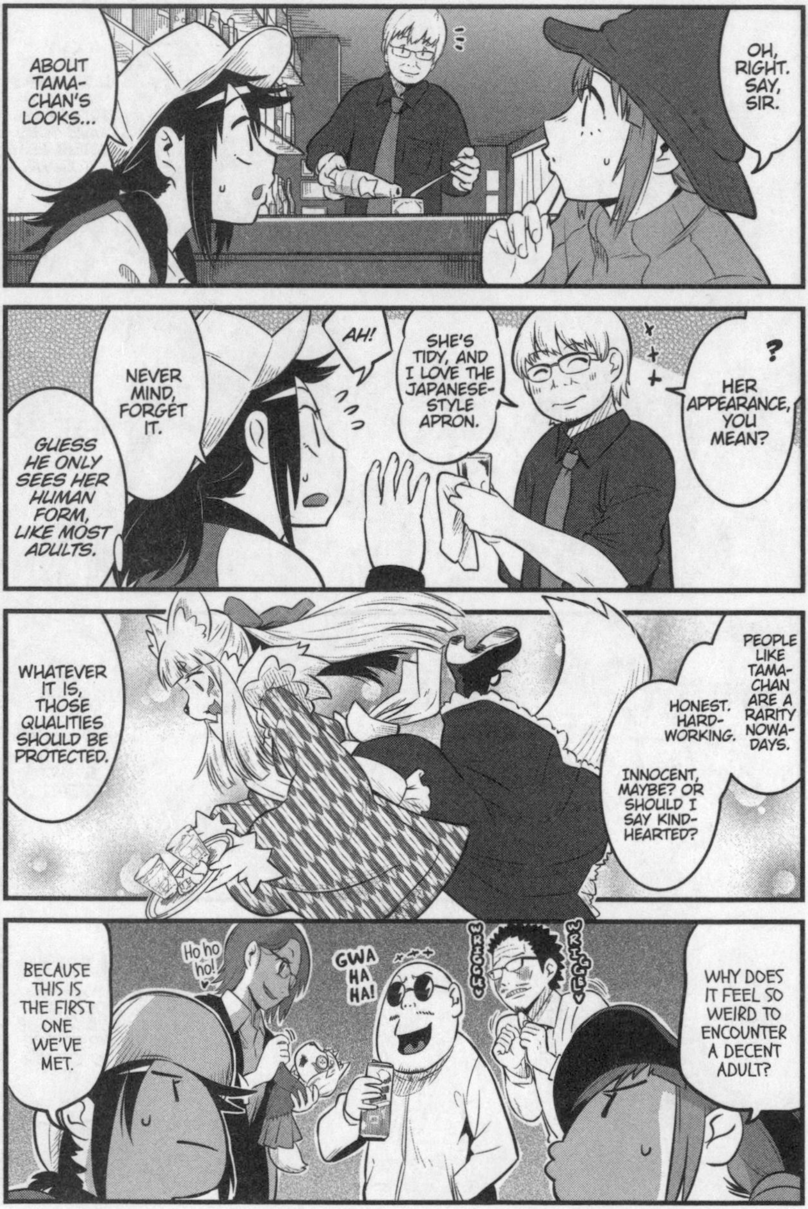
OH, RIGHT. SAY, SIR.
ABOUT TAMA-CHAN'S LOOKS...
HER APPEARANCE, YOU MEAN?
SHE'S TIDY, AND I LOVE THE JAPANESE-STYLE APRON.
AH!
NEVER MIND, FORGET IT.
GUESS HE ONLY SEES HER HUMAN FORM, LIKE MOST ADULTS.
PEOPLE LIKE TAMA-CHAN ARE A RARITY NOWADAYS.
HONEST. HARD-WORKING.
INNOCENT, MAYBE? OR SHOULD I SAY KIND-HEARTED?
WHATEVER IT IS, THOSE QUALITIES SHOULD BE PROTECTED.
WHY DOES IT FEEL SO WEIRD TO ENCOUNTER A DECENT ADULT?
WRIGGLE
WRIGGLE
GWA HA HA!
Ho ho ho!
BECAUSE THIS IS THE FIRST ONE WE'VE MET.

CAFÉ ORIGINALLY JUST COFFEE SHOPS, MOST CAFÉS ARE NOW SPOTS WHERE YOU CAN ENJOY A LIGHT MEAL. IN ITALY AND SPAIN, CAFÉS ARE SOMETIMES CALLED "BARS," INDICATING THAT THEY ALSO SERVE ALCOHOL.

They don't consider their teachers to be decent adults.

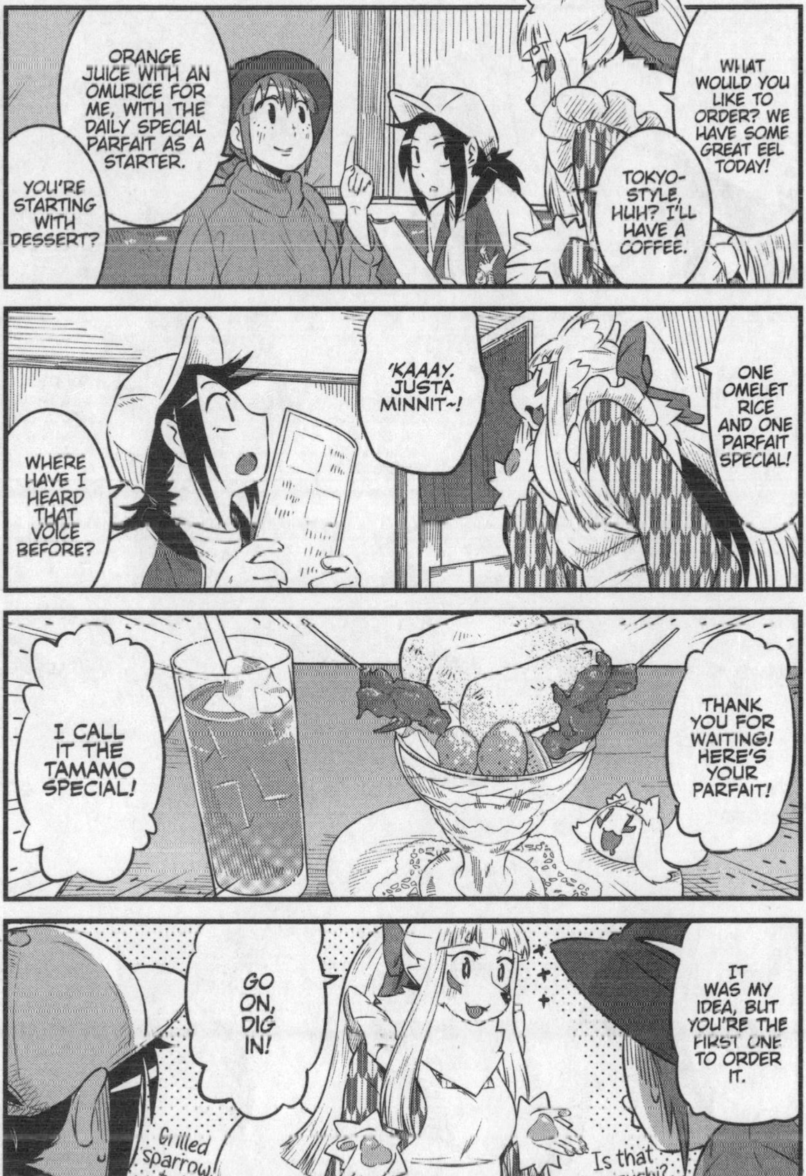
WHAT WOULD YOU LIKE TO ORDER? WE HAVE SOME GREAT EEL TODAY!
TOKYO-STYLE, HUH? I'LL HAVE A COFFEE.
ORANGE JUICE WITH AN OMURICE FOR ME, WITH THE DAILY SPECIAL PARFAIT AS A STARTER.
YOU'RE STARTING WITH DESSERT?
ONE OMELET RICE AND ONE PARFAIT SPECIAL!
'KAAAY. JUSTA MINNIT~!
WHERE HAVE I HEARD THAT VOICE BEFORE?
THANK YOU FOR WAITING! HERE'S YOUR PARFAIT!
I CALL IT THE TAMAMO SPECIAL!
IT WAS MY IDEA, BUT YOU'RE THE FIRST ONE TO ORDER IT.
GO ON, DIG IN!
Is that inarizushi?
Grilled sparrow, too.

PARFAIT THE WORD COMES FROM THE FRENCH AND MEANS A DESSERT MADE WITH ICE CREAM, FRUIT, AND OTHER GOODIES. IN AMERICA, THEY'RE CALLED "SUNDAES."

Individually they all taste great, but together...

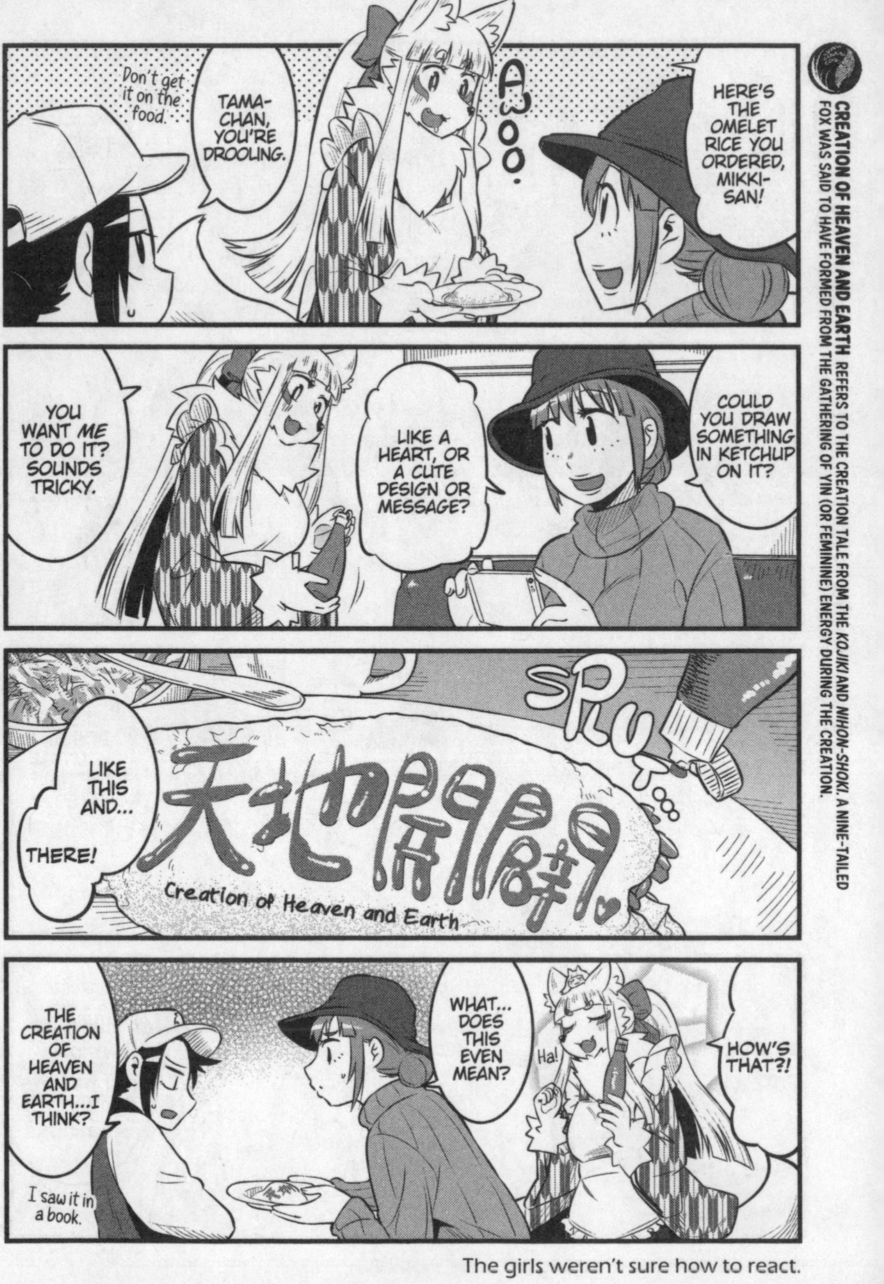
HERE'S THE OMELET RICE YOU ORDERED, MIKKI-SAN!
AWOOO.
TAMA-CHAN, YOU'RE DROOLING.
Don't get it on the food.
COULD YOU DRAW SOMETHING IN KETCHUP ON IT?
LIKE A HEART, OR A CUTE DESIGN OR MESSAGE?
YOU WANT *ME* TO DO IT? SOUNDS TRICKY.
SPLUT...
天地開闢
LIKE THIS AND...
THERE!
Creation of Heaven and Earth
HOW'S THAT?!
Ha!
WHAT... DOES THIS EVEN MEAN?
THE CREATION OF HEAVEN AND EARTH...I THINK?
I saw it in a book.

CREATION OF HEAVEN AND EARTH REFERS TO THE CREATION TALE FROM THE *KOJIKI* AND *NIHON-SHOKI*. A NINE-TAILED FOX WAS SAID TO HAVE FORMED FROM THE GATHERING OF YIN (OR FEMININE) ENERGY DURING THE CREATION.

The girls weren't sure how to react.

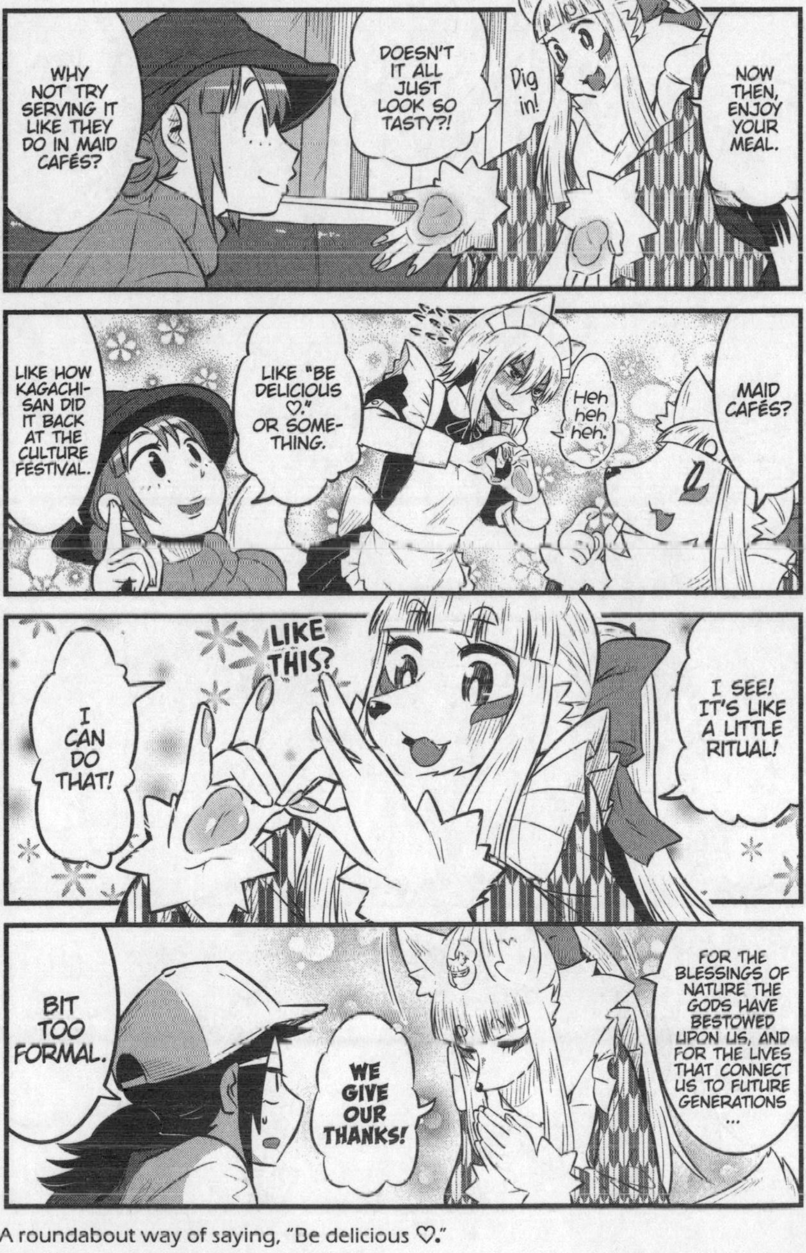
NOW THEN, ENJOY YOUR MEAL.
Dig in!
DOESN'T IT ALL JUST LOOK SO TASTY?!
WHY NOT TRY SERVING IT LIKE THEY DO IN MAID CAFÉS?
MAID CAFÉS?
Heh heh heh.
LIKE "BE DELICIOUS ♡." OR SOME-THING.
LIKE HOW KAGACHI-SAN DID IT BACK AT THE CULTURE FESTIVAL.
I SEE! IT'S LIKE A LITTLE RITUAL!
LIKE THIS?
I CAN DO THAT!
FOR THE BLESSINGS OF NATURE THE GODS HAVE BESTOWED UPON US, AND FOR THE LIVES THAT CONNECT US TO FUTURE GENERATIONS ...
WE GIVE OUR THANKS!
BIT TOO FORMAL.

GRATITUDE SINCE ANCIENT TIMES, PEOPLE HAVE PRAYED TO THE GODS FOR GOOD HARVESTS, AND AFTER THE RICE WAS GATHERED, THEY OFFERED A PORTION TO THE GODS TO SHOW THEIR GRATITUDE. SINCE THEN, PRAYER AND GRATITUDE HAVE BECOME A BASIC TENANT OF JAPANESE RELIGIOUS IDEOLOGY.

A roundabout way of saying, "Be delicious ♡."

FIRST PART-TIME JOB! I NORMALLY JUST STAND BESIDE A GATE, SO THIS IS MY FIRST TIME DOING SOMETHING LIKE THIS. IT'S SO MUCH FUN! I BET CUSTOMERS WOULD LIKE IT IF I WORE MY SHRINE MAIDEN OUTFIT!

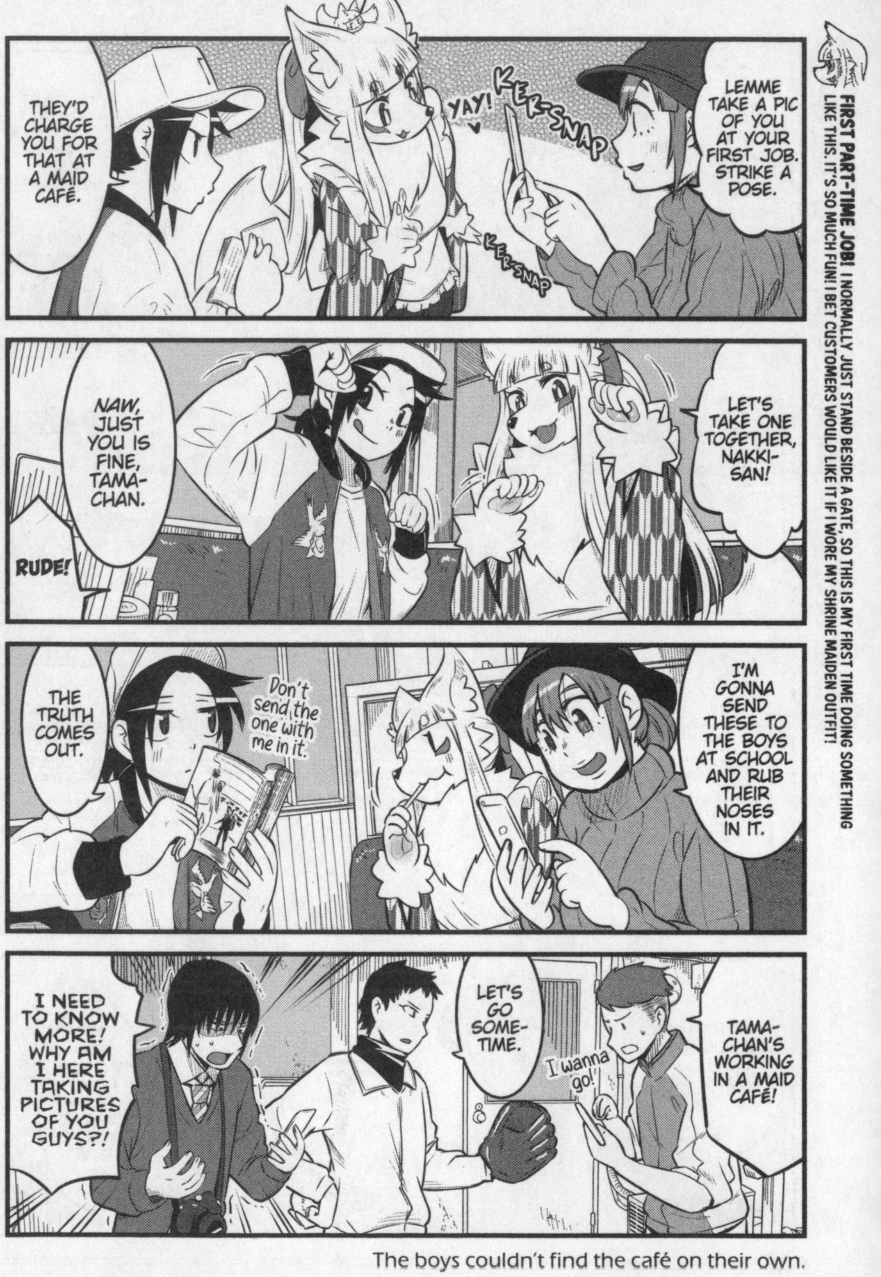
LEMME TAKE A PIC OF YOU AT YOUR FIRST JOB. STRIKE A POSE.
KER-SNAP
YAY! ♥
KER-SNAP
THEY'D CHARGE YOU FOR THAT AT A MAID CAFÉ.
LET'S TAKE ONE TOGETHER, NAKKI-SAN!
NAW, JUST YOU IS FINE, TAMA-CHAN.
RUDE!
I'M GONNA SEND THESE TO THE BOYS AT SCHOOL AND RUB THEIR NOSES IN IT.
Don't send the one with me in it.
THE TRUTH COMES OUT.
TAMA-CHAN'S WORKING IN A MAID CAFÉ!
I wanna go!
LET'S GO SOMETIME.
I NEED TO KNOW MORE! WHY AM I HERE TAKING PICTURES OF YOU GUYS?!

The boys couldn't find the café on their own.

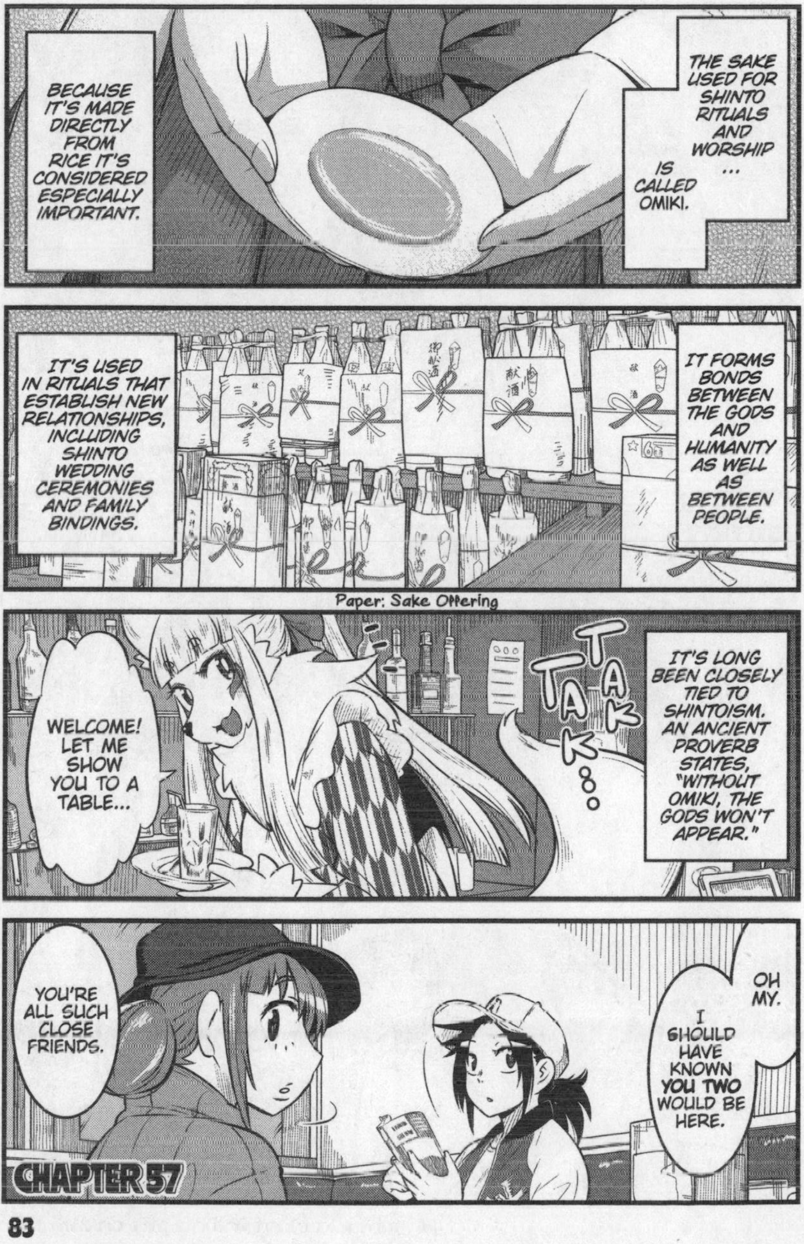
THE SAKE USED FOR SHINTO RITUALS AND WORSHIP ...
IS CALLED OMIKI.
BECAUSE IT'S MADE DIRECTLY FROM RICE IT'S CONSIDERED ESPECIALLY IMPORTANT.
IT FORMS BONDS BETWEEN THE GODS AND HUMANITY AS WELL AS BETWEEN PEOPLE.
IT'S USED IN RITUALS THAT ESTABLISH NEW RELATIONSHIPS, INCLUDING SHINTO WEDDING CEREMONIES AND FAMILY BINDINGS.
Paper: Sake Offering
IT'S LONG BEEN CLOSELY TIED TO SHINTOISM. AN ANCIENT PROVERB STATES, "WITHOUT OMIKI, THE GODS WON'T APPEAR."
TAK TAK
WELCOME! LET ME SHOW YOU TO A TABLE...
OH MY.
I SHOULD HAVE KNOWN YOU TWO WOULD BE HERE.
YOU'RE ALL SUCH CLOSE FRIENDS.
CHAPTER 57

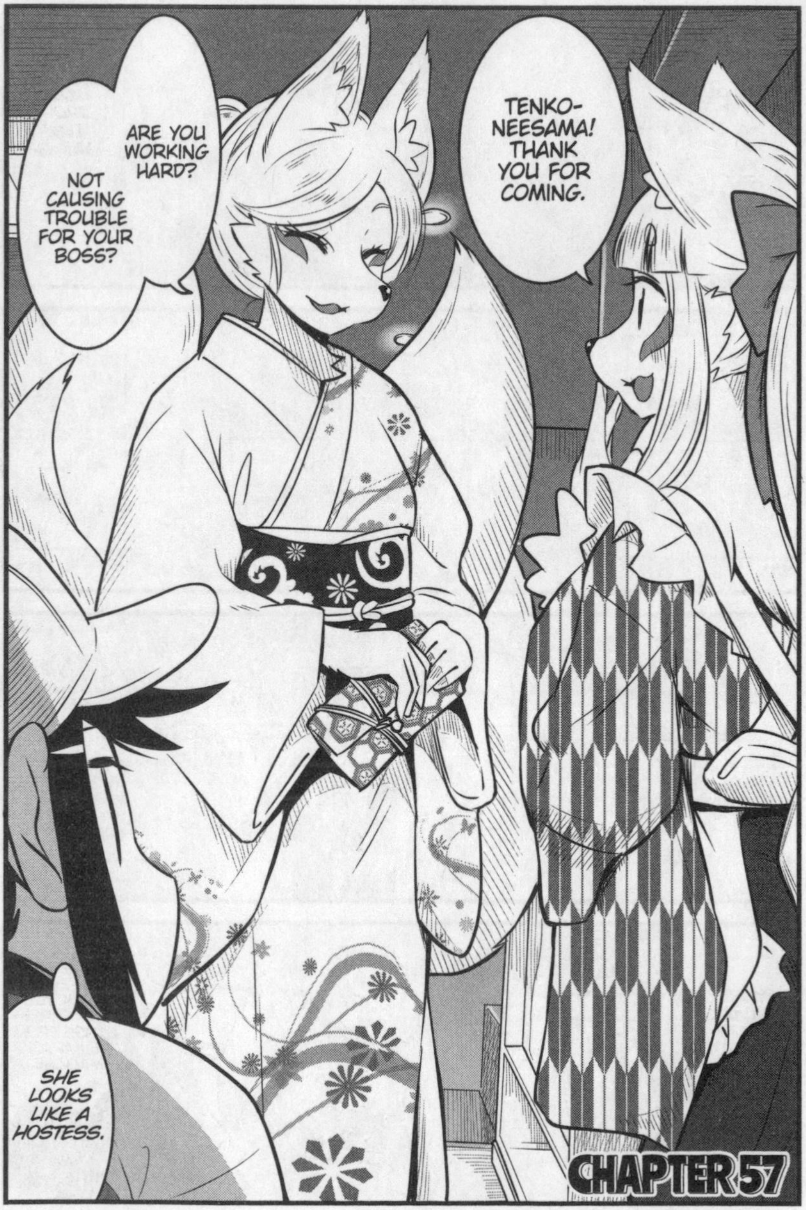
CHAPTER 57
TENKO-NEESAMA! THANK YOU FOR COMING.
ARE YOU WORKING HARD?
NOT CAUSING TROUBLE FOR YOUR BOSS?
SHE LOOKS LIKE A HOSTESS.
Like she should be running a place of her own.

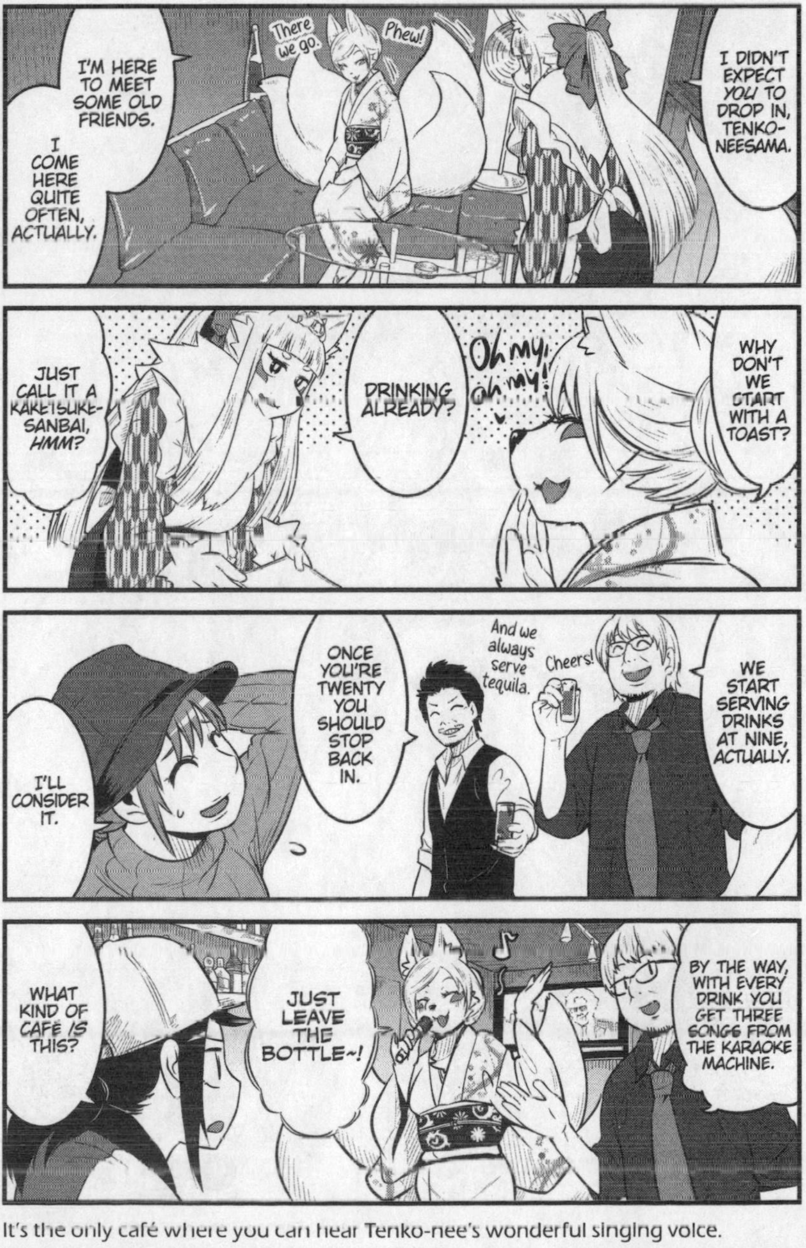
I DIDN'T EXPECT *YOU* TO DROP IN, TENKO-NEESAMA.
Phew!
There we go.
I'M HERE TO MEET SOME OLD FRIENDS.
I COME HERE QUITE OFTEN, ACTUALLY.
WHY DON'T WE START WITH A TOAST?
Oh my, oh my!
DRINKING ALREADY?
JUST CALL IT A KAKETSUKE-SANBAI, *HMM?*
WE START SERVING DRINKS AT NINE, ACTUALLY.
Cheers!
And we always serve tequila.
ONCE YOU'RE TWENTY YOU SHOULD STOP BACK IN.
I'LL CONSIDER IT.
BY THE WAY, WITH EVERY DRINK YOU GET THREE SONGS FROM THE KARAOKE MACHINE.
JUST LEAVE THE BOTTLE~!
WHAT KIND OF CAFÉ *IS* THIS?

KAKETSUKE-SANBAI A TERM REFERRING TO THE THREE DRINKS THAT LATECOMERS TO A PARTY ARE FORCED TO DOWN IN SUCCESSION AS A PUNISHMENT FOR THEIR TARDINESS. BUT IN THIS CASE TENKO-NEE IS JUST LOOKING FOR A DRINK.

It's the only café where you can hear Tenko-nee's wonderful singing voice.

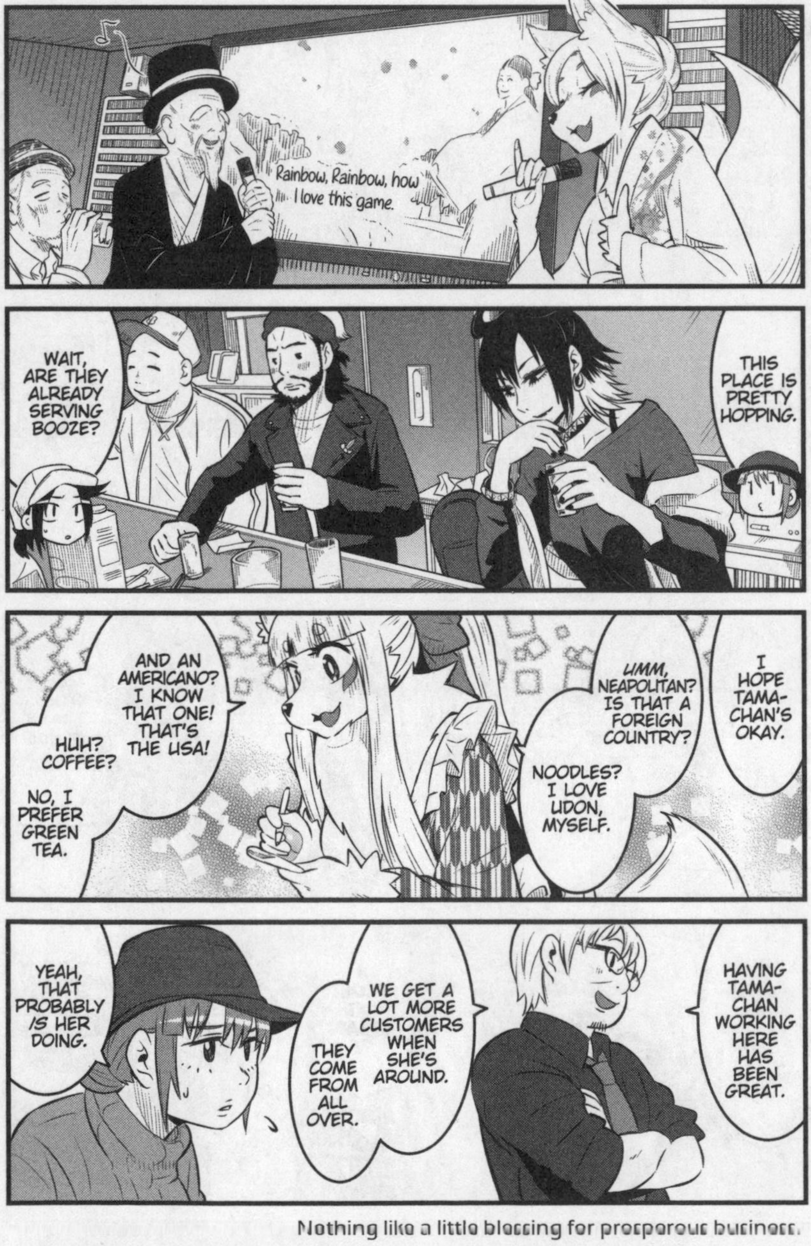
Rainbow, Rainbow, how I love this game.
THIS PLACE IS PRETTY HOPPING.
WAIT, ARE THEY ALREADY SERVING BOOZE?
I HOPE TAMA-CHAN'S OKAY.
UMM, NEAPOLITAN? IS THAT A FOREIGN COUNTRY?
NOODLES? I LOVE UDON, MYSELF.
AND AN AMERICANO? I KNOW THAT ONE! THAT'S THE USA!
HUH? COFFEE?
NO, I PREFER GREEN TEA.
HAVING TAMA-CHAN WORKING HERE HAS BEEN GREAT.
WE GET A LOT MORE CUSTOMERS WHEN SHE'S AROUND.
THEY COME FROM ALL OVER.
YEAH, THAT PROBABLY IS HER DOING.

DRINKING SPOTS IN JAPAN, WESTERN-STYLE DRINKING SPOTS ARE CALLED PUBS OR BARS. THE NAME DEPENDS ON WHAT'S OFFERED TO EAT AND DRINK.

Nothing like a little blessing for prosperous business.

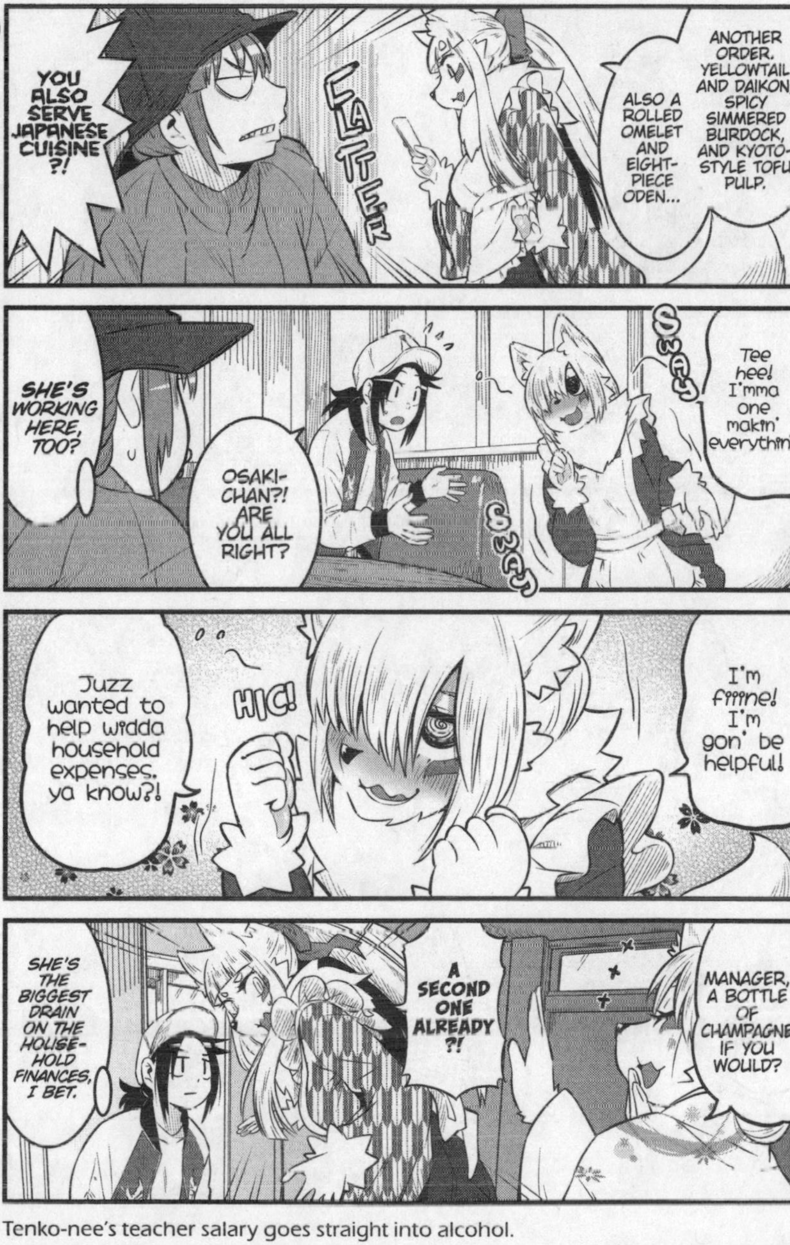
ANOTHER ORDER. YELLOWTAIL AND DAIKON, SPICY SIMMERED BURDOCK, AND KYOTO-STYLE TOFU PULP.
ALSO A ROLLED OMELET AND EIGHT-PIECE ODEN...
CLATTER
YOU ALSO SERVE JAPANESE CUISINE?!
Tee hee! I'mma one makin' everythin'!
SWAY
SWAY
OSAKI-CHAN?! ARE YOU ALL RIGHT?
SHE'S WORKING HERE, TOO?
I'm fiiine! I'm gon' be helpful!
HIC!
Juzz wanted to help widda household expenses. ya know?!
MANAGER, A BOTTLE OF CHAMPAGNE IF YOU WOULD?
A SECOND ONE ALREADY?!
SHE'S THE BIGGEST DRAIN ON THE HOUSEHOLD FINANCES, I BET.

Tenko-nee's teacher salary goes straight into alcohol.

JAPANESE CUISINE LOCAL DISHES BASED ON JAPAN'S CLIMATE AND CULTURE. CHARACTERIZED BY AN EMPHASIS ON SEASONAL INGREDIENTS, IT WAS REGISTERED AS AN INTANGIBLE CULTURAL HERITAGE IN 2013.

ARTICULATION THE JAPANESE WORD FOR "ARTICULATION," *RORETSU*, COMES FROM AN OLD COURT MUSIC TERM, *RYORITSU*, THAT CAME FROM CHINA. THE PHRASE "WANDERING ARTICULATION" REFERS TO SOMEONE WITH SLURRED SPEECH.

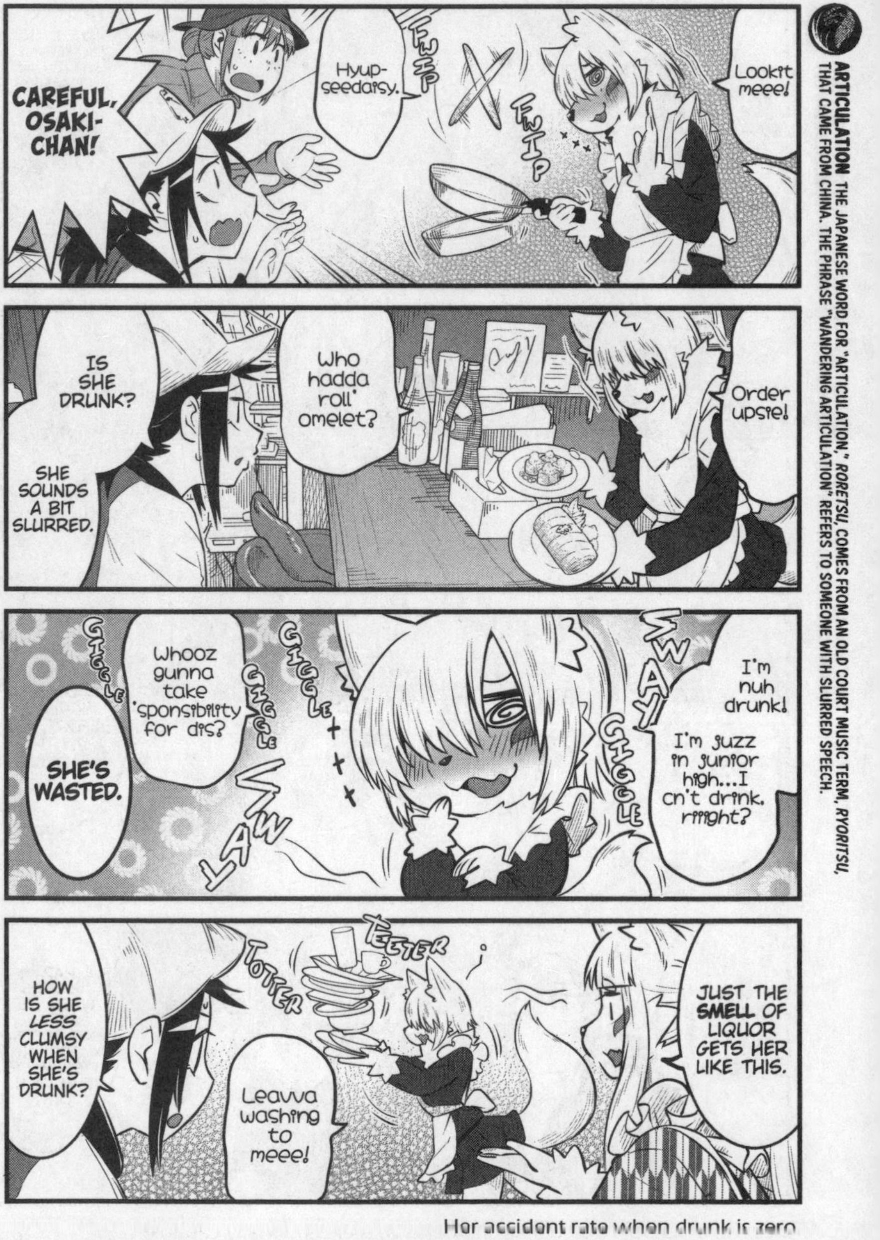
Lookit meee!
FWIP
FWIP
Hyup-seedaisy.
CAREFUL, OSAKI-CHAN!
Order upsie!
Who hadda roll' omelet?
IS SHE DRUNK?
SHE SOUNDS A BIT SLURRED.
SWAY
I'm nuh drunk!
I'm juzz in junior high...I cn't drink. riiight?
GIGGLE
GIGGLE
GIGGLE
Whooz gunna take 'sponsibility for dis?
GIGGLE
SHE'S WASTED.
JUST THE SMELL OF LIQUOR GETS HER LIKE THIS.
TEETER
TOTTER
Leavva washing to meee!
HOW IS SHE *LESS* CLUMSY WHEN SHE'S DRUNK?

Her accident rate when drunk is zero

HELPING OUT I REMEMBER GOING OUT TO HELP TAMAMO-NEESAMA BUT THE NEXT THING I KNEW I WAS ASLEEP BACK AT HOME.

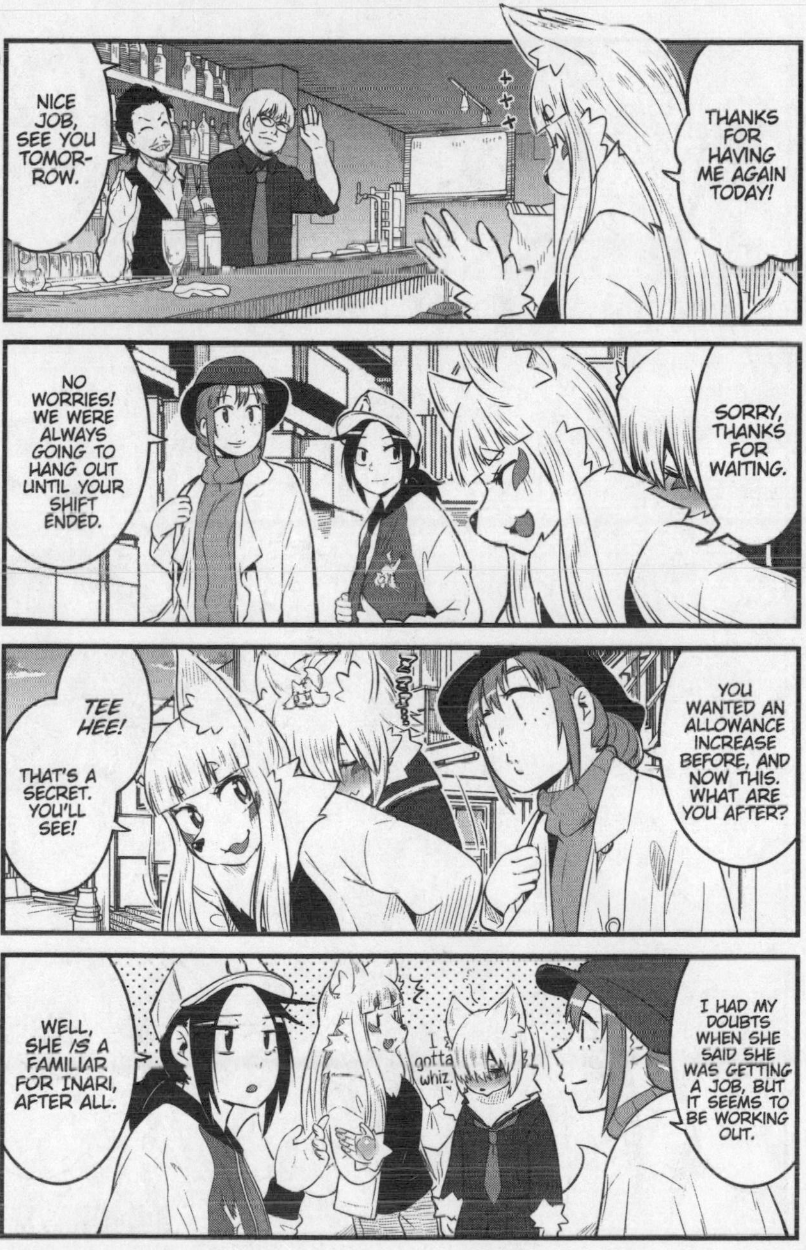
THANKS FOR HAVING ME AGAIN TODAY!
NICE JOB, SEE YOU TOMOR-ROW.
SORRY, THANKS FOR WAITING.
NO WORRIES! WE WERE ALWAYS GOING TO HANG OUT UNTIL YOUR SHIFT ENDED.
YOU WANTED AN ALLOWANCE INCREASE BEFORE, AND NOW THIS. WHAT ARE YOU AFTER?
TEE HEE!
THAT'S A SECRET. YOU'LL SEE!
I HAD MY DOUBTS WHEN SHE SAID SHE WAS GETTING A JOB, BUT IT SEEMS TO BE WORKING OUT.
I gotta whiz.
WELL, SHE *IS* A FAMILIAR FOR INARI, AFTER ALL.

Outside of school-related matters, Tamamo is exceptionally capable.

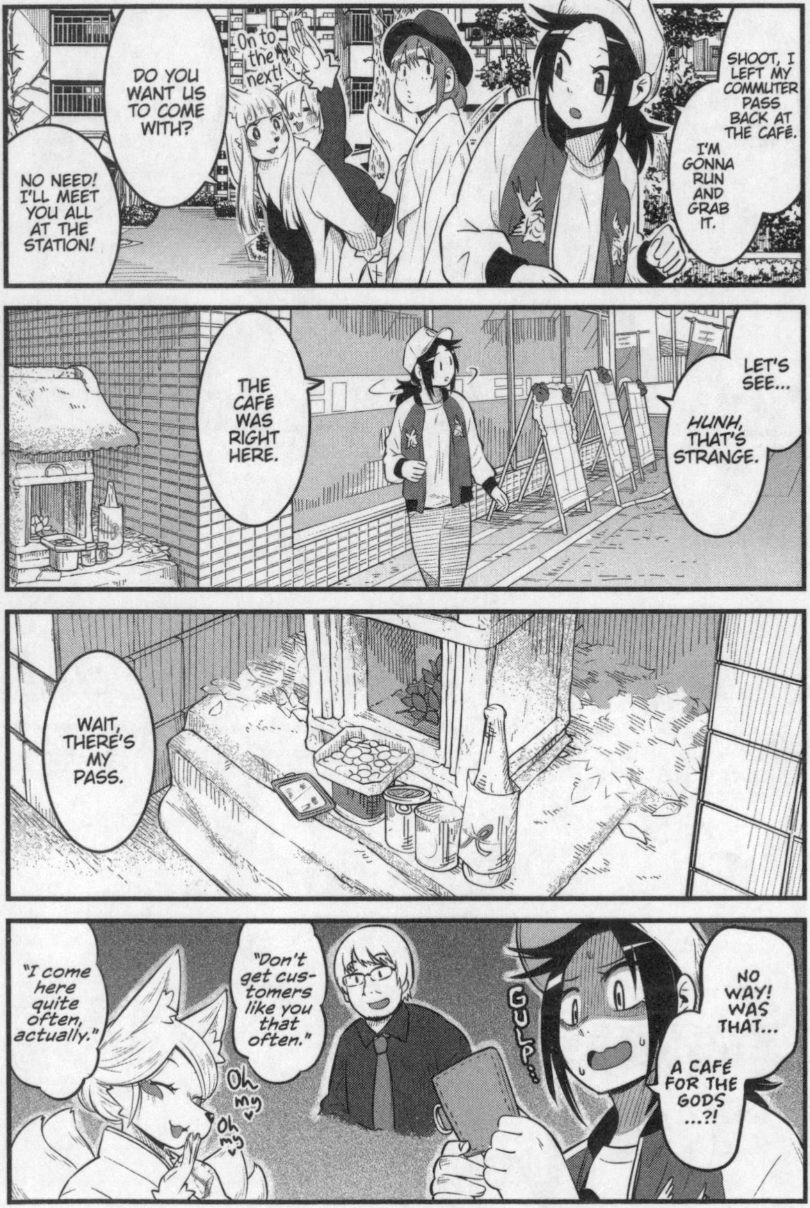
SHOOT, I LEFT MY COMMUTER PASS BACK AT THE CAFÉ.
I'M GONNA RUN AND GRAB IT.
On to the next!
DO YOU WANT US TO COME WITH?
NO NEED! I'LL MEET YOU ALL AT THE STATION!
LET'S SEE...
HUNH, THAT'S STRANGE.
THE CAFÉ WAS RIGHT HERE.
WAIT, THERE'S MY PASS.
NO WAY! WAS THAT...
A CAFÉ FOR THE GODS ...?!
GULP...
"Don't get customers like you that often."
"I come here quite often, actually."
Oh my
Oh my

CAFÉ THE SHOP IS ACTUALLY IN KAWARAMACHI IN KYOTO BUT THE SHRINE LETS ME COMMUTE FROM TOKYO!

Tamamo's workplace is very mysterious.

Tamamo-chan's a FOX!

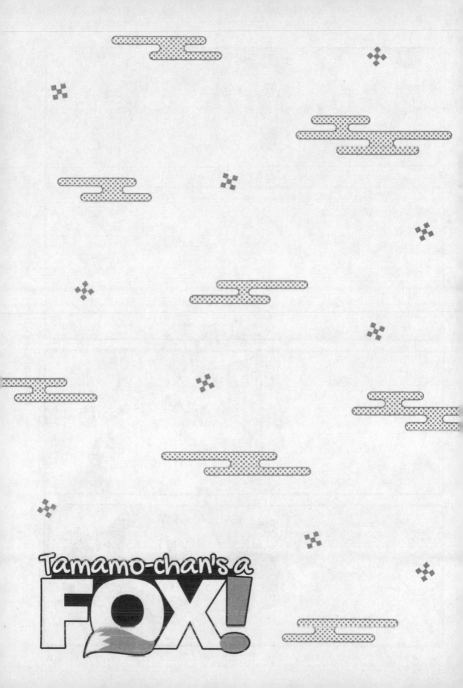

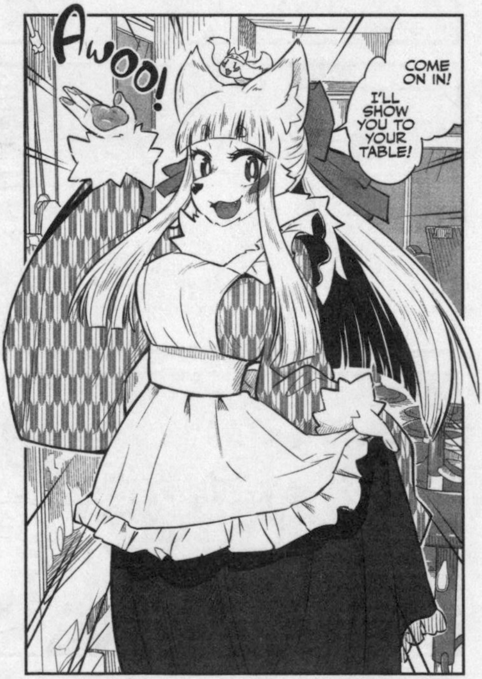
AWOO!
COME ON IN!
I'LL SHOW YOU TO YOUR TABLE!

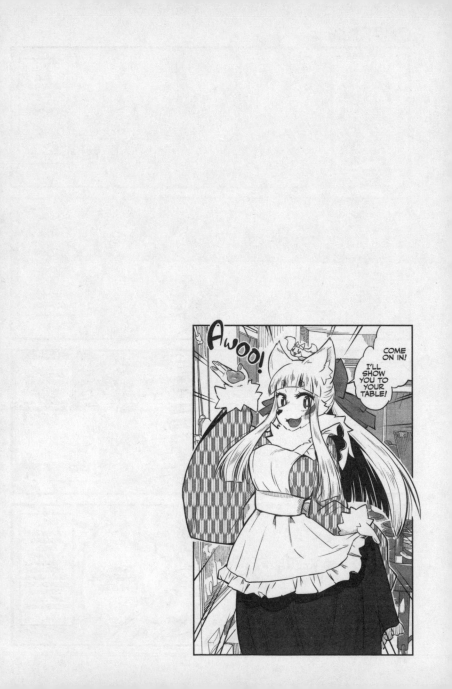

CHAPTER 58

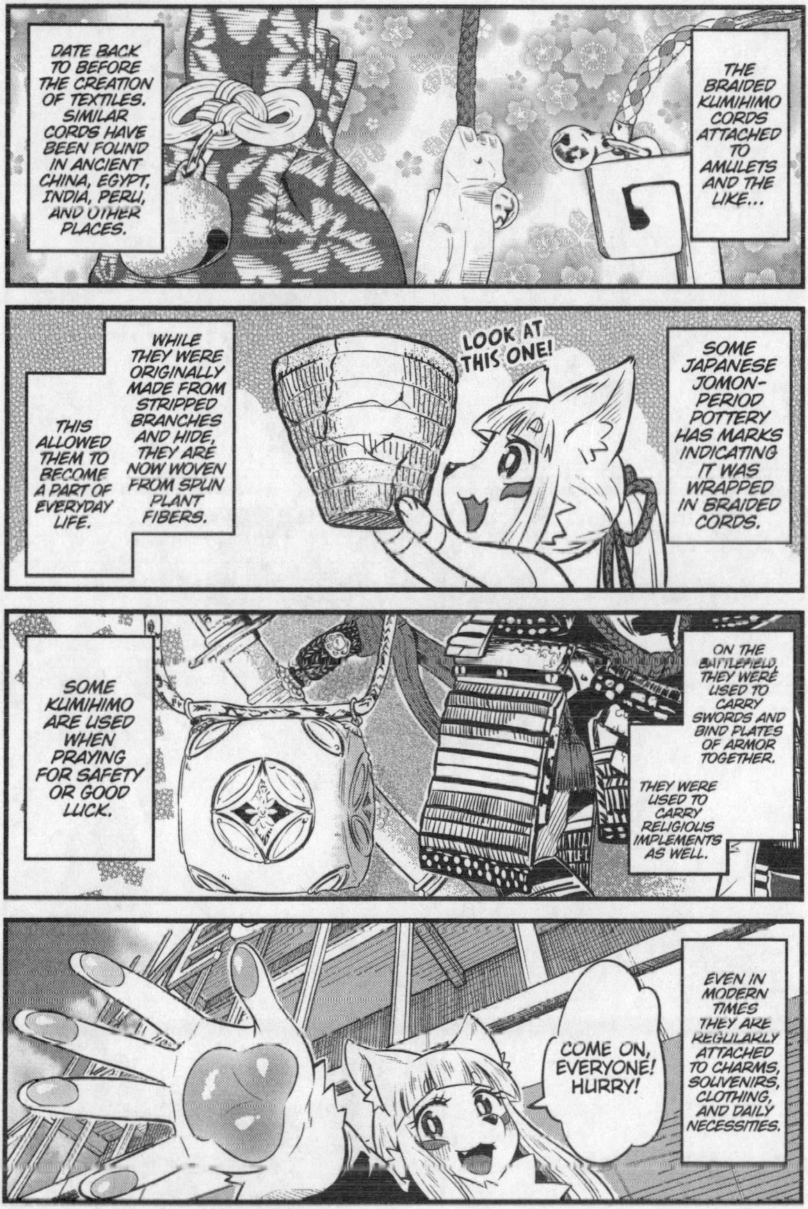
THE BRAIDED KUMIHIMO CORDS ATTACHED TO AMULETS AND THE LIKE...
DATE BACK TO BEFORE THE CREATION OF TEXTILES. SIMILAR CORDS HAVE BEEN FOUND IN ANCIENT CHINA, EGYPT, INDIA, PERU, AND OTHER PLACES.
SOME JAPANESE JOMON-PERIOD POTTERY HAS MARKS INDICATING IT WAS WRAPPED IN BRAIDED CORDS.
LOOK AT THIS ONE!
WHILE THEY WERE ORIGINALLY MADE FROM STRIPPED BRANCHES AND HIDE, THEY ARE NOW WOVEN FROM SPUN PLANT FIBERS.
THIS ALLOWED THEM TO BECOME A PART OF EVERYDAY LIFE.
ON THE BATTLEFIELD, THEY WERE USED TO CARRY SWORDS AND BIND PLATES OF ARMOR TOGETHER.
THEY WERE USED TO CARRY RELIGIOUS IMPLEMENTS AS WELL.
SOME KUMIHIMO ARE USED WHEN PRAYING FOR SAFETY OR GOOD LUCK.
EVEN IN MODERN TIMES THEY ARE REGULARLY ATTACHED TO CHARMS, SOUVENIRS, CLOTHING, AND DAILY NECESSITIES.
COME ON, EVERYONE! HURRY!

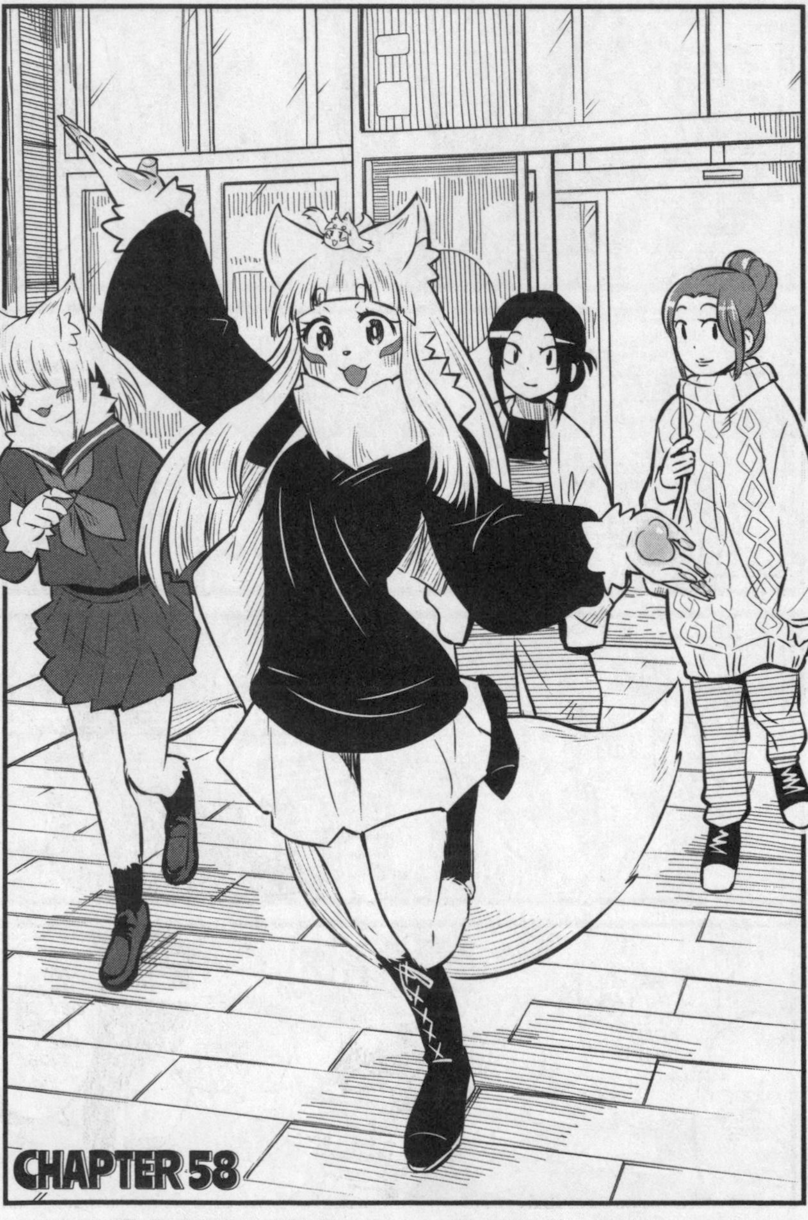
CHAPTER 58

To Tamamo and Osaki, even an ordinary shopping trip is an adventure.

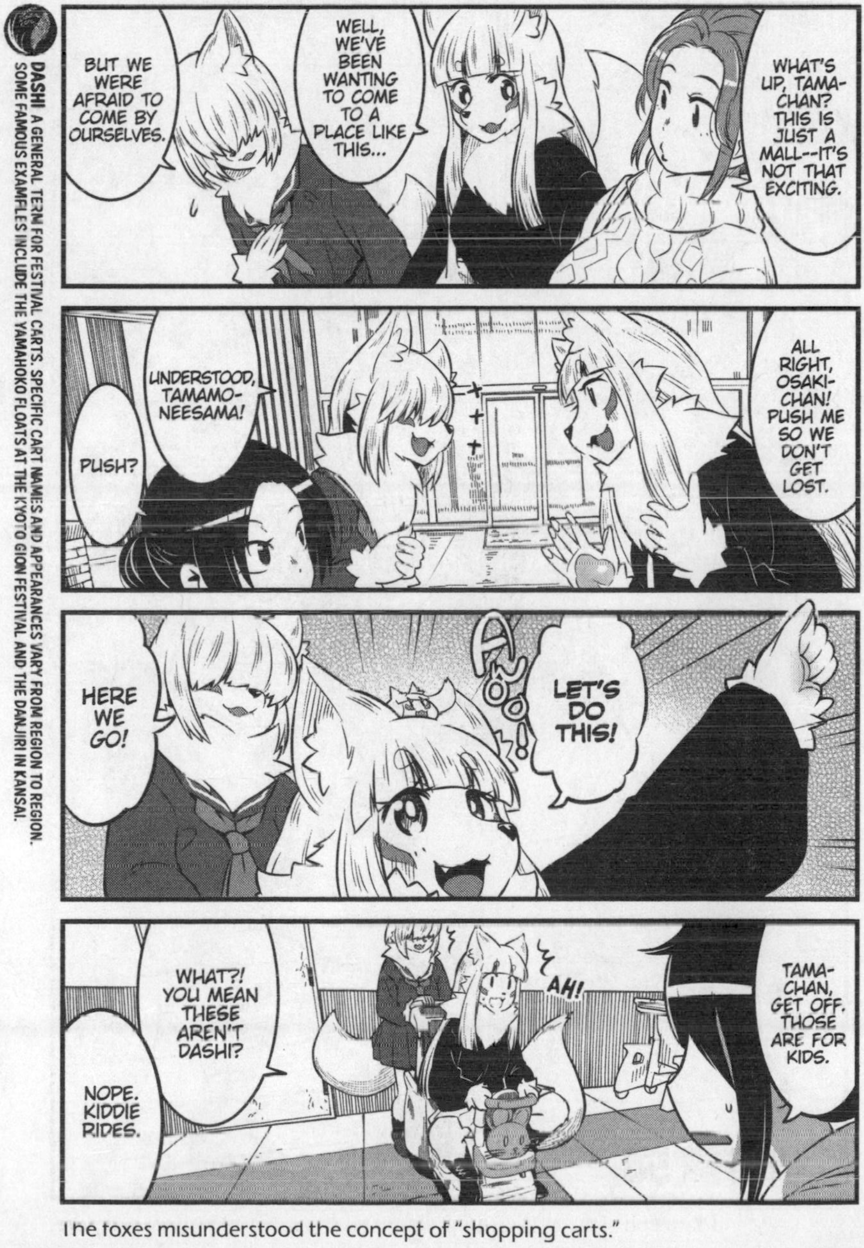
WHAT'S UP, TAMA-CHAN? THIS IS JUST A MALL--IT'S NOT THAT EXCITING.
WELL, WE'VE BEEN WANTING TO COME TO A PLACE LIKE THIS...
BUT WE WERE AFRAID TO COME BY OURSELVES.
ALL RIGHT, OSAKI-CHAN! PUSH ME SO WE DON'T GET LOST.
UNDERSTOOD, TAMAMO-NEESAMA!
PUSH?
AWOOO!
LET'S DO THIS!
HERE WE GO!
TAMA-CHAN, GET OFF. THOSE ARE FOR KIDS.
AH!
WHAT?! YOU MEAN THESE AREN'T DASHI?
NOPE. KIDDIE RIDES.

The foxes misunderstood the concept of "shopping carts."

DASHI A GENERAL TERM FOR FESTIVAL CARTS. SPECIFIC CART NAMES AND APPEARANCES VARY FROM REGION TO REGION. SOME FAMOUS EXAMPLES INCLUDE THE YAMAHOKO FLOATS AT THE KYOTO GION FESTIVAL AND THE DANJIRI IN KANSAI.

FIVE-STORY PAGODA THERE ARE FOUR FIVE-STORY PAGODAS IN KYOTO AT TOJI TEMPLE, NINNAJI TEMPLE, DAIGOJI TEMPLE, AND HOKANJI TEMPLE. THEY CAN BE SEEN FROM VARIOUS TRAINS INCLUDING THE BULLET TRAIN.

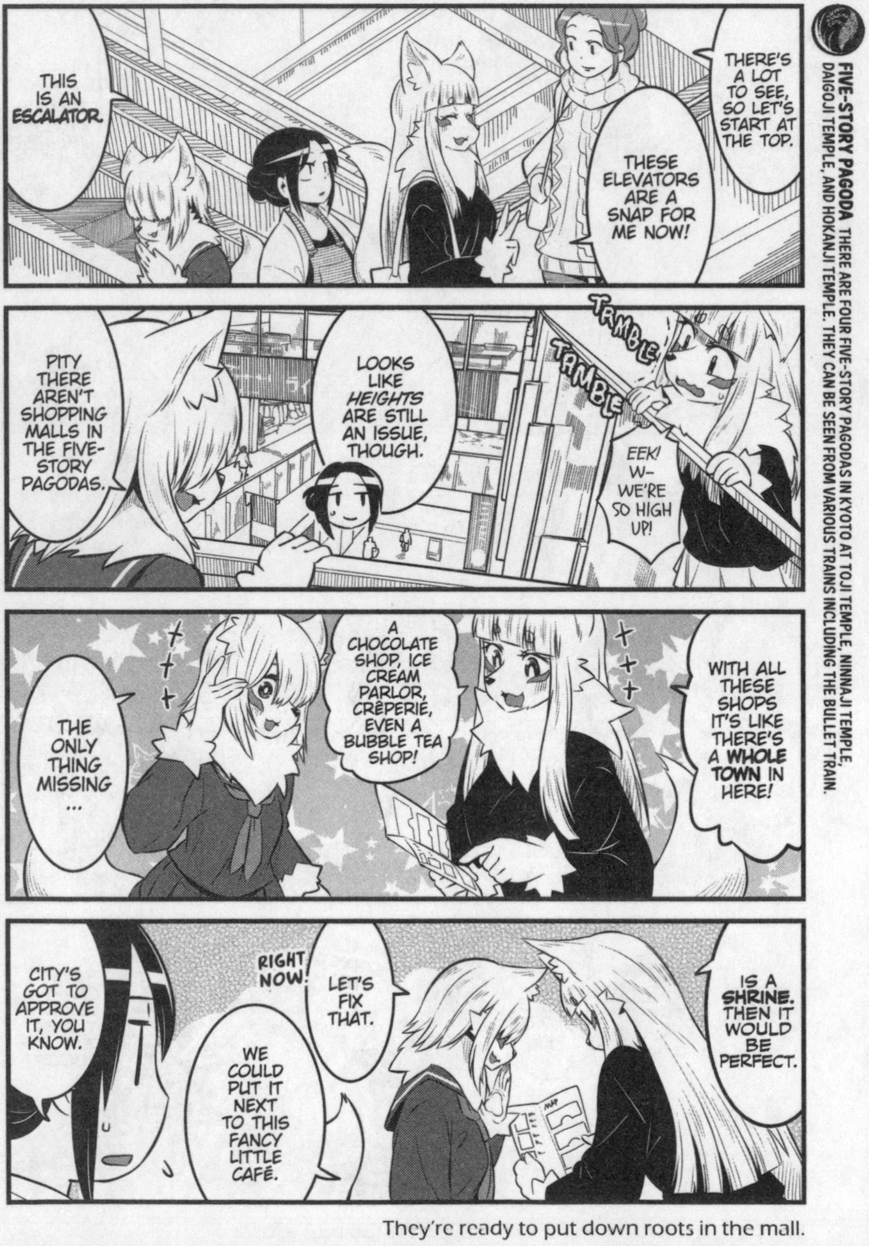
THERE'S A LOT TO SEE, SO LET'S START AT THE TOP.
THESE ELEVATORS ARE A SNAP FOR ME NOW!
THIS IS AN ESCALATOR.
TAMBLE
TAMBLE
EEK! W–WE'RE SO HIGH UP!
LOOKS LIKE HEIGHTS ARE STILL AN ISSUE, THOUGH.
PITY THERE AREN'T SHOPPING MALLS IN THE FIVE-STORY PAGODAS.
WITH ALL THESE SHOPS IT'S LIKE THERE'S A WHOLE TOWN IN HERE!
A CHOCOLATE SHOP, ICE CREAM PARLOR, CRÊPERIE, EVEN A BUBBLE TEA SHOP!
THE ONLY THING MISSING ...
IS A SHRINE. THEN IT WOULD BE PERFECT.
LET'S FIX THAT.
RIGHT NOW!
WE COULD PUT IT NEXT TO THIS FANCY LITTLE CAFÉ.
CITY'S GOT TO APPROVE IT, YOU KNOW.

They're ready to put down roots in the mall.

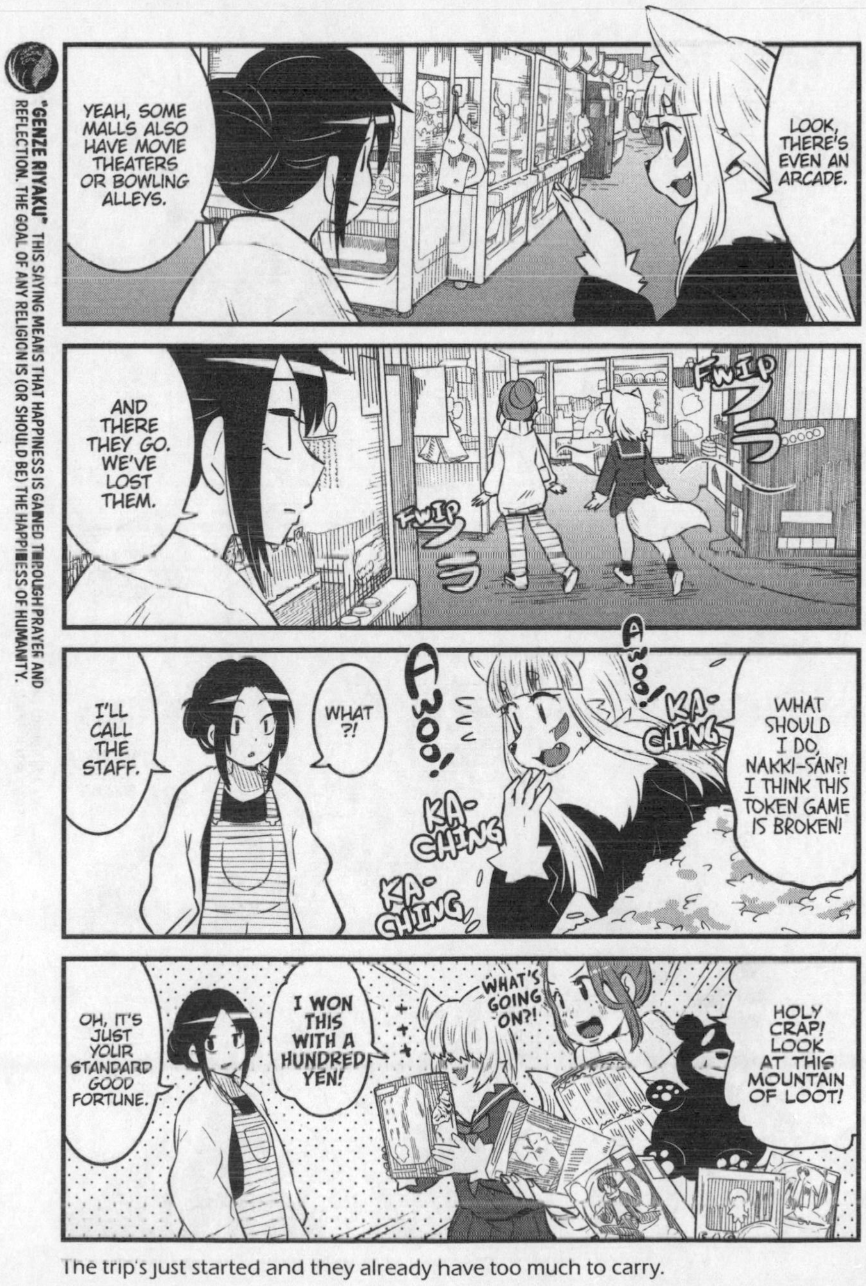
LOOK, THERE'S EVEN AN ARCADE.
YEAH, SOME MALLS ALSO HAVE MOVIE THEATERS OR BOWLING ALLEYS.
FWIP
FWIP
AND THERE THEY GO. WE'VE LOST THEM.
WHAT SHOULD I DO, NAKKI-SAN?! I THINK THIS TOKEN GAME IS BROKEN!
KA-CHING
AWOO!
AWOO!
KA-CHING
KA-CHING
WHAT ?!
I'LL CALL THE STAFF.
HOLY CRAP! LOOK AT THIS MOUNTAIN OF LOOT!
WHAT'S GOING ON?!
I WON THIS WITH A HUNDRED YEN!
OH, IT'S JUST YOUR STANDARD GOOD FORTUNE.

"GENZE RIYAKU" THIS SAYING MEANS THAT HAPPINESS IS GAINED THROUGH PRAYER AND REFLECTION. THE GOAL OF ANY RELIGION IS (OR SHOULD BE) THE HAPPINESS OF HUMANITY.

The trip's just started and they already have too much to carry.

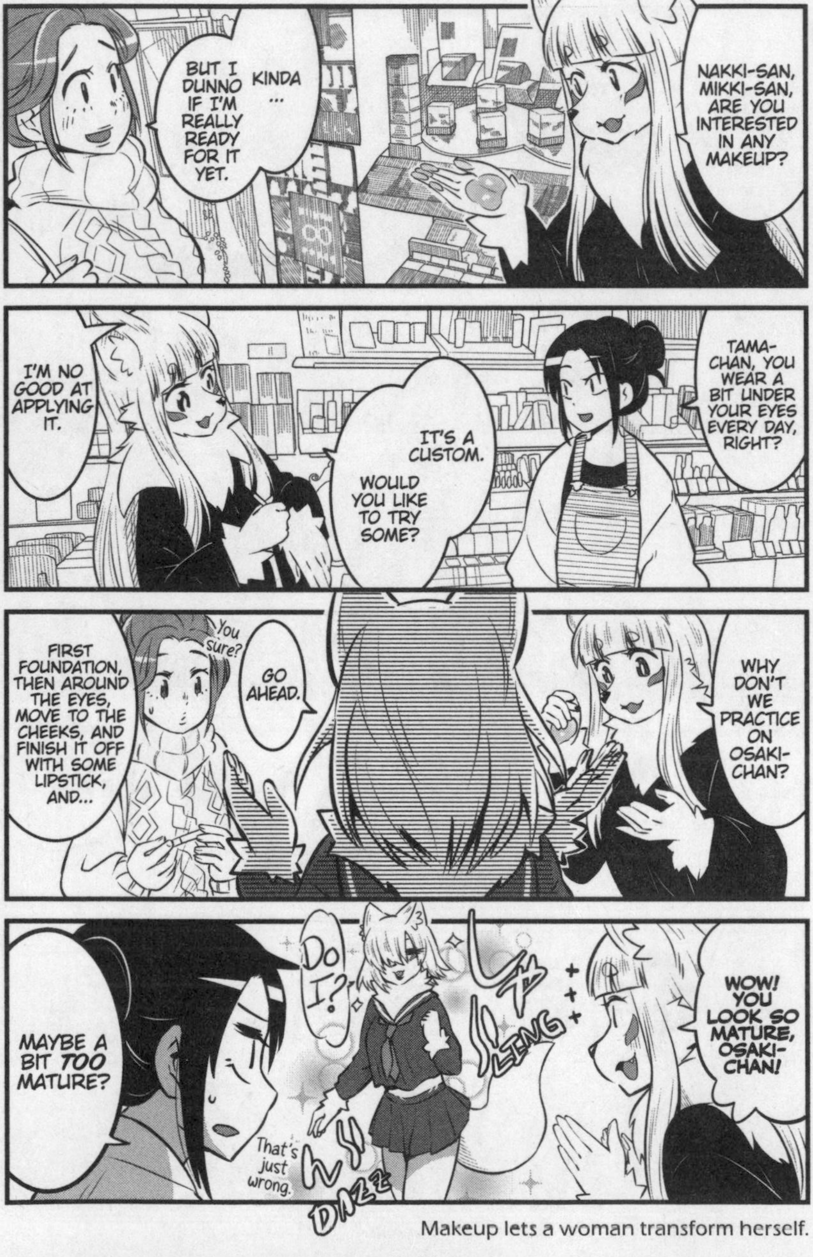
NAKKI-SAN, MIKKI-SAN, ARE YOU INTERESTED IN ANY MAKEUP?
KINDA ...
BUT I DUNNO IF I'M REALLY READY FOR IT YET.
TAMA-CHAN, YOU WEAR A BIT UNDER YOUR EYES EVERY DAY, RIGHT?
IT'S A CUSTOM.
WOULD YOU LIKE TO TRY SOME?
I'M NO GOOD AT APPLYING IT.
WHY DON'T WE PRACTICE ON OSAKI-CHAN?
GO AHEAD.
You sure?
FIRST FOUNDATION, THEN AROUND THE EYES, MOVE TO THE CHEEKS, AND FINISH IT OFF WITH SOME LIPSTICK, AND...
WOW! YOU LOOK SO MATURE, OSAKI-CHAN!
LING
Do I?
MAYBE A BIT *TOO* MATURE?
That's just wrong.
DAZZ

Makeup lets a woman transform herself.

MAKEUP MAKEUP IS APPLIED TO RITUAL DANCERS, AND ON SPECIAL OCCASIONS IT CAN BE QUITE HEAVY. IT'S ALSO USED TO DECORATE THE PARTICIPANTS IN FESTIVAL PARADES AND TRADITIONAL CHIGOMAI CHILDREN'S PERFORMANCES.

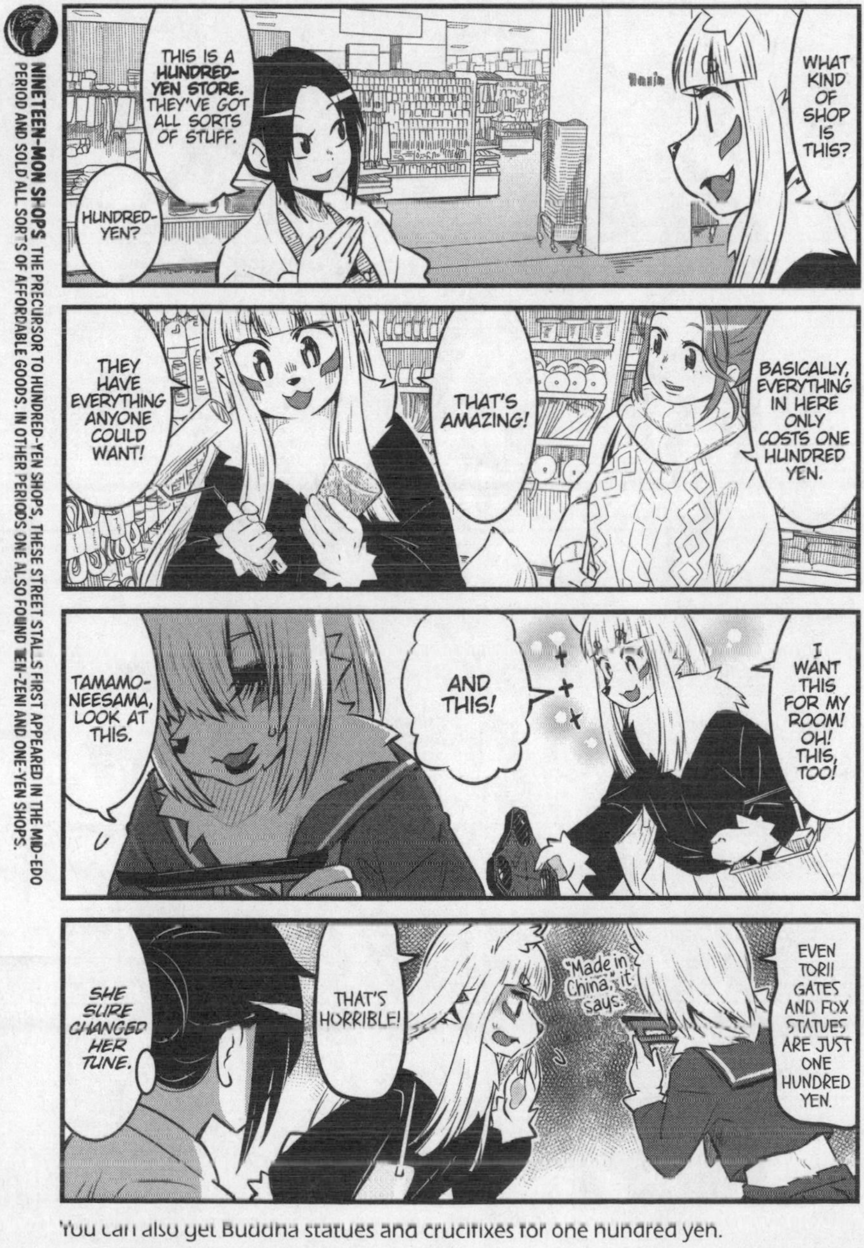
WHAT KIND OF SHOP IS THIS?
THIS IS A HUNDRED-YEN STORE. THEY'VE GOT ALL SORTS OF STUFF.
HUNDRED-YEN?
BASICALLY, EVERYTHING IN HERE ONLY COSTS ONE HUNDRED YEN.
THAT'S AMAZING!
THEY HAVE EVERYTHING ANYONE COULD WANT!
I WANT THIS FOR MY ROOM! OH! THIS, TOO!
AND THIS!
TAMAMO-NEESAMA, LOOK AT THIS.
EVEN TORII GATES AND FOX STATUES ARE JUST ONE HUNDRED YEN.
"Made in China," it says.
THAT'S HORRIBLE!
SHE SURE CHANGED HER TUNE.

You can also get Buddha statues and crucifixes for one hundred yen.

NINETEEN-MON SHOPS THE PRECURSOR TO HUNDRED-YEN SHOPS, THESE STREET STALLS FIRST APPEARED IN THE MID-EDO PERIOD AND SOLD ALL SORTS OF AFFORDABLE GOODS. IN OTHER PERIODS ONE ALSO FOUND TEN-ZENI AND ONE-YEN SHOPS.

FURNITURE! WITH FURNITURE, FOOD, AND CLOTHING ALL IN ONE PLACE, I'M READY TO MOVE IN! WE SHOULD SET UP A SHRINE IMMEDIATELY!

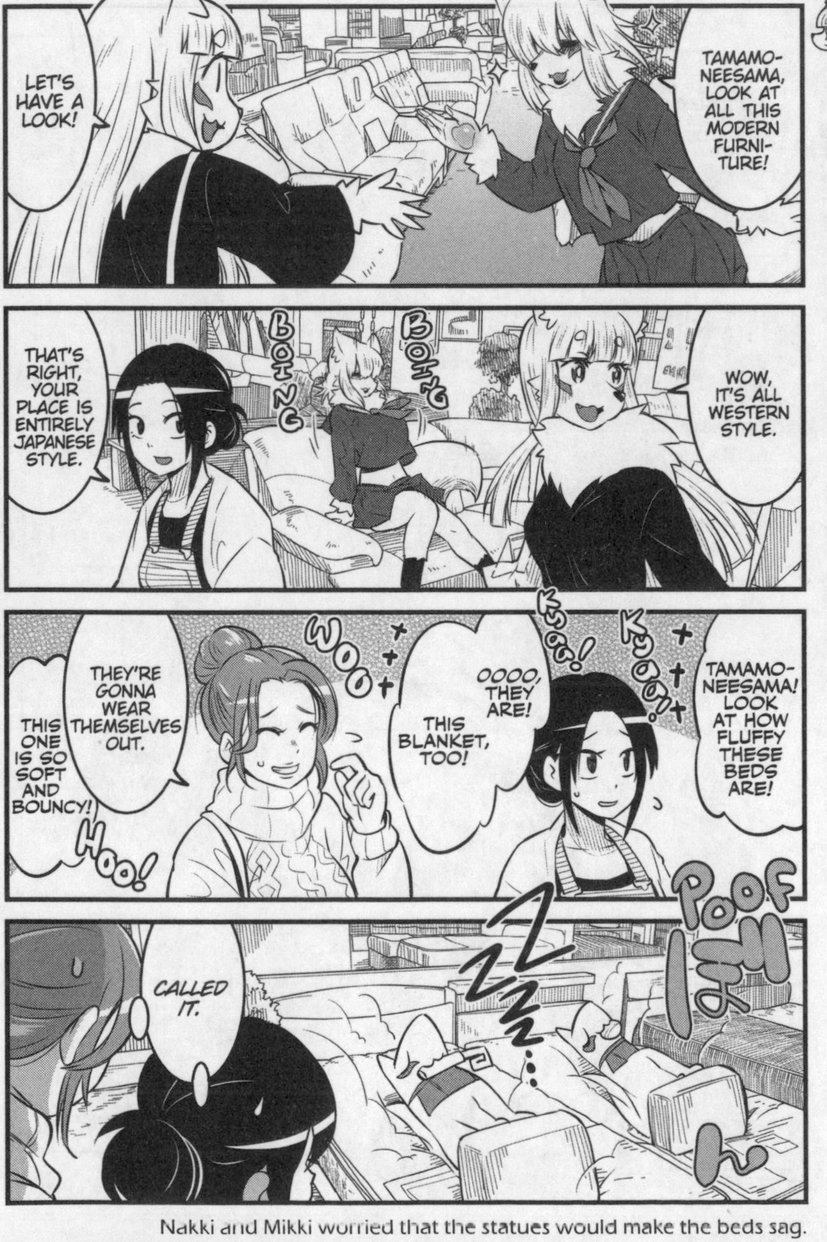
TAMAMO-NEESAMA, LOOK AT ALL THIS MODERN FURNI-TURE!
LET'S HAVE A LOOK!
WOW, IT'S ALL WESTERN STYLE.
BOING
BOING
THAT'S RIGHT, YOUR PLACE IS ENTIRELY JAPANESE STYLE.
TAMAMO-NEESAMA! LOOK AT HOW FLUFFY THESE BEDS ARE!
Kyaa!
Kyaa!
OOOO, THEY ARE!
THIS BLANKET, TOO!
WOO
HOO!
THIS ONE IS SO SOFT AND BOUNCY!
THEY'RE GONNA WEAR THEMSELVES OUT.
POOF
ZZZ
CALLED IT.

Nakki and Mikki worried that the statues would make the beds sag.

CHAPTER 59

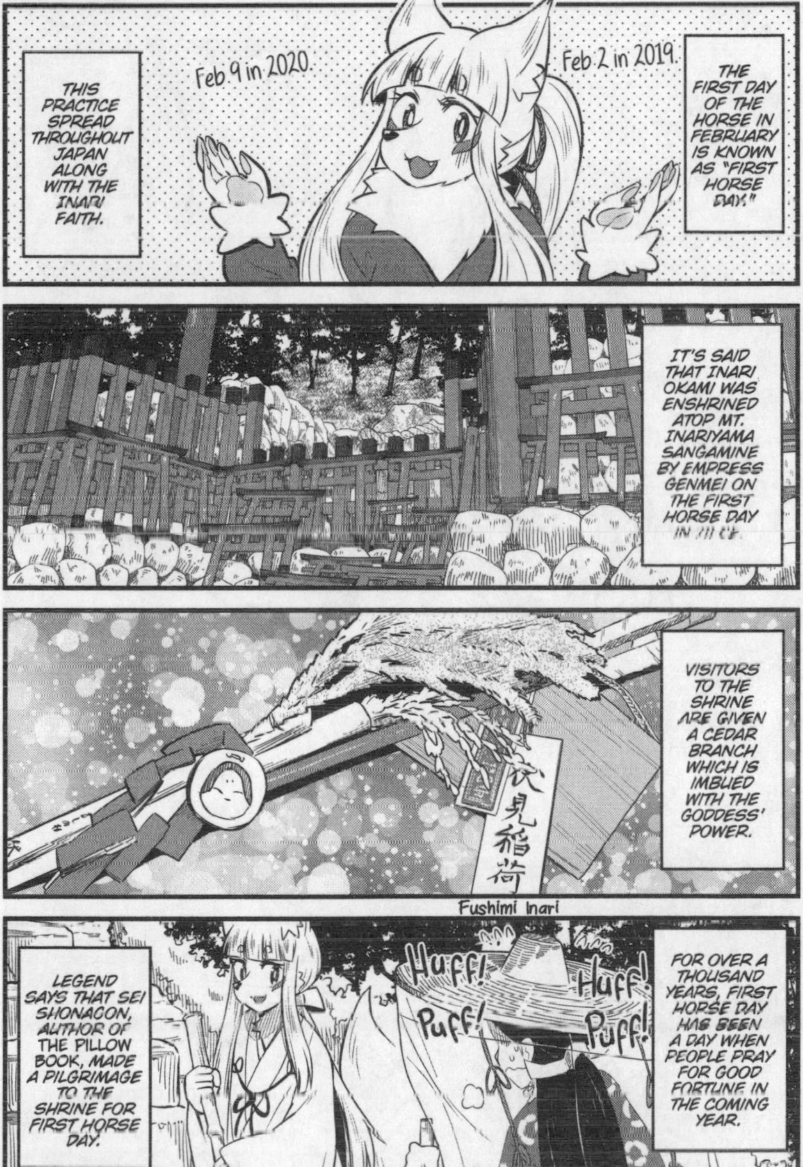
THE FIRST DAY OF THE HORSE IN FEBRUARY IS KNOWN AS "FIRST HORSE DAY."
Feb 2 in 2019.
Feb 9 in 2020.
THIS PRACTICE SPREAD THROUGHOUT JAPAN ALONG WITH THE INARI FAITH.
IT'S SAID THAT INARI OKAMI WAS ENSHRINED ATOP MT. INARIYAMA SANGAMINE BY EMPRESS GENMEI ON THE FIRST HORSE DAY IN 711 CE.
VISITORS TO THE SHRINE ARE GIVEN A CEDAR BRANCH WHICH IS IMBUED WITH THE GODDESS' POWER.
伏見稲荷
Fushimi Inari
FOR OVER A THOUSAND YEARS, FIRST HORSE DAY HAS BEEN A DAY WHEN PEOPLE PRAY FOR GOOD FORTUNE IN THE COMING YEAR.
Huff! Huff!
Puff! Puff!
LEGEND SAYS THAT SEI SHONAGON, AUTHOR OF THE PILLOW BOOK, MADE A PILGRIMAGE TO THE SHRINE FOR FIRST HORSE DAY.

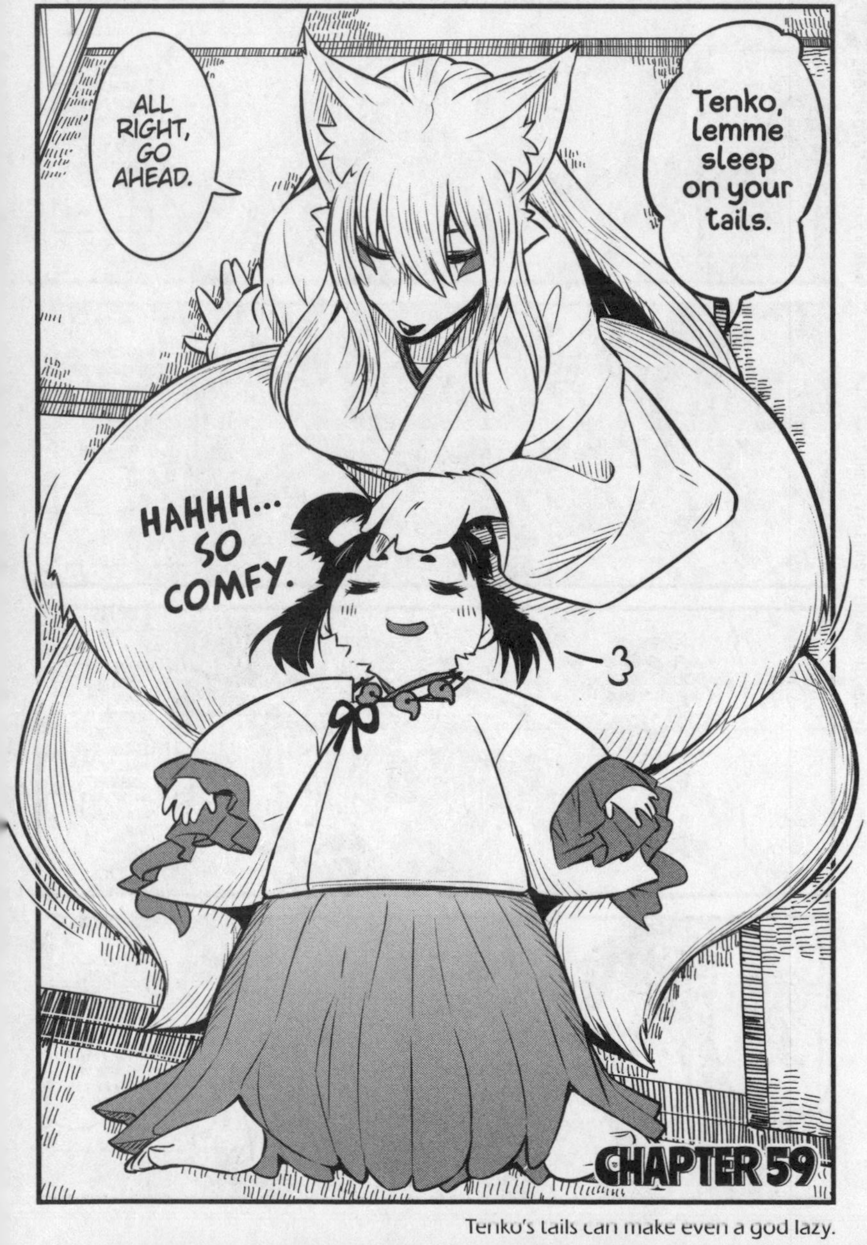
Tenko, lemme sleep on your tails.
ALL RIGHT, GO AHEAD.
HAHHH... SO COMFY.
CHAPTER 59
Tenko's tails can make even a god lazy.

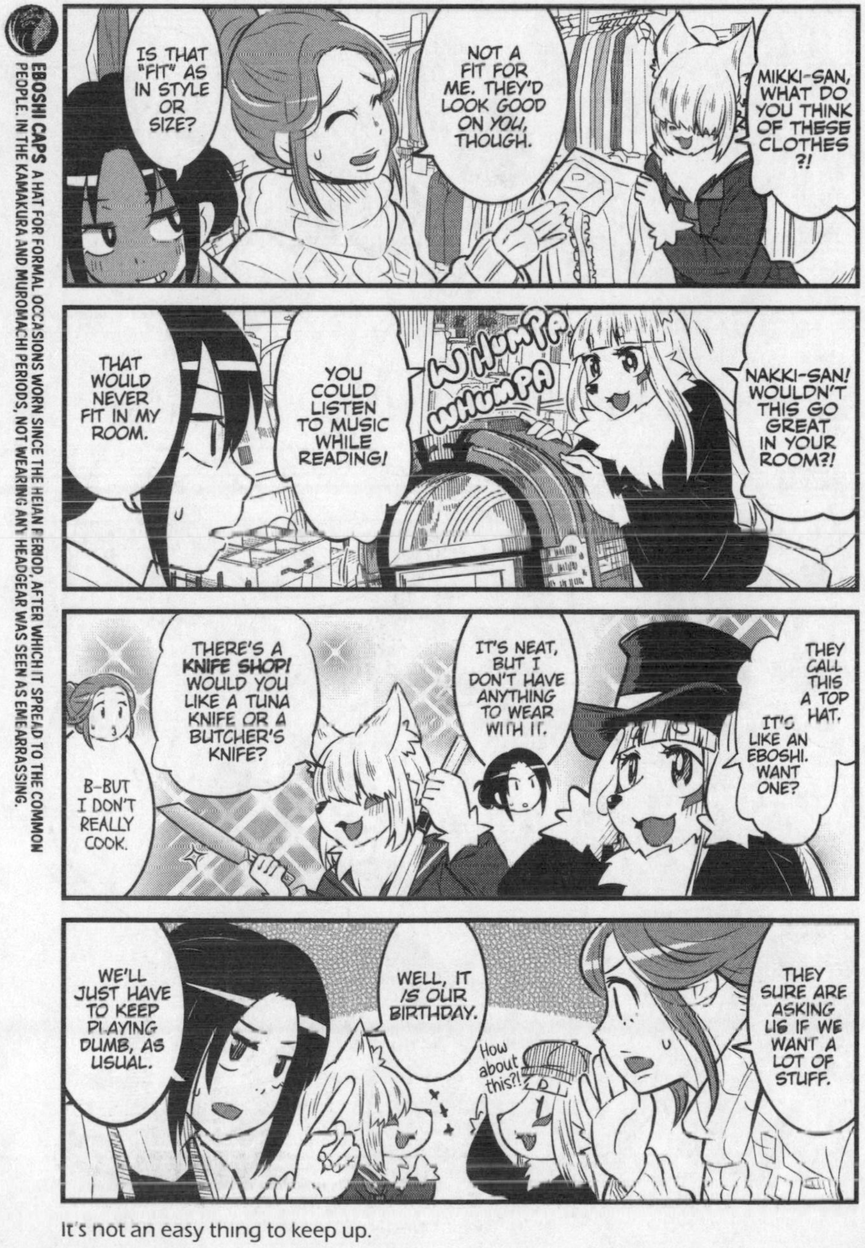
MIKKI-SAN, WHAT DO YOU THINK OF THESE CLOTHES?!
NOT A FIT FOR ME. THEY'D LOOK GOOD ON *YOU*, THOUGH.
IS THAT "FIT" AS IN STYLE OR SIZE?
NAKKI-SAN! WOULDN'T THIS GO GREAT IN YOUR ROOM?!
WHUMPA WHUMPA
YOU COULD LISTEN TO MUSIC WHILE READING!
THAT WOULD NEVER FIT IN MY ROOM.
THEY CALL THIS A TOP HAT.
IT'S LIKE AN EBOSHI. WANT ONE?
IT'S NEAT, BUT I DON'T HAVE ANYTHING TO WEAR WITH IT.
THERE'S A **KNIFE SHOP!** WOULD YOU LIKE A TUNA KNIFE OR A BUTCHER'S KNIFE?
B-BUT I DON'T REALLY COOK.
THEY SURE ARE ASKING US IF WE WANT A LOT OF STUFF.
How about this?!
WELL, IT *IS* OUR BIRTHDAY.
WE'LL JUST HAVE TO KEEP PLAYING DUMB, AS USUAL.

It's not an easy thing to keep up.

EBOSHI CAPS A HAT FOR FORMAL OCCASIONS WORN SINCE THE HEIAN PERIOD, AFTER WHICH IT SPREAD TO THE COMMON PEOPLE. IN THE KAMAKURA AND MUROMACHI PERIODS, NOT WEARING ANY HEADGEAR WAS SEEN AS EMBARRASSING.

SERICULTURE RAISING SILKWORMS. SOME FAMILIES MAINTAIN SECRET TECHNIQUES, AND IN ONE LEGEND, A FAMILY THAT GAINED SUDDEN PROSPERITY VIA SILKWORMS WAS LABELED AS POSSESSED.

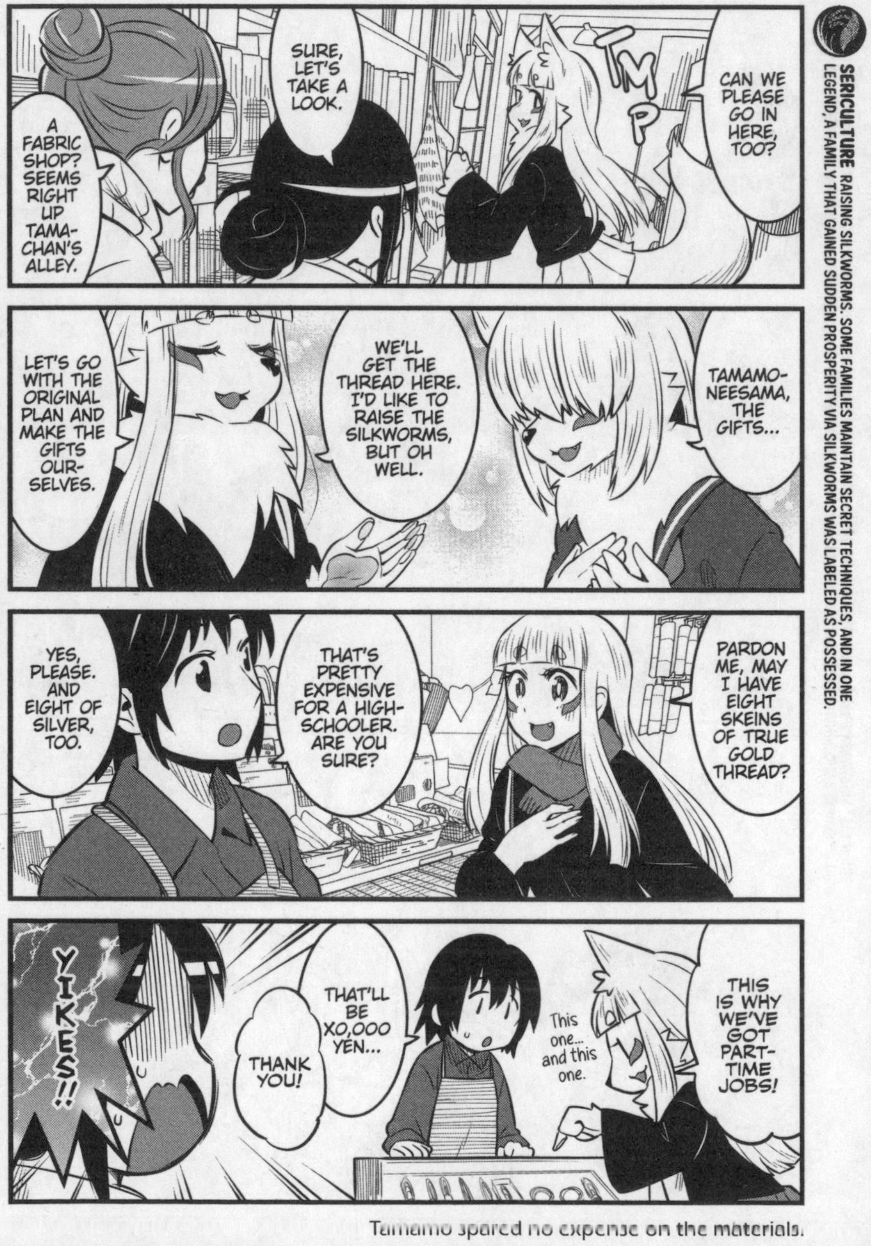

CAN WE PLEASE GO IN HERE, TOO?
TMP
SURE, LET'S TAKE A LOOK.
A FABRIC SHOP? SEEMS RIGHT UP TAMA-CHAN'S ALLEY.
TAMAMO-NEESAMA, THE GIFTS...
WE'LL GET THE THREAD HERE. I'D LIKE TO RAISE THE SILKWORMS, BUT OH WELL.
LET'S GO WITH THE ORIGINAL PLAN AND MAKE THE GIFTS OURSELVES.
PARDON ME, MAY I HAVE EIGHT SKEINS OF TRUE GOLD THREAD?
THAT'S PRETTY EXPENSIVE FOR A HIGH-SCHOOLER. ARE YOU SURE?
YES, PLEASE. AND EIGHT OF SILVER, TOO.
THIS IS WHY WE'VE GOT PART-TIME JOBS!
This one... and this one.
THAT'LL BE X0,000 YEN...
THANK YOU!
YIKES!!

Tamamo spared no expense on the materials.

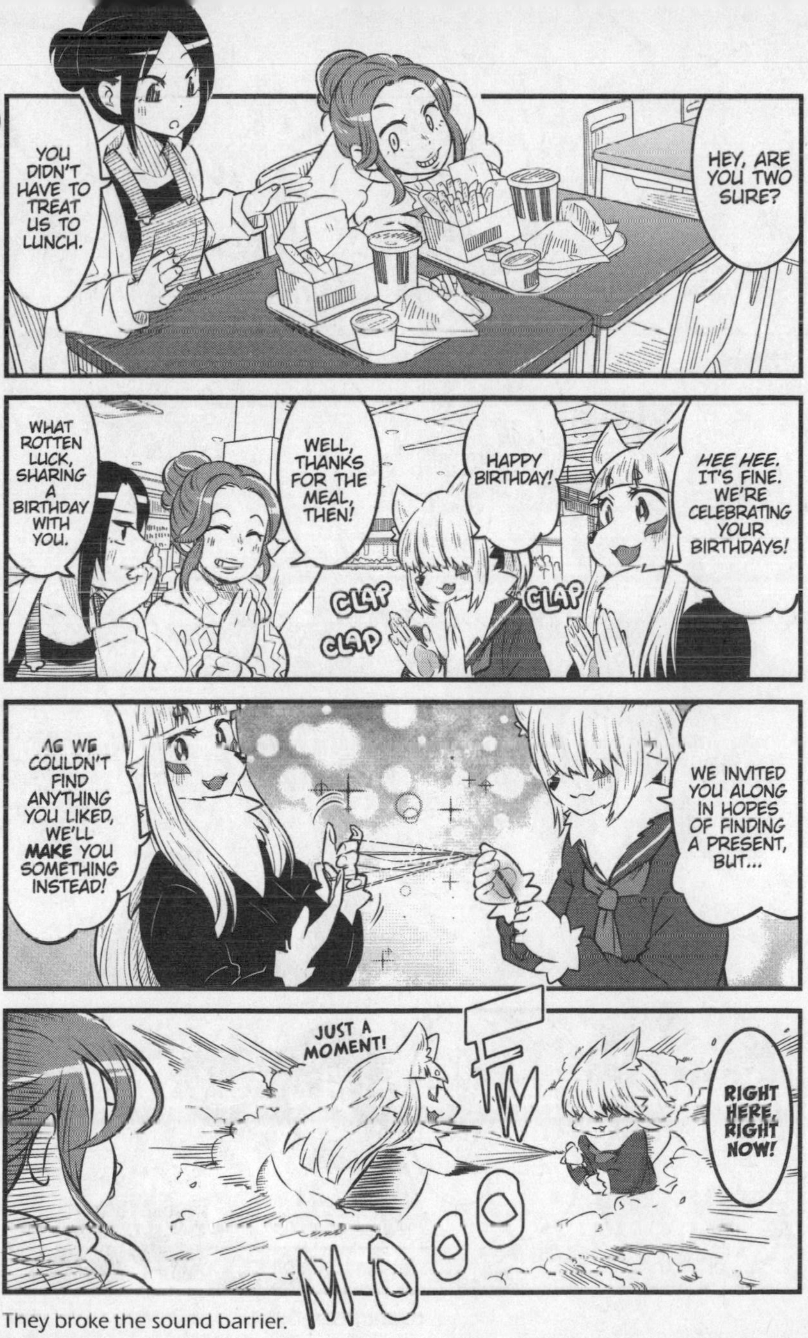
HEY, ARE YOU TWO SURE?
YOU DIDN'T HAVE TO TREAT US TO LUNCH.
HEE HEE. IT'S FINE. WE'RE CELEBRATING YOUR BIRTHDAYS!
HAPPY BIRTHDAY!
CLAP
CLAP
CLAP
WELL, THANKS FOR THE MEAL, THEN!
WHAT ROTTEN LUCK, SHARING A BIRTHDAY WITH YOU.
WE INVITED YOU ALONG IN HOPES OF FINDING A PRESENT, BUT...
AS WE COULDN'T FIND ANYTHING YOU LIKED, WE'LL **MAKE** YOU SOMETHING INSTEAD!
RIGHT HERE, RIGHT NOW!
FWW
JUST A MOMENT!
MOOOO

They broke the sound barrier.

KUTEUCHI AN ANCIENT METHOD OF HAND-BRAIDING THREADS INTO A PATTERNED KUMIHIMO CORD. SINCE THE EDO PERIOD, BRAIDING STANDS AND OTHER TOOLS WERE DEVELOPED, AND FROM THE MEIJI PERIOD ON, VERY FEW PEOPLE STILL KNEW THIS TECHNIQUE.

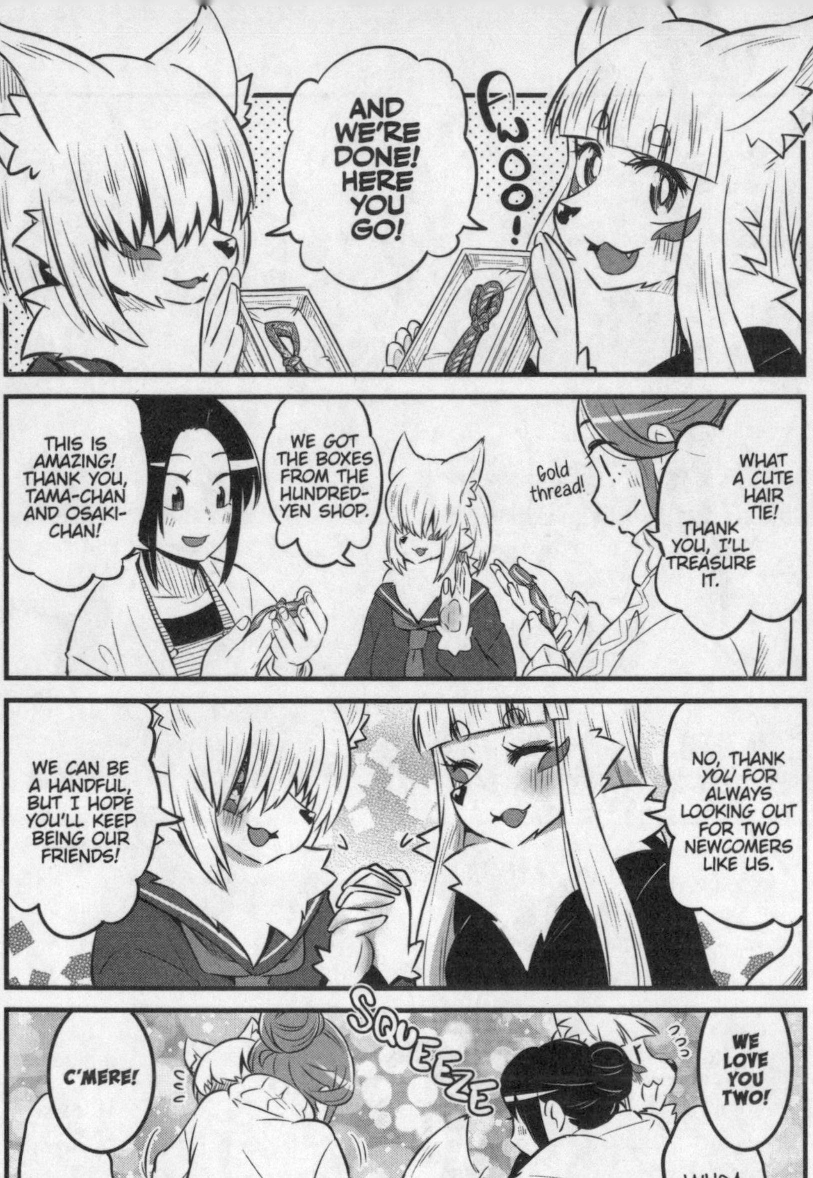
WOO!
AND WE'RE DONE! HERE YOU GO!
WHAT A CUTE HAIR TIE!
THANK YOU, I'LL TREASURE IT.
Gold thread!
WE GOT THE BOXES FROM THE HUNDRED-YEN SHOP.
THIS IS AMAZING! THANK YOU, TAMA-CHAN AND OSAKI-CHAN!
NO, THANK *YOU* FOR ALWAYS LOOKING OUT FOR TWO NEWCOMERS LIKE US.
WE CAN BE A HANDFUL, BUT I HOPE YOU'LL KEEP BEING OUR FRIENDS!
WE LOVE YOU TWO!
SQUEEEZE
C'MERE!
WHOA, NAKKI!?!
MIKKI!?!

TRUE GOLD THREAD THIS GOLDEN THREAD IS MADE BY LACQUERING JAPANESE PAPER WITH GOLD OR PLATINUM LEAF, CUTTING IT INTO THIN STRIPS, AND WRAPPING IT IN A SPIRAL AROUND A CORE THREAD.

The dropped honorifics show how close they've grown.

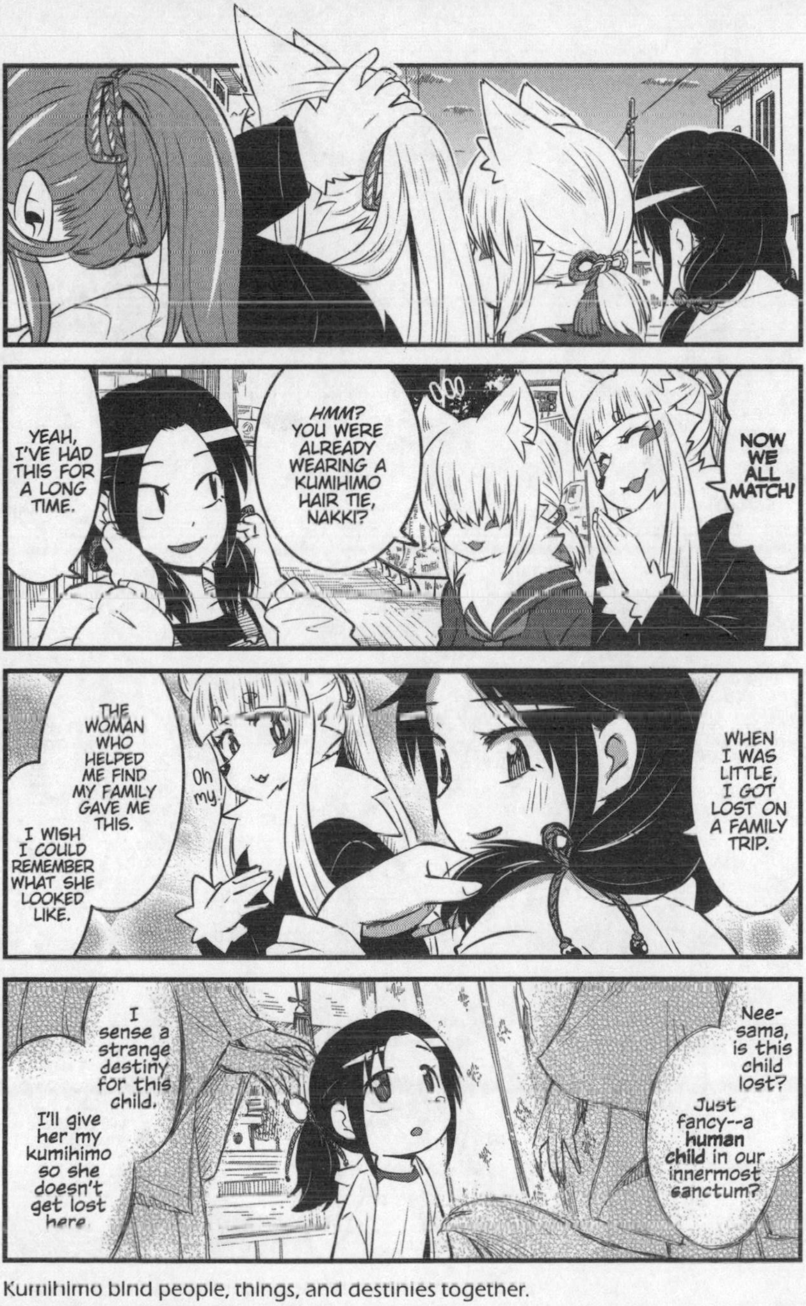
NOW WE ALL MATCH!
HMM? YOU WERE ALREADY WEARING A KUMIHIMO HAIR TIE, NAKKI?
YEAH, I'VE HAD THIS FOR A LONG TIME.
WHEN I WAS LITTLE, I GOT LOST ON A FAMILY TRIP.
Oh my.
THE WOMAN WHO HELPED ME FIND MY FAMILY GAVE ME THIS.
I WISH I COULD REMEMBER WHAT SHE LOOKED LIKE.
Nee-sama, is this child lost?
Just fancy--a **human child** in our innermost sanctum?
I sense a strange destiny for this child.
I'll give her my kumihimo so she doesn't get lost here.

KUMIHIMO THESE CORDS HAVE BEEN USED TO DECORATE BUDDHIST TOOLS AND SUTRAS. IN THE NARA PERIOD THEY WERE USED AS BELTS IN CEREMONIAL DRESS, IN THE KAMAKURA PERIOD THEY WERE USED TO BIND ARMOR TOGETHER AND SINCE THEN THEY'VE ADORNED TEA-CEREMONY TOOLS AS WELL.

Kumihimo bind people, things, and destinies together.

PRESENTS! THE GIFTS FOR NAKKI AND MIKKI COST ALMOST EVERYTHING WE EARNED FROM OUR JOBS, SO WE SCROUNGED UP WHAT WE HAD LEFT FOR SOME SWEETS!

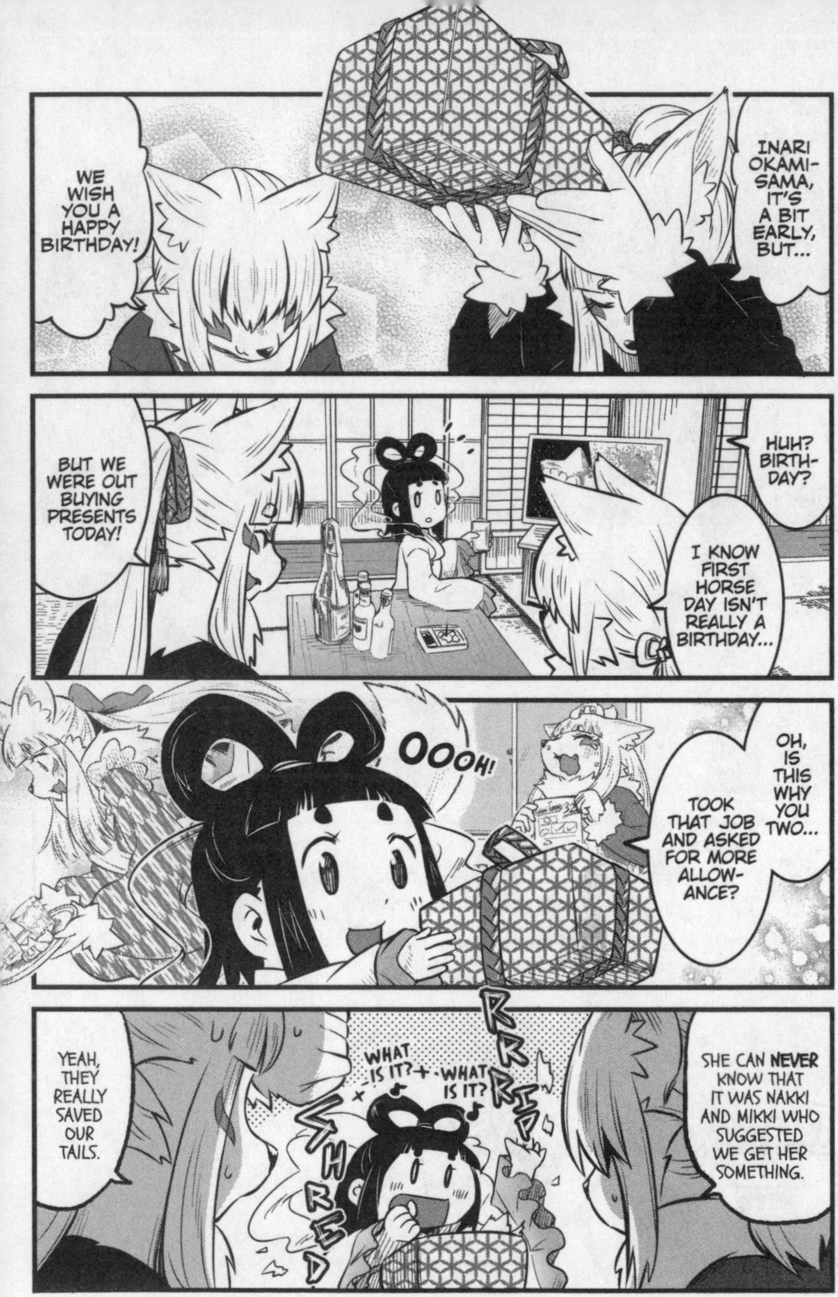
INARI OKAMI-SAMA, IT'S A BIT EARLY, BUT...
WE WISH YOU A HAPPY BIRTHDAY!
HUH? BIRTH-DAY?
I KNOW FIRST HORSE DAY ISN'T REALLY A BIRTHDAY...
BUT WE WERE OUT BUYING PRESENTS TODAY!
OH, IS THIS WHY YOU TWO...
TOOK THAT JOB AND ASKED FOR MORE ALLOW-ANCE?
OOOH!
SHE CAN **NEVER** KNOW THAT IT WAS NAKKI AND MIKKI WHO SUGGESTED WE GET HER SOMETHING.
RRRIP
WHAT IS IT?
WHAT IS IT?
SHRED
YEAH, THEY REALLY SAVED OUR TAILS.

The bountiful winter harvest and fishing season kept going on strong.

Tamamo-chan's a FOX!

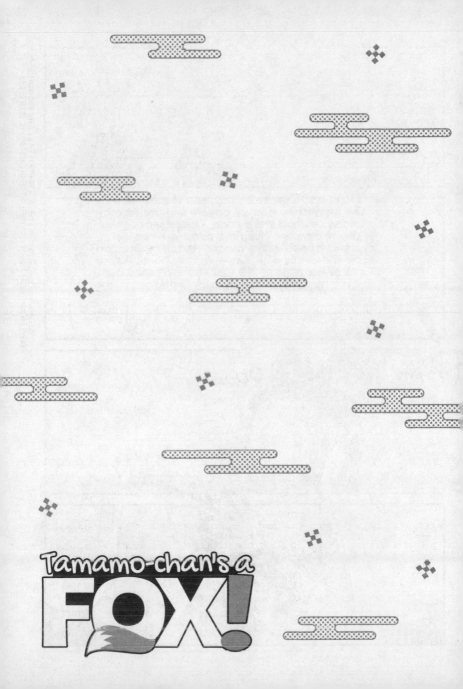

✱ P. 101, panel 2: Empress Genmei ✱
The forty-third ruler of Japan, and the fourth woman to hold the throne. Under her reign, Japan developed its first currency--copper coins with holes in the center--and she directed scribes to write down Japan's traditions. At the end of her reign in 715 CE, she abdicated the throne to her daughter, Gensho.

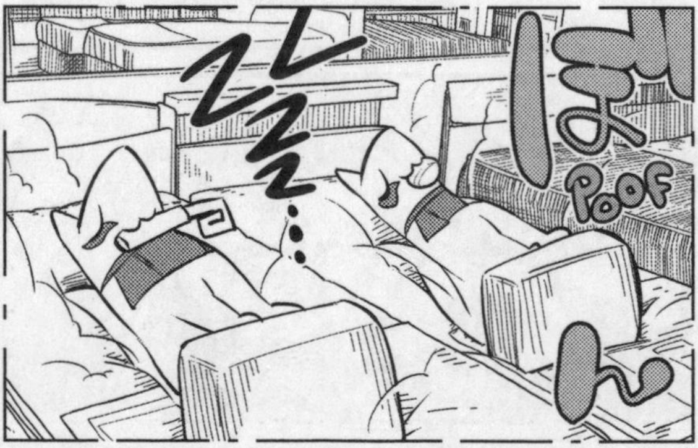
Poof

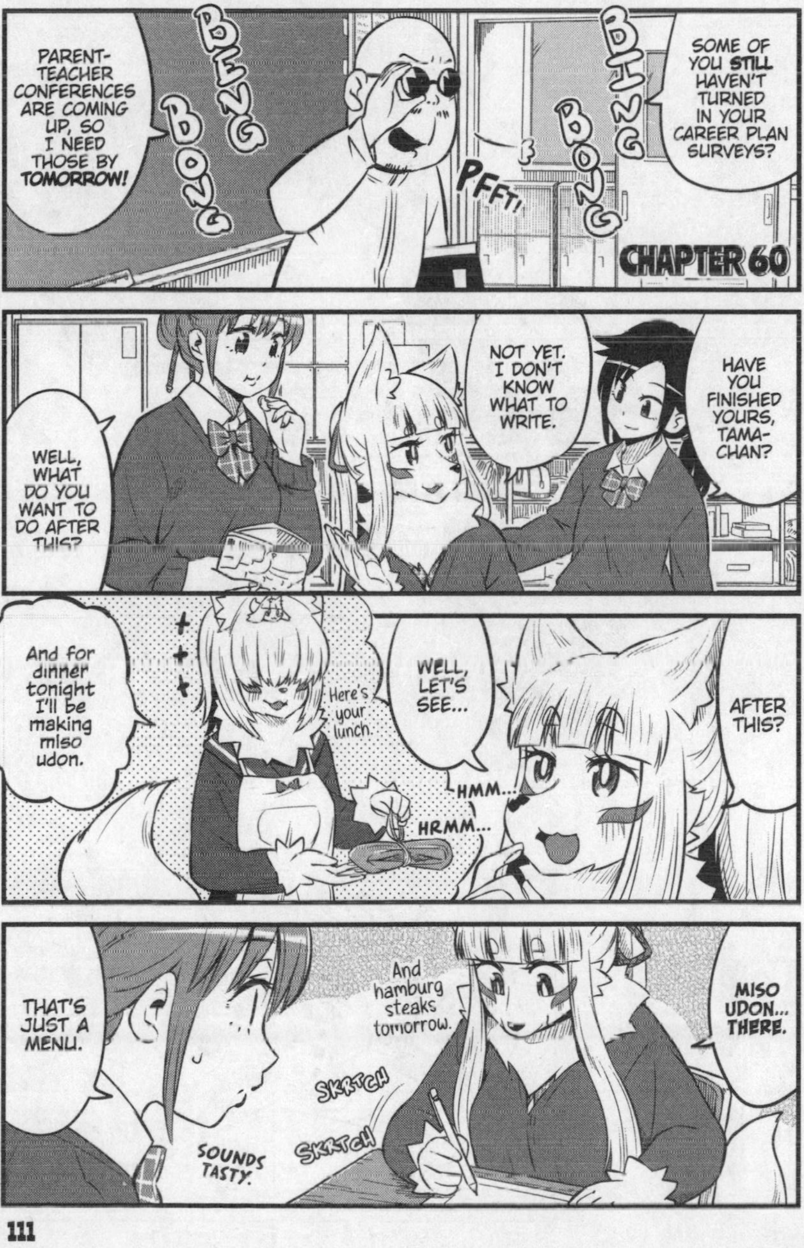
CHAPTER 60
SOME OF YOU STILL HAVEN'T TURNED IN YOUR CAREER PLAN SURVEYS?
BING BONG
PFFT
BENG BONG
PARENT-TEACHER CONFERENCES ARE COMING UP, SO I NEED THOSE BY TOMORROW!
HAVE YOU FINISHED YOURS, TAMA-CHAN?
NOT YET. I DON'T KNOW WHAT TO WRITE.
WELL, WHAT DO YOU WANT TO DO AFTER THIS?
AFTER THIS?
HMM...
HRMM...
WELL, LET'S SEE...
Here's your lunch.
And for dinner tonight I'll be making miso udon.
MISO UDON... THERE.
And hamburg steaks tomorrow.
SKRTCH
SKRTCH
THAT'S JUST A MENU.
SOUNDS TASTY.

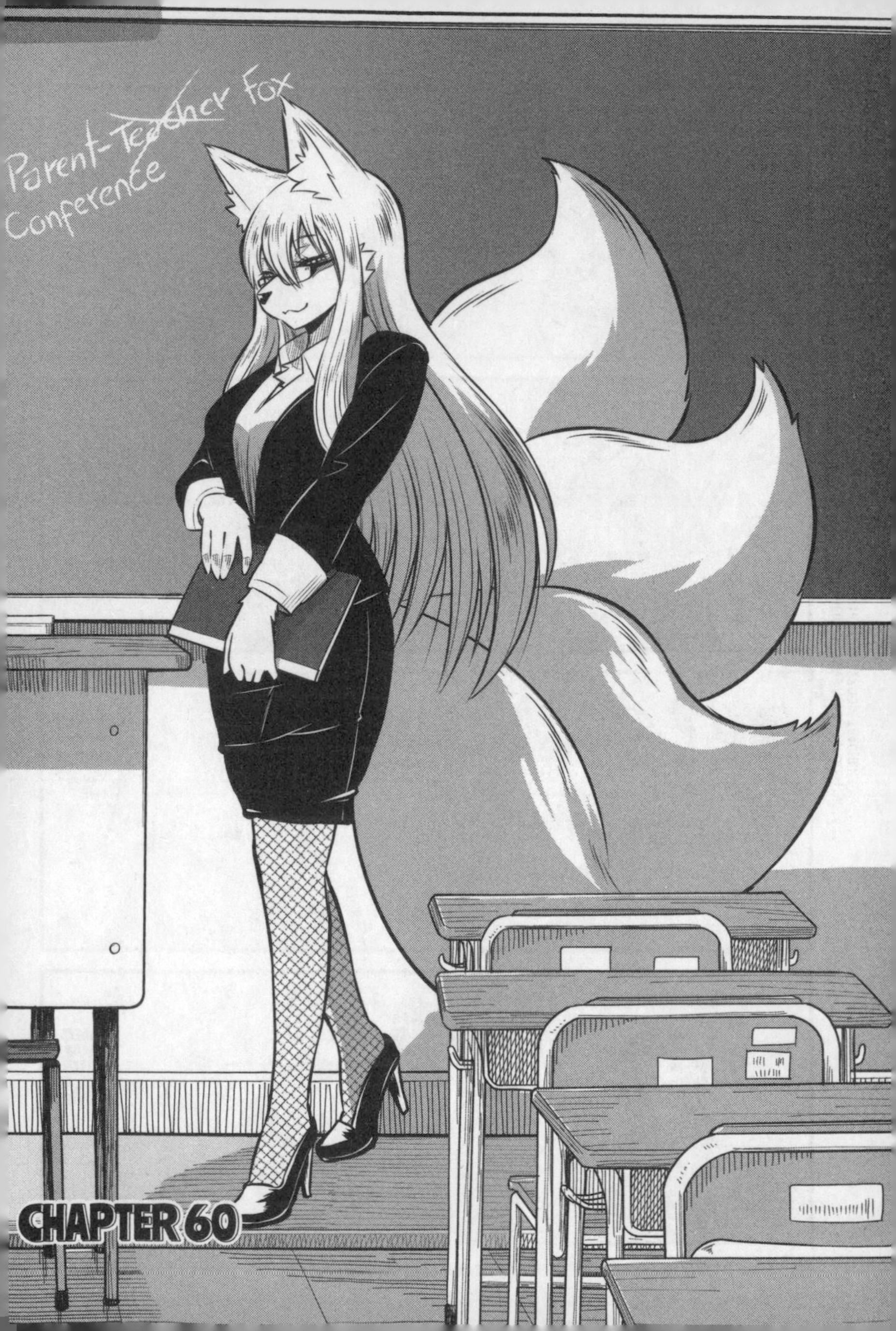
Parent-Teacher Fox
Conference
CHAPTER 60

GUIDANCE COUNSELING PROVIDING STUDENTS WITH ADVICE ABOUT THEIR OPTIONS AFTER GRADUATING. PERFORMED IN JAPANESE SCHOOLS BY A STUDENT'S HOMEROOM OR ASSISTANT HOMEROOM TEACHER.

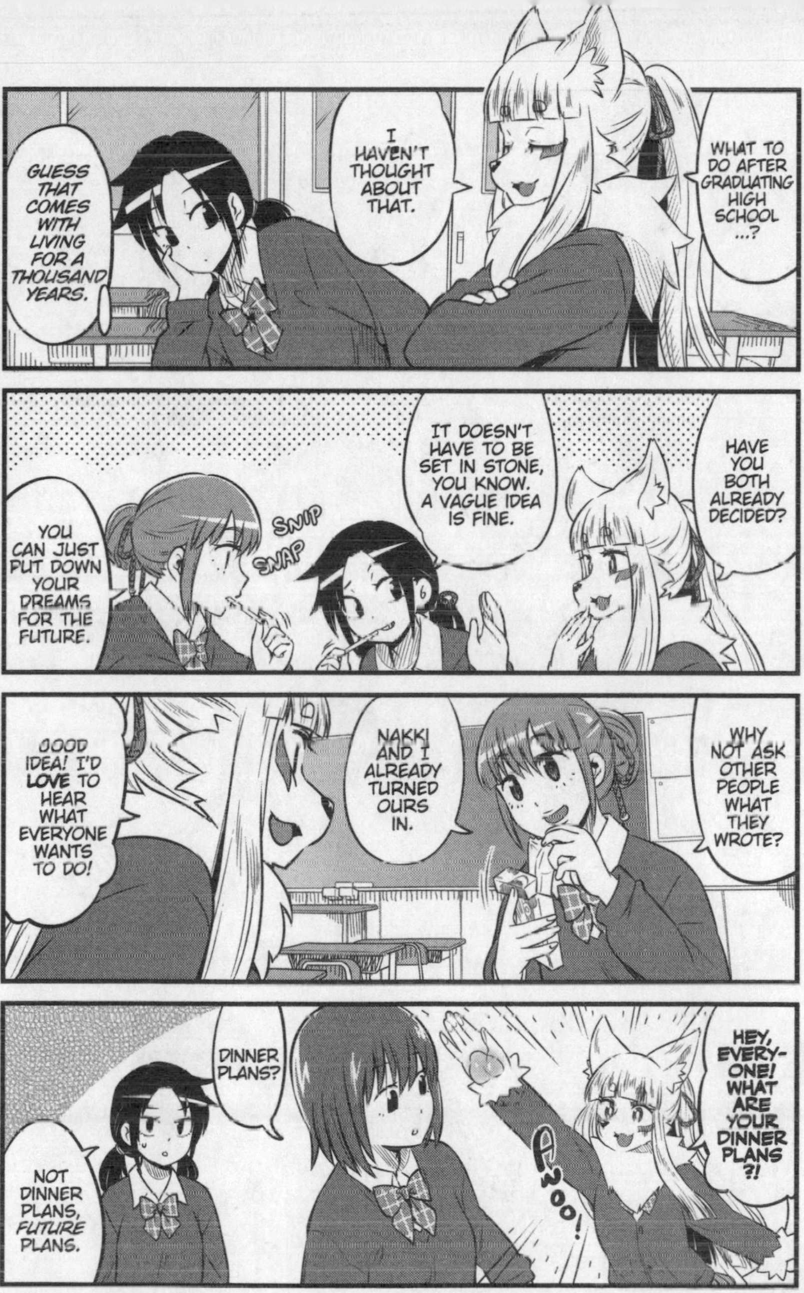
WHAT TO DO AFTER GRADUATING HIGH SCHOOL ...?
I HAVEN'T THOUGHT ABOUT THAT.
GUESS THAT COMES WITH LIVING FOR A THOUSAND YEARS.
HAVE YOU BOTH ALREADY DECIDED?
IT DOESN'T HAVE TO BE SET IN STONE, YOU KNOW. A VAGUE IDEA IS FINE.
SNIP
SNAP
YOU CAN JUST PUT DOWN YOUR DREAMS FOR THE FUTURE.
WHY NOT ASK OTHER PEOPLE WHAT THEY WROTE?
NAKKI AND I ALREADY TURNED OURS IN.
GOOD IDEA! I'D LOVE TO HEAR WHAT EVERYONE WANTS TO DO!
HEY, EVERYONE! WHAT ARE YOUR DINNER PLANS?!
AWOO!
DINNER PLANS?
NOT DINNER PLANS, FUTURE PLANS.

All she found out was everyone's menus for that night.

FUTURE PLANS I ASKED EVERYONE WHAT THEY WANTED TO DO AFTER GRADUATING. I THINK IT'S WONDERFUL THAT THEY ALL HAVE THEIR OWN DREAM! THEY CAN DO ANYTHING THEY PUT THEIR MINDS TO!

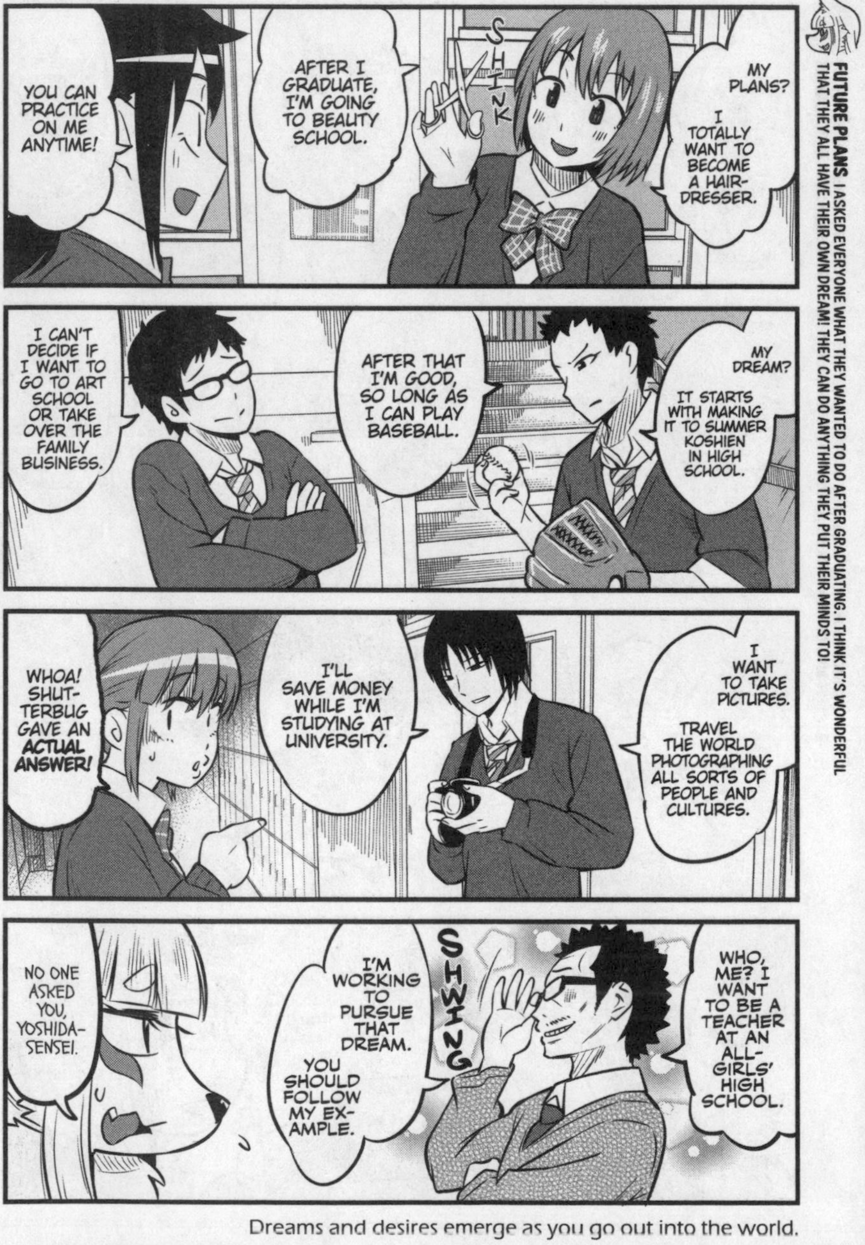

MY PLANS?
I TOTALLY WANT TO BECOME A HAIR-DRESSER.
SHINK
AFTER I GRADUATE, I'M GOING TO BEAUTY SCHOOL.
YOU CAN PRACTICE ON ME ANYTIME!
MY DREAM?
IT STARTS WITH MAKING IT TO SUMMER KOSHIEN IN HIGH SCHOOL.
AFTER THAT I'M GOOD, SO LONG AS I CAN PLAY BASEBALL.
I CAN'T DECIDE IF I WANT TO GO TO ART SCHOOL OR TAKE OVER THE FAMILY BUSINESS.
I WANT TO TAKE PICTURES.
TRAVEL THE WORLD PHOTOGRAPHING ALL SORTS OF PEOPLE AND CULTURES.
I'LL SAVE MONEY WHILE I'M STUDYING AT UNIVERSITY.
WHOA! SHUTTERBUG GAVE AN ACTUAL ANSWER!
WHO, ME? I WANT TO BE A TEACHER AT AN ALL-GIRLS' HIGH SCHOOL.
SHWING
I'M WORKING TO PURSUE THAT DREAM.
YOU SHOULD FOLLOW MY EXAMPLE.
NO ONE ASKED YOU, YOSHIDA-SENSEI.

Dreams and desires emerge as you go out into the world.

SCHOOL LIFE WHETHER YOU'RE STUDYING FOR UNIVERSITY OR DEVOTING YOUR TIME TO CLUB ACTIVITIES, FIND OPPORTUNITIES TO GROW AND APPLY YOUR EXPERIENCES TOWARDS YOUR FUTURE!

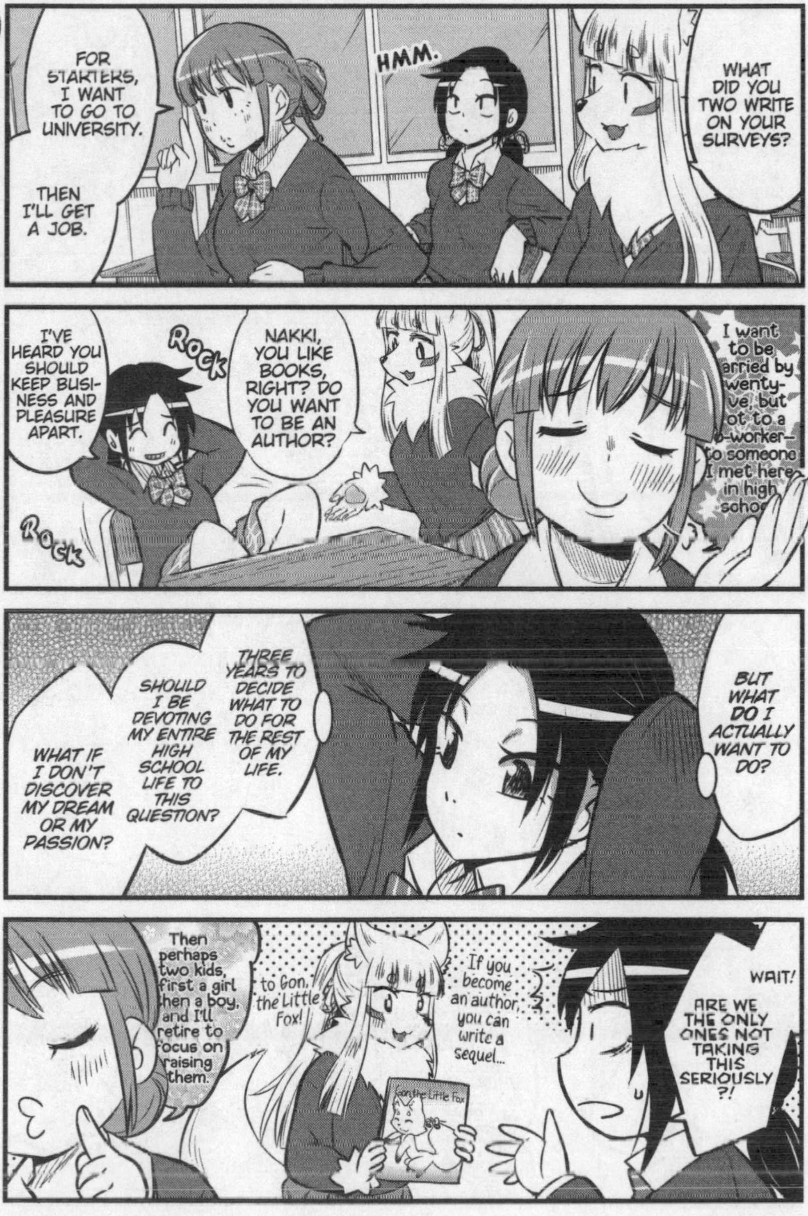
WHAT DID YOU TWO WRITE ON YOUR SURVEYS?
HMM.
FOR STARTERS, I WANT TO GO TO UNIVERSITY.
THEN I'LL GET A JOB.
I want to be arried by wenty-ve, but ot to a o-worker—to someone I met here in high schoo
NAKKI, YOU LIKE BOOKS, RIGHT? DO YOU WANT TO BE AN AUTHOR?
ROCK
I'VE HEARD YOU SHOULD KEEP BUSINESS AND PLEASURE APART.
ROCK
BUT WHAT DO I ACTUALLY WANT TO DO?
THREE YEARS TO DECIDE WHAT TO DO FOR THE REST OF MY LIFE.
SHOULD I BE DEVOTING MY ENTIRE HIGH SCHOOL LIFE TO THIS QUESTION?
WHAT IF I DON'T DISCOVER MY DREAM OR MY PASSION?
WAIT!
ARE WE THE ONLY ONES NOT TAKING THIS SERIOUSLY?!
If you become an author, you can write a sequel...
to Gon, the Little Fox!
Gon the Little Fox
Then perhaps two kids, first a girl then a boy, and I'll retire to focus on raising them.

Your teen years end just when they get going.

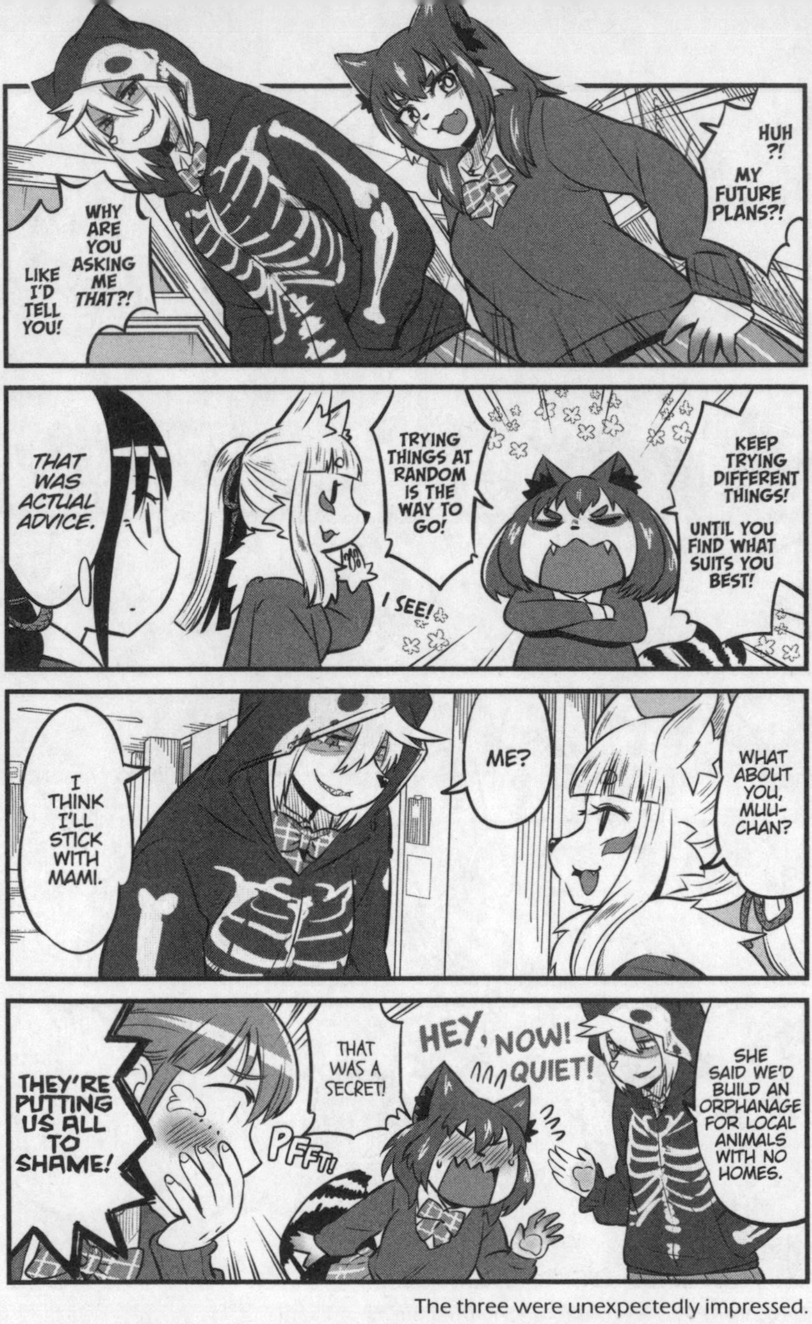
HUH?!
MY FUTURE PLANS?!
WHY ARE YOU ASKING ME THAT?!
LIKE I'D TELL YOU!
KEEP TRYING DIFFERENT THINGS!
UNTIL YOU FIND WHAT SUITS YOU BEST!
TRYING THINGS AT RANDOM IS THE WAY TO GO!
I SEE!
THAT WAS ACTUAL ADVICE.
WHAT ABOUT YOU, MUU-CHAN?
ME?
I THINK I'LL STICK WITH MAMI.
SHE SAID WE'D BUILD AN ORPHANAGE FOR LOCAL ANIMALS WITH NO HOMES.
HEY, NOW! QUIET!
THAT WAS A SECRET!
PFFT!
THEY'RE PUTTING US ALL TO SHAME!

ORPHANAGE A HOME FOR CHILDREN WHO DON'T HAVE PARENTS OR ANYONE ELSE TO LOOK AFTER THEM. HIDEN-IN TEMPLE, BUILT IN 593 CE ON THE ORDERS OF PRINCE SHOTOKU, WAS FOUNDED AS AN ORPHANAGE.

The three were unexpectedly impressed.

TAMAMO'S DREAM AT FIRST IT WAS JUST ATTENDING SCHOOL LIKE SHE'D ALWAYS LONGED FOR, BUT AFTER SPENDING TIME THERE, HER DREAM BECAME FOCUSED ON THE PEOPLE INSTEAD OF THE PLACE.

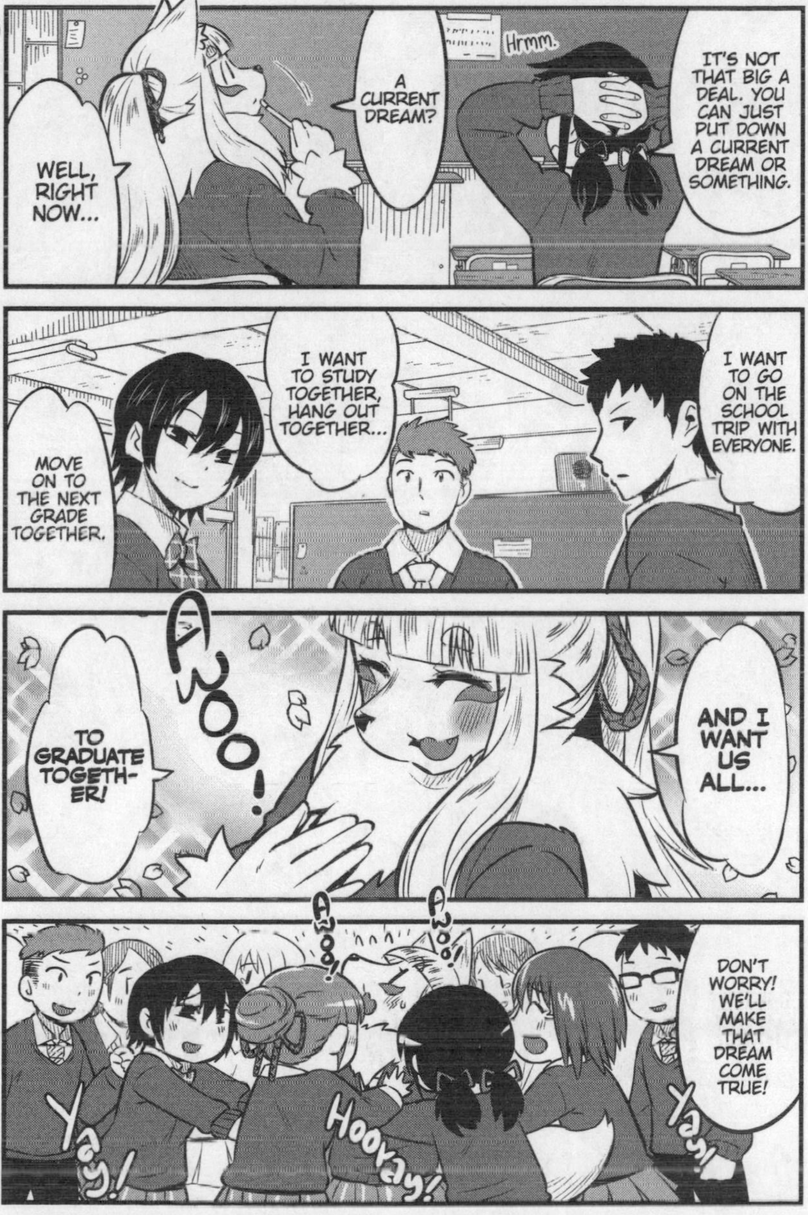
IT'S NOT THAT BIG A DEAL. YOU CAN JUST PUT DOWN A CURRENT DREAM OR SOMETHING.
Hrmm.
A CURRENT DREAM?
WELL, RIGHT NOW...
I WANT TO GO ON THE SCHOOL TRIP WITH EVERYONE.
I WANT TO STUDY TOGETHER, HANG OUT TOGETHER...
MOVE ON TO THE NEXT GRADE TOGETHER.
AND I WANT US ALL...
AWOO!
TO GRADUATE TOGETH-ER!
DON'T WORRY! WE'LL MAKE THAT DREAM COME TRUE!
Yay!
Awoo!
Awoo!
Hooray!
Yay!

Everyone was worried about Tamamo's future plans.

MY FUTURE I FINALLY DECIDE AND HE TELLS ME IT'S NO GOOD. I GUESS I'LL GO TO UNIVERSITY... WAIT, WAS MIURA-SENSEI DRINKING?

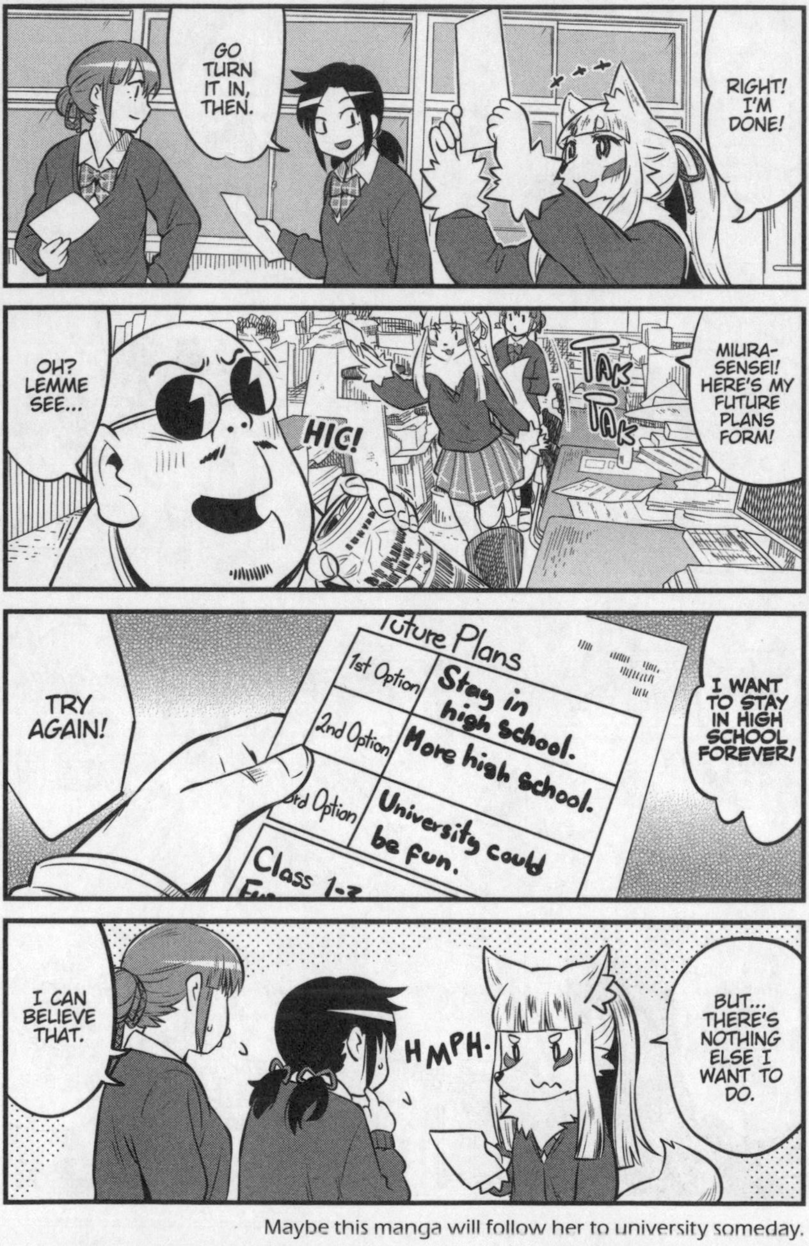
RIGHT! I'M DONE!
GO TURN IT IN, THEN.
MIURA-SENSEI! HERE'S MY FUTURE PLANS FORM!
TAK TAK
HIC!
OH? LEMME SEE...
I WANT TO STAY IN HIGH SCHOOL FOREVER!
uture Plans
1st Option
Stay in high school.
2nd Option
More high school.
rd Option
University could be fun.
Class 1-3
TRY AGAIN!
BUT... THERE'S NOTHING ELSE I WANT TO DO.
HMPH.
I CAN BELIEVE THAT.

Maybe this manga will follow her to university someday.

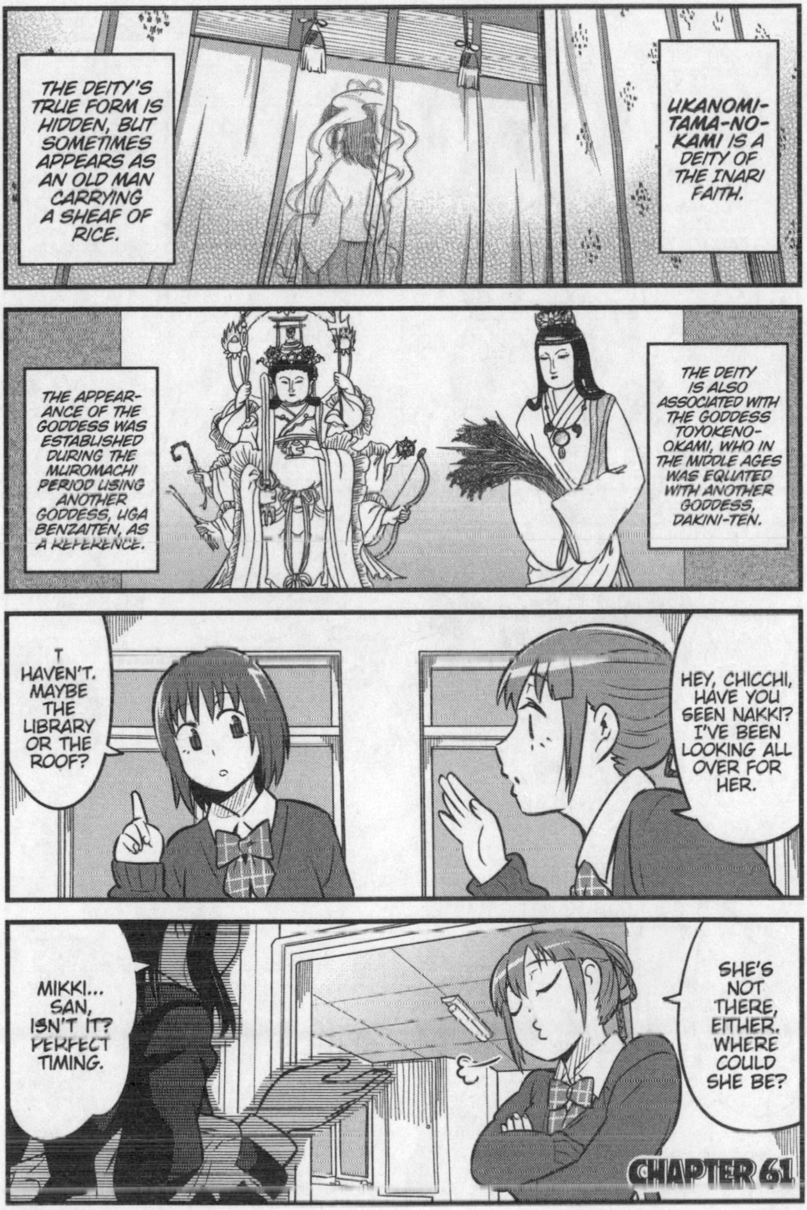
UKANOMI-TAMA-NO-KAMI IS A DEITY OF THE INARI FAITH.
THE DEITY'S TRUE FORM IS HIDDEN, BUT SOMETIMES APPEARS AS AN OLD MAN CARRYING A SHEAF OF RICE.
THE DEITY IS ALSO ASSOCIATED WITH THE GODDESS TOYOKENO-OKAMI, WHO IN THE MIDDLE AGES WAS EQUATED WITH ANOTHER GODDESS, DAKINI-TEN.
THE APPEARANCE OF THE GODDESS WAS ESTABLISHED DURING THE MUROMACHI PERIOD USING ANOTHER GODDESS, UGA BENZAITEN, AS A REFERENCE.
HEY, CHICCHI, HAVE YOU SEEN NAKKI? I'VE BEEN LOOKING ALL OVER FOR HER.
I HAVEN'T. MAYBE THE LIBRARY OR THE ROOF?
SHE'S NOT THERE, EITHER. WHERE COULD SHE BE?
MIKKI... SAN, ISN'T IT? PERFECT TIMING.
CHAPTER 61

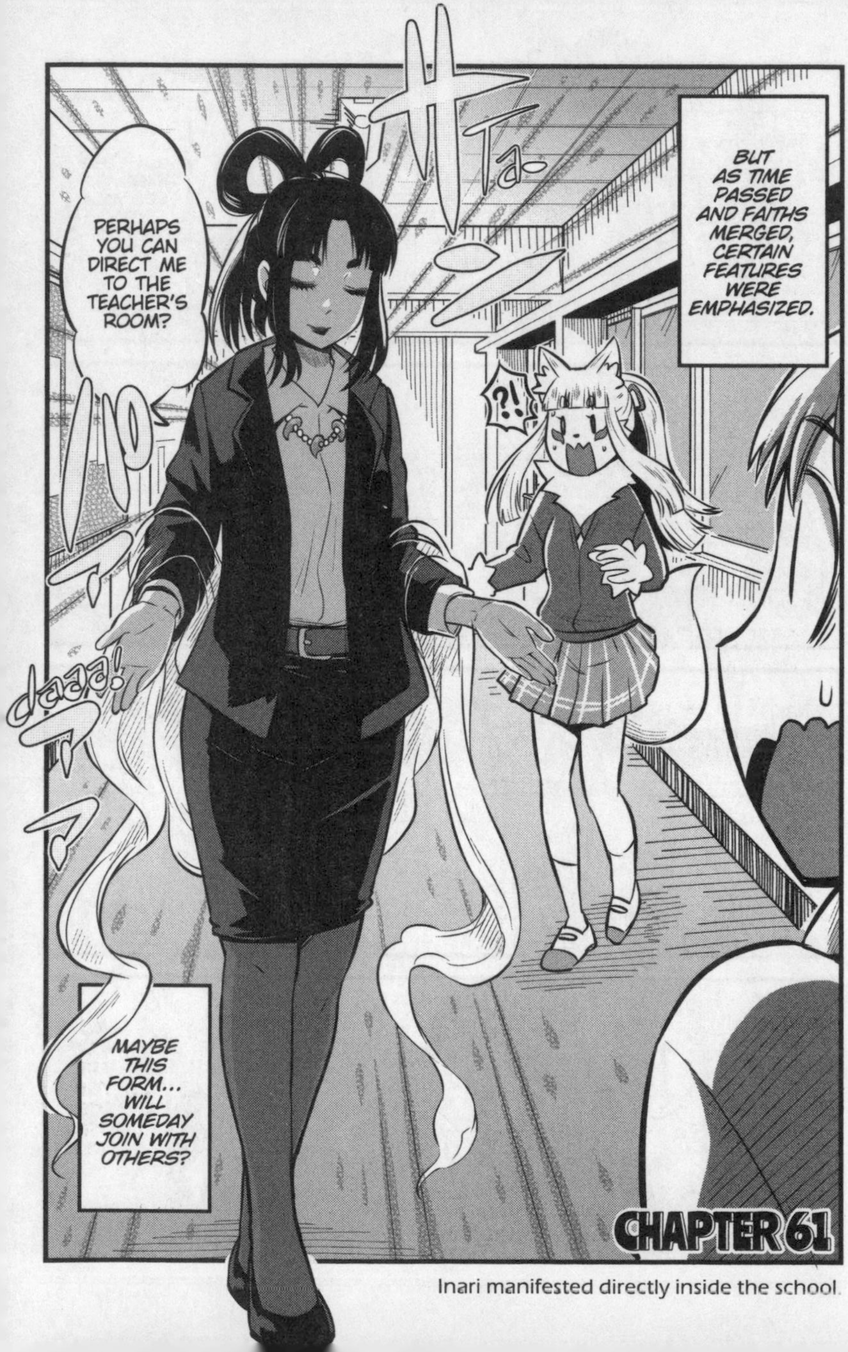
BUT AS TIME PASSED AND FAITHS MERGED, CERTAIN FEATURES WERE EMPHASIZED.
Ta-
?!
PERHAPS YOU CAN DIRECT ME TO THE TEACHER'S ROOM?
daaa!
MAYBE THIS FORM... WILL SOMEDAY JOIN WITH OTHERS?
CHAPTER 61
Inari manifested directly inside the school.

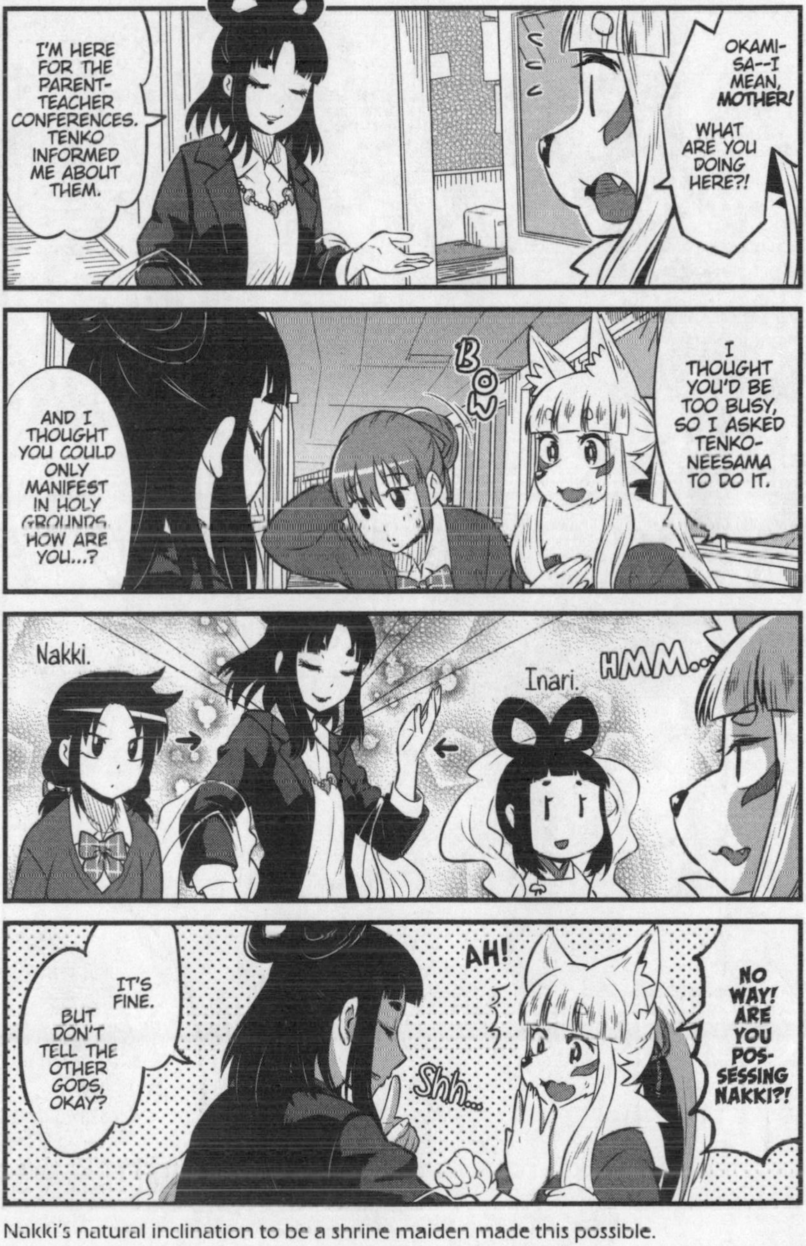
OKAMI-SA--I MEAN, MOTHER!
WHAT ARE YOU DOING HERE?!
I'M HERE FOR THE PARENT-TEACHER CONFERENCES. TENKO INFORMED ME ABOUT THEM.
I THOUGHT YOU'D BE TOO BUSY, SO I ASKED TENKO-NEESAMA TO DO IT.
BOW
AND I THOUGHT YOU COULD ONLY MANIFEST IN HOLY GROUNDS. HOW ARE YOU...?
HMM...
Inari.
Nakki.
NO WAY! ARE YOU POSSESSING NAKKI?!
AH!
Shh...
IT'S FINE.
BUT DON'T TELL THE OTHER GODS, OKAY?

Nakki's natural inclination to be a shrine maiden made this possible.

INVOKING A DEITY THE ACT OF CALLING UPON A DEITY TO DESCEND FROM THE HEAVENS INTO AN ALTAR AND THEN ASSIGNING A SHRINE MAIDEN TO ACT AS AN ORACLE. ON THIS OCCASION THE GODDESS DESCENDED WITHOUT BEING CALLED.

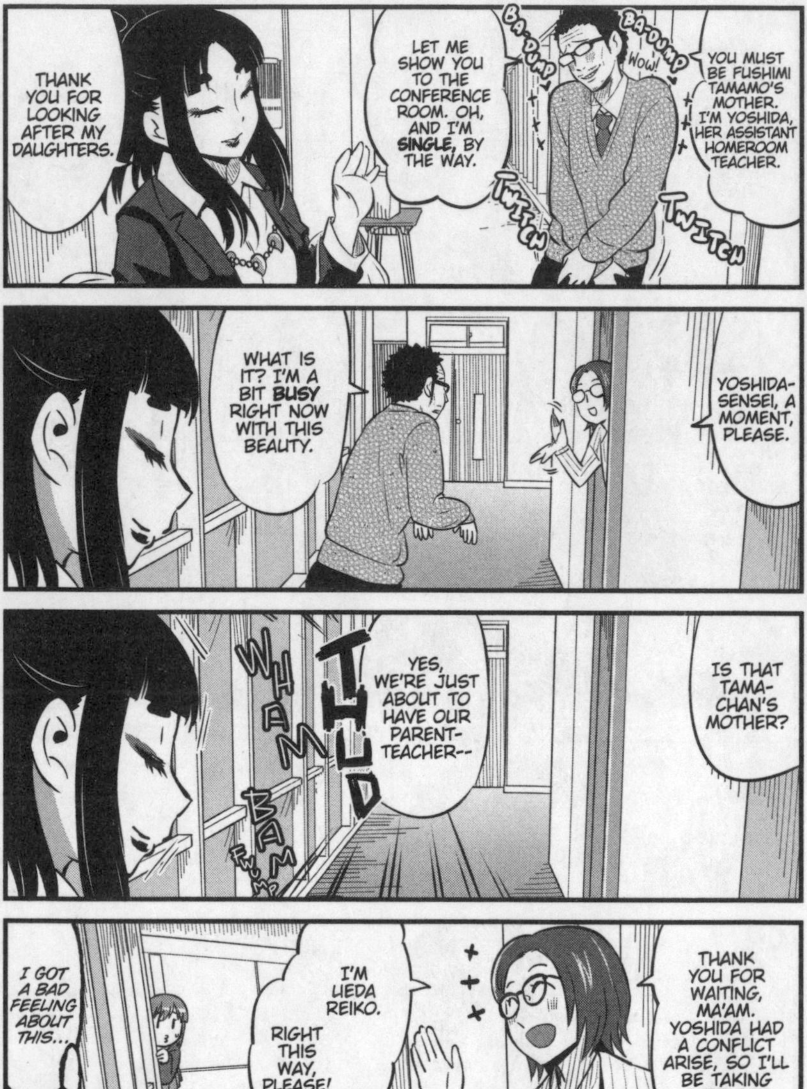
YOU MUST BE FUSHIMI TAMAMO'S MOTHER. I'M YOSHIDA, HER ASSISTANT HOMEROOM TEACHER.
BA-DUMP
WOW!
BA-DUMP
TWITCH
TWITCH
LET ME SHOW YOU TO THE CONFERENCE ROOM. OH, AND I'M **SINGLE**, BY THE WAY.
THANK YOU FOR LOOKING AFTER MY DAUGHTERS.
YOSHIDA-SENSEI, A MOMENT, PLEASE.
WHAT IS IT? I'M A BIT **BUSY** RIGHT NOW WITH THIS BEAUTY.
IS THAT TAMA-CHAN'S MOTHER?
YES, WE'RE JUST ABOUT TO HAVE OUR PARENT-TEACHER--
THUD
WHAM
BAM
THANK YOU FOR WAITING, MA'AM. YOSHIDA HAD A CONFLICT ARISE, SO I'LL BE TAKING OVER FOR HIM.
I'M UEDA REIKO.
RIGHT THIS WAY, PLEASE! ♡
I GOT A BAD FEELING ABOUT THIS...

KAKUREMI THE WORD *KAMI* STEMS FROM THE WORD *KAMU*, WHICH MEANS "HIDDEN IN COMPLEXITY" AND "PROFOUND," AND IS SAID TO HAVE COME FROM THE WORD *KAKUREMI* IN ANCIENT SHINTO TEXTS, WHICH MEANS "HIDDEN FORM."

By the time Yoshida-sensei came to, the day was over

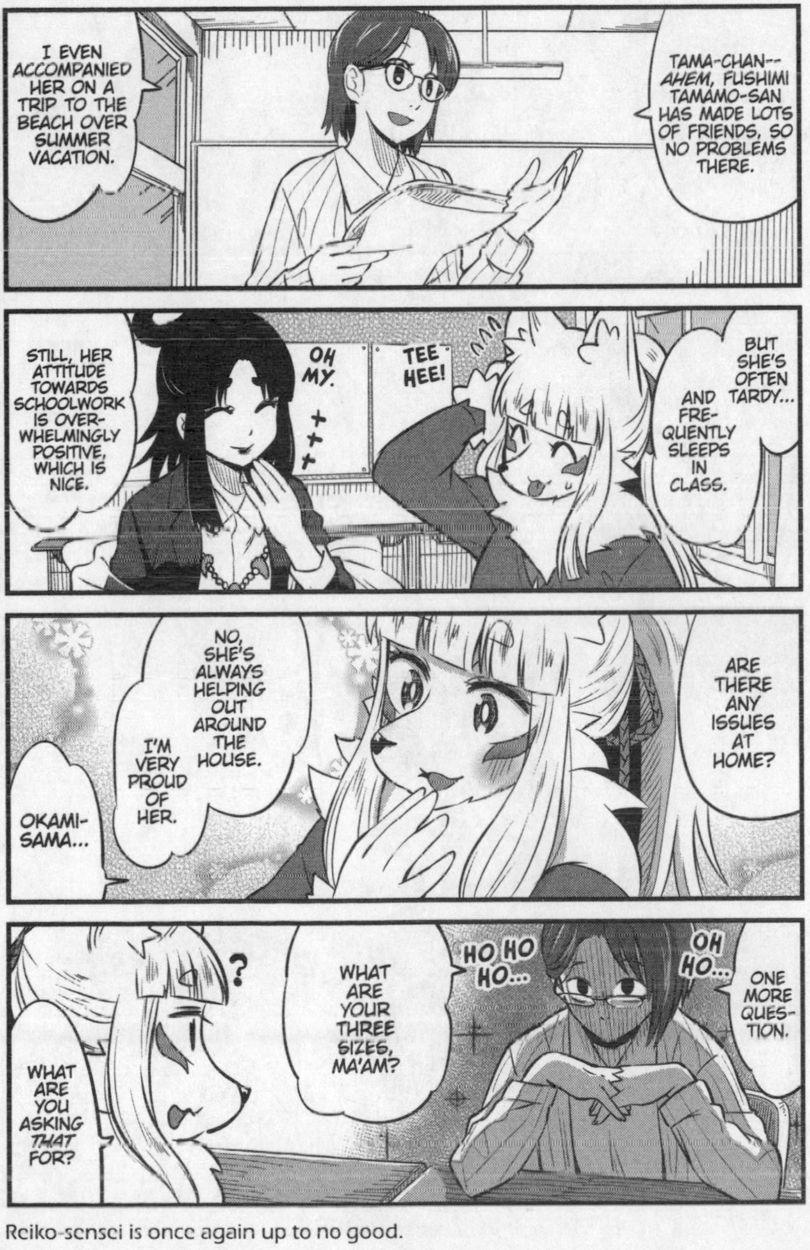
TAMA-CHAN-- *AHEM*, FUSHIMI TAMAMO-SAN HAS MADE LOTS OF FRIENDS, SO NO PROBLEMS THERE.
I EVEN ACCOMPANIED HER ON A TRIP TO THE BEACH OVER SUMMER VACATION.
BUT SHE'S OFTEN TARDY...
AND FRE-QUENTLY SLEEPS IN CLASS.
TEE HEE!
OH MY.
STILL, HER ATTITUDE TOWARDS SCHOOLWORK IS OVER-WHELMINGLY POSITIVE, WHICH IS NICE.
ARE THERE ANY ISSUES AT HOME?
NO, SHE'S ALWAYS HELPING OUT AROUND THE HOUSE.
I'M VERY PROUD OF HER.
OKAMI-SAMA...
ONE MORE QUES-TION.
OH HO...
HO HO HO...
WHAT ARE YOUR THREE SIZES, MA'AM?
?
WHAT ARE YOU ASKING *THAT* FOR?

PARENT/CHILD/TEACHER MEETINGS ONE FORM OF PARENT-TEACHER CONFERENCE IN WHICH THE STUDENT IS ALSO PRESENT. THEY ALL DISCUSS VARIOUS TOPICS, INCLUDING POSSIBLE CAREER PATHS, HOME LIFE, AND SCHOOL PERFORMANCE.

Reiko-sensei is once again up to no good.

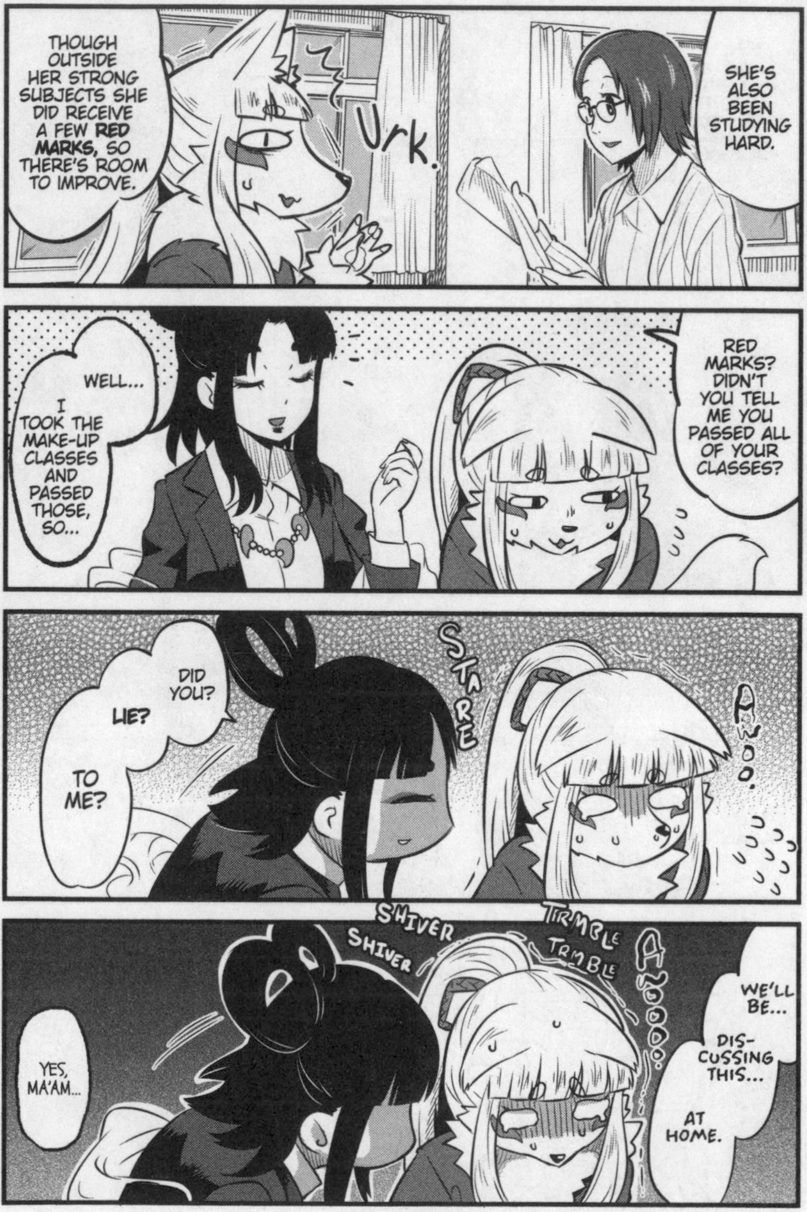
SHE'S ALSO BEEN STUDYING HARD.
THOUGH OUTSIDE HER STRONG SUBJECTS SHE DID RECEIVE A FEW **RED MARKS,** SO THERE'S ROOM TO IMPROVE.
Urk.
RED MARKS? DIDN'T YOU TELL ME YOU PASSED ALL OF YOUR CLASSES?
WELL... I TOOK THE MAKE-UP CLASSES AND PASSED THOSE, SO...
STARE
AWOO.
DID YOU?
LIE?
TO ME?
WE'LL BE... DIS-CUSSING THIS... AT HOME.
AWOOOOO.
TRMBLE TRMBLE
SHIVER SHIVER
YES, MA'AM...

RED MARK A TERM THAT MEANS FAILING GRADES ON HIGH SCHOOL FINALS. TAMAMO WILL HAVE TO WRITE REPORTS AND TAKE MAKE-UP EXAMS AND LESSONS TO COMPENSATE.

Not even divine messengers are spared from Inari's wrath.

7

AUTHORITY AN OVERWHELMING DIGNITY THAT EVOKES FEELINGS OF AWE IN PEOPLE. IT'S SAID THAT THE GODS GROW IN AUTHORITY AS PEOPLE VENERATE THEM.

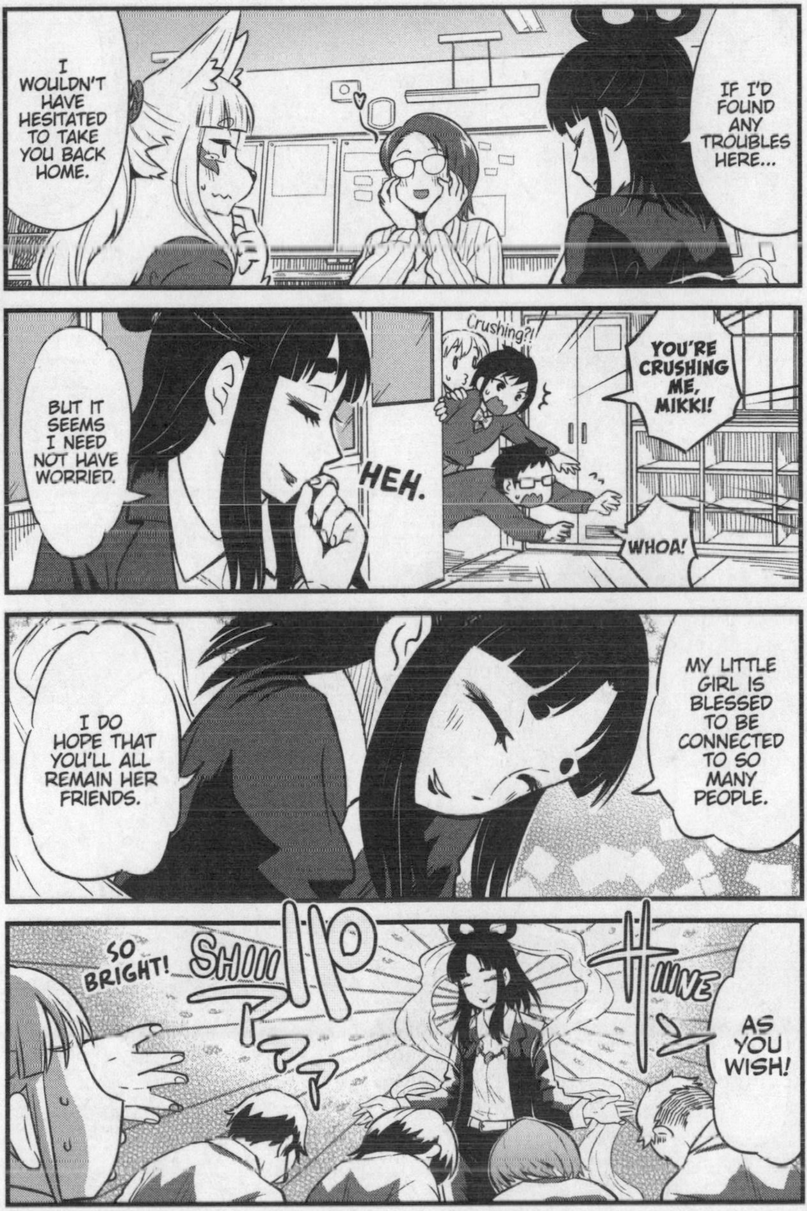
IF I'D FOUND ANY TROUBLES HERE...
I WOULDN'T HAVE HESITATED TO TAKE YOU BACK HOME.
YOU'RE CRUSHING ME, MIKKI!
Crushing?!
WHOA!
HEH.
BUT IT SEEMS I NEED NOT HAVE WORRIED.
MY LITTLE GIRL IS BLESSED TO BE CONNECTED TO SO MANY PEOPLE.
I DO HOPE THAT YOU'LL ALL REMAIN HER FRIENDS.
AS YOU WISH!
SHIIII
HIIINE
SO BRIGHT!

They bowed before her unconcealable divine authority.

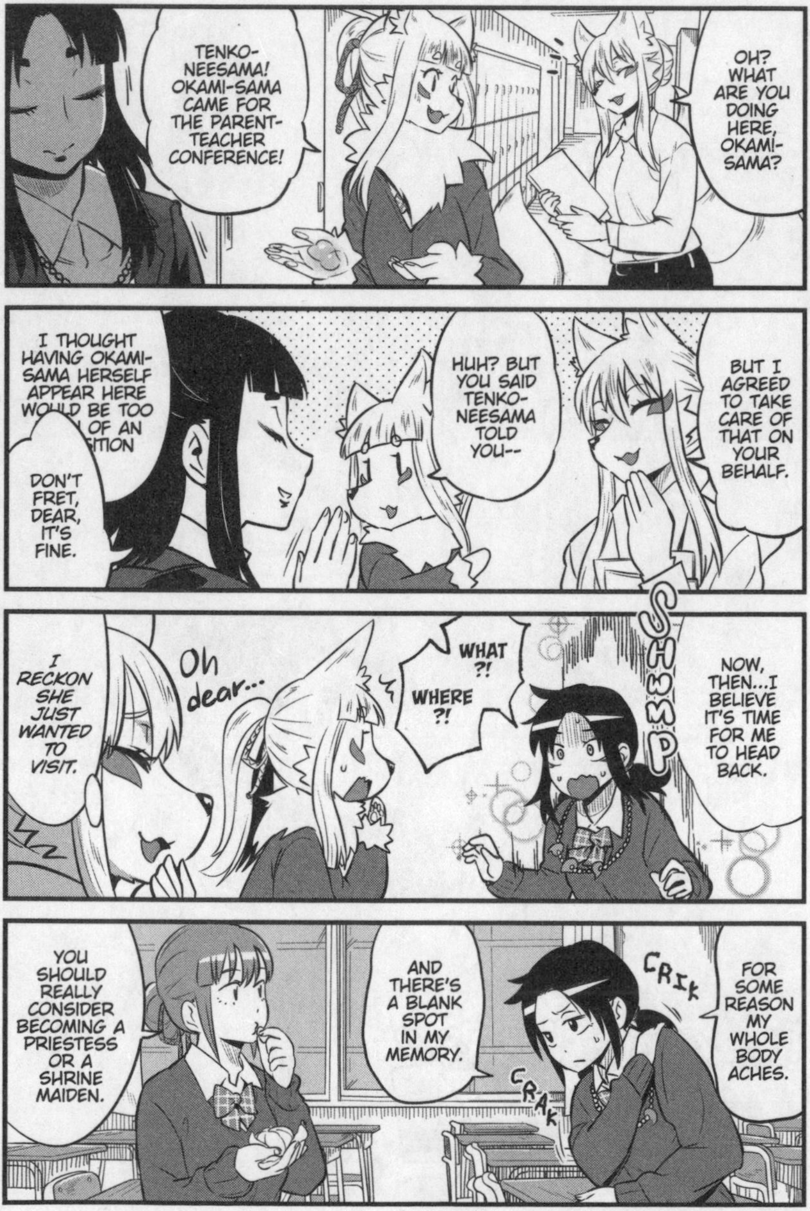
OH? WHAT ARE YOU DOING HERE, OKAMI-SAMA?
TENKO-NEESAMA! OKAMI-SAMA CAME FOR THE PARENT-TEACHER CONFERENCE!
BUT I AGREED TO TAKE CARE OF THAT ON YOUR BEHALF.
HUH? BUT YOU SAID TENKO-NEESAMA TOLD YOU--
I THOUGHT HAVING OKAMI-SAMA HERSELF APPEAR HERE WOULD BE TOO OF AN
DON'T FRET, DEAR, IT'S FINE.
SHWMP
NOW, THEN...I BELIEVE IT'S TIME FOR ME TO HEAD BACK.
WHAT?!
WHERE?!
Oh dear...
I RECKON SHE JUST WANTED TO VISIT.
FOR SOME REASON MY WHOLE BODY ACHES.
CRIK
CRAK
AND THERE'S A BLANK SPOT IN MY MEMORY.
YOU SHOULD REALLY CONSIDER BECOMING A PRIESTESS OR A SHRINE MAIDEN.

VISITING? COMING ALL THIS WAY JUST TO VISIT...I GUESS I CAN UNDERSTAND THAT! MAYBE SHE NEEDED A BREAK FROM HER DAILY ROUTINE. JUST LIKE ME!

Inari left her divine necklace behind, so Nakki's keeping it safe for her.

Tamamo-chan's a FOX!

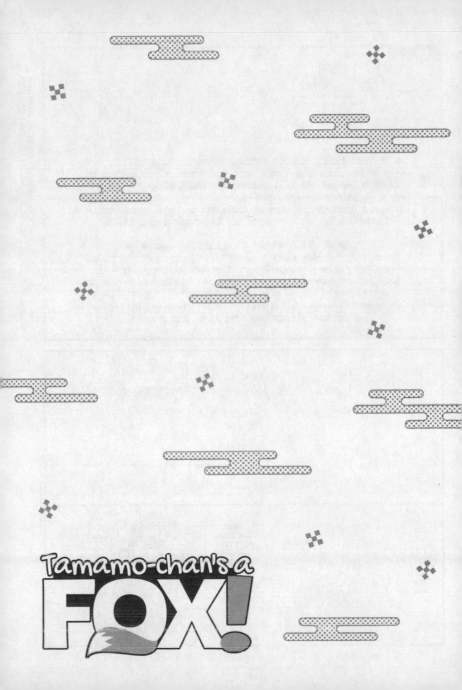

✻ P. 116, side caption: Prince Shotoku and Hiden-in ✻
Prince Shotoku is a legendary figure who ruled during the Asuka period. He is regarded as the "father of Japanese Buddhism." He built a number of important Buddhist temples, including Hiden-in, believed to have been built in Osaka to be a sanctuary for the poor and orphans.

✻ P. 119, panels 1 and 2: Deities ✻
Ukanomitama-no-Kami is a harvest deity, described as both female and male. Dakini-Ten was originally a Hindu goddess of farming, but became associated with sexual desire, and is known for devouring human hearts. Uga Benzaiten is one of the Seven Gods of Luck, as well as a patron of music, literature, and geisha.

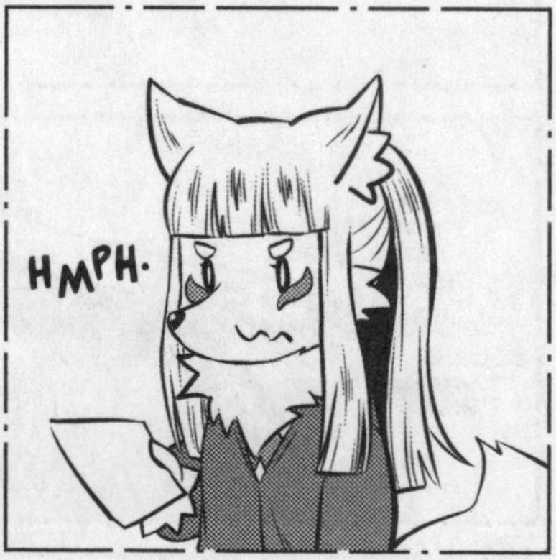
HMPH.

CHAPTER 62

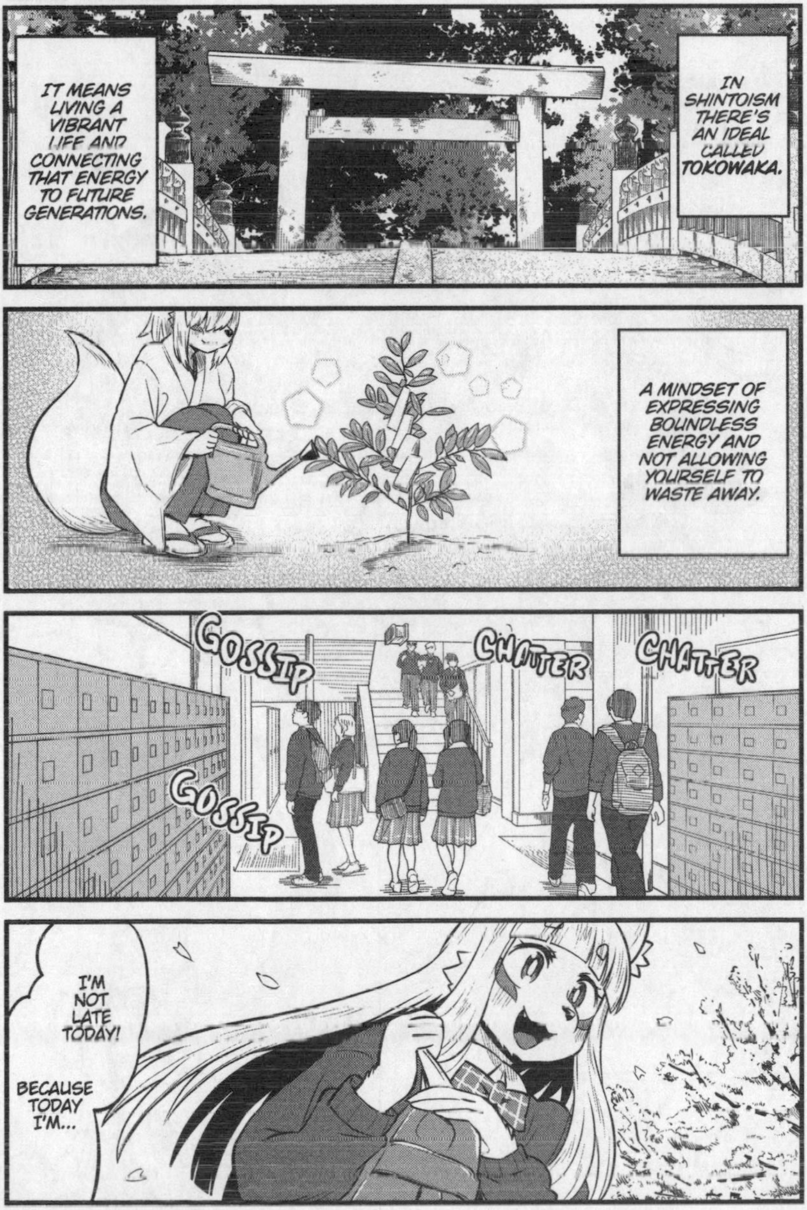

IN SHINTOISM THERE'S AN IDEAL CALLED TOKOWAKA.
IT MEANS LIVING A VIBRANT LIFE AND CONNECTING THAT ENERGY TO FUTURE GENERATIONS.
A MINDSET OF EXPRESSING BOUNDLESS ENERGY AND NOT ALLOWING YOURSELF TO WASTE AWAY.
CHATTER
CHATTER
GOSSIP
GOSSIP
I'M NOT LATE TODAY!
BECAUSE TODAY I'M...

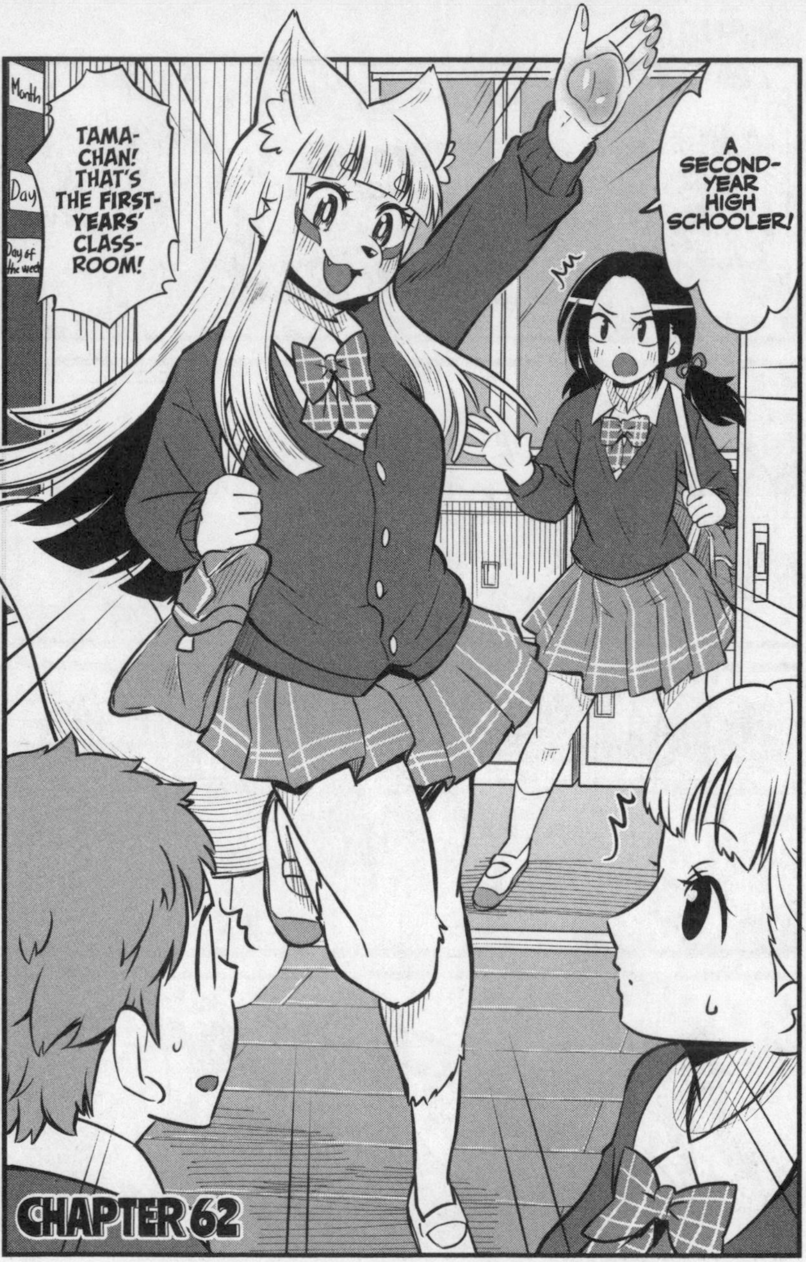
A SECOND-YEAR HIGH SCHOOLER!
TAMA-CHAN! THAT'S THE FIRST-YEARS' CLASSROOM!
Month
Day
Day of the week
CHAPTER 62
Over a thousand years old but still a high school girl at heart.

CLASS CHANGE A GREAT CHANCE TO MEET NEW PEOPLE. CLASSES ARE USUALLY ASSIGNED BASED ON ACADEMIC PERFORMANCE, BUT EVERYONE WITH A LINK TO TAMAMO WOUND UP IN THE SAME CLASS.

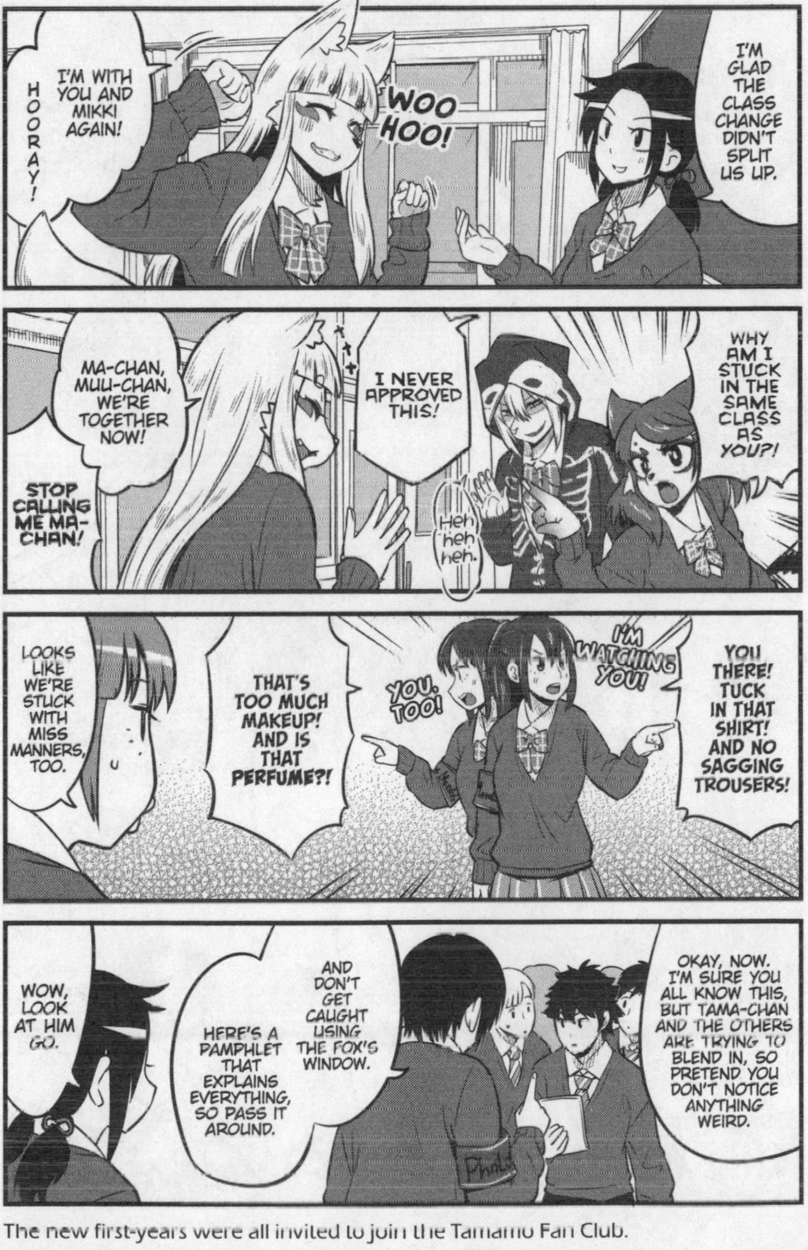

I'M GLAD THE CLASS CHANGE DIDN'T SPLIT US UP.
WOO HOO!
I'M WITH YOU AND MIKKI AGAIN!
HOORAY!
WHY AM I STUCK IN THE SAME CLASS AS YOU?!
I NEVER APPROVED THIS!
Heh heh heh.
MA-CHAN, MUU-CHAN, WE'RE TOGETHER NOW!
STOP CALLING ME MA-CHAN!
YOU THERE! TUCK IN THAT SHIRT! AND NO SAGGING TROUSERS!
I'M WATCHING YOU!
YOU, TOO!
THAT'S TOO MUCH MAKEUP! AND IS THAT PERFUME?!
LOOKS LIKE WE'RE STUCK WITH MISS MANNERS, TOO.
OKAY, NOW. I'M SURE YOU ALL KNOW THIS, BUT TAMA-CHAN AND THE OTHERS ARE TRYING TO BLEND IN, SO PRETEND YOU DON'T NOTICE ANYTHING WEIRD.
AND DON'T GET CAUGHT USING THE FOX'S WINDOW.
HERE'S A PAMPHLET THAT EXPLAINS EVERYTHING, SO PASS IT AROUND.
WOW, LOOK AT HIM GO.

The new first-years were all invited to join the Tamamo Fan Club.

TSUNDERE A PERSON WHO HIDES A SOFT SIDE (*DEREDERE* IN JAPANESE) BEHIND A PRICKLY ATTITUDE (*TSUNTSUN* IN JAPANESE). IT'S UNKNOWN WHETHER MAMI HAS A SOFT SIDE.

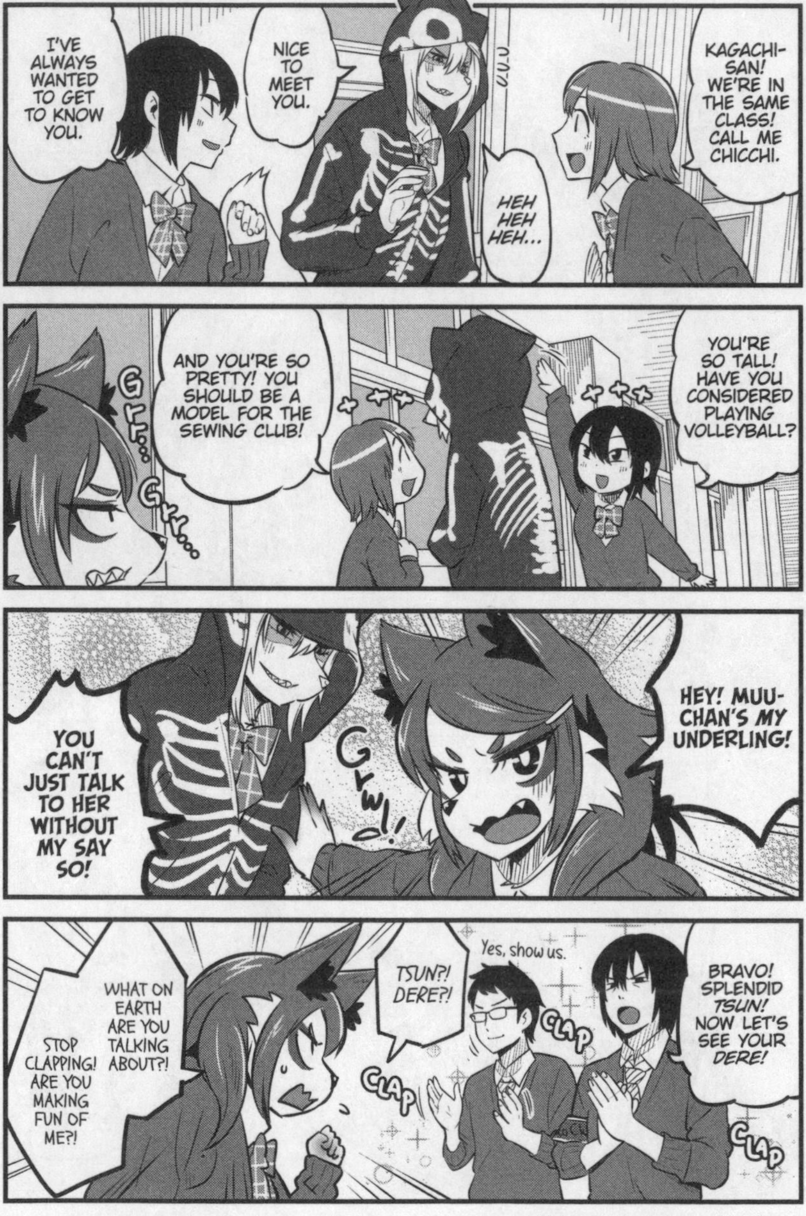
KAGACHI-SAN! WE'RE IN THE SAME CLASS! CALL ME CHICCHI.
HEH HEH HEH...
NICE TO MEET YOU.
I'VE ALWAYS WANTED TO GET TO KNOW YOU.
YOU'RE SO TALL! HAVE YOU CONSIDERED PLAYING VOLLEYBALL?
AND YOU'RE SO PRETTY! YOU SHOULD BE A MODEL FOR THE SEWING CLUB!
HEY! MUU-CHAN'S MY UNDERLING!
YOU CAN'T JUST TALK TO HER WITHOUT MY SAY SO!
BRAVO! SPLENDID *TSUN*! NOW LET'S SEE YOUR *DERE*!
CLAP
CLAP
Yes, show us.
TSUN?! *DERE*?!
CLAP
WHAT ON EARTH ARE YOU TALKING ABOUT?!
STOP CLAPPING! ARE YOU MAKING FUN OF ME?!

Her soft side is well hidden.

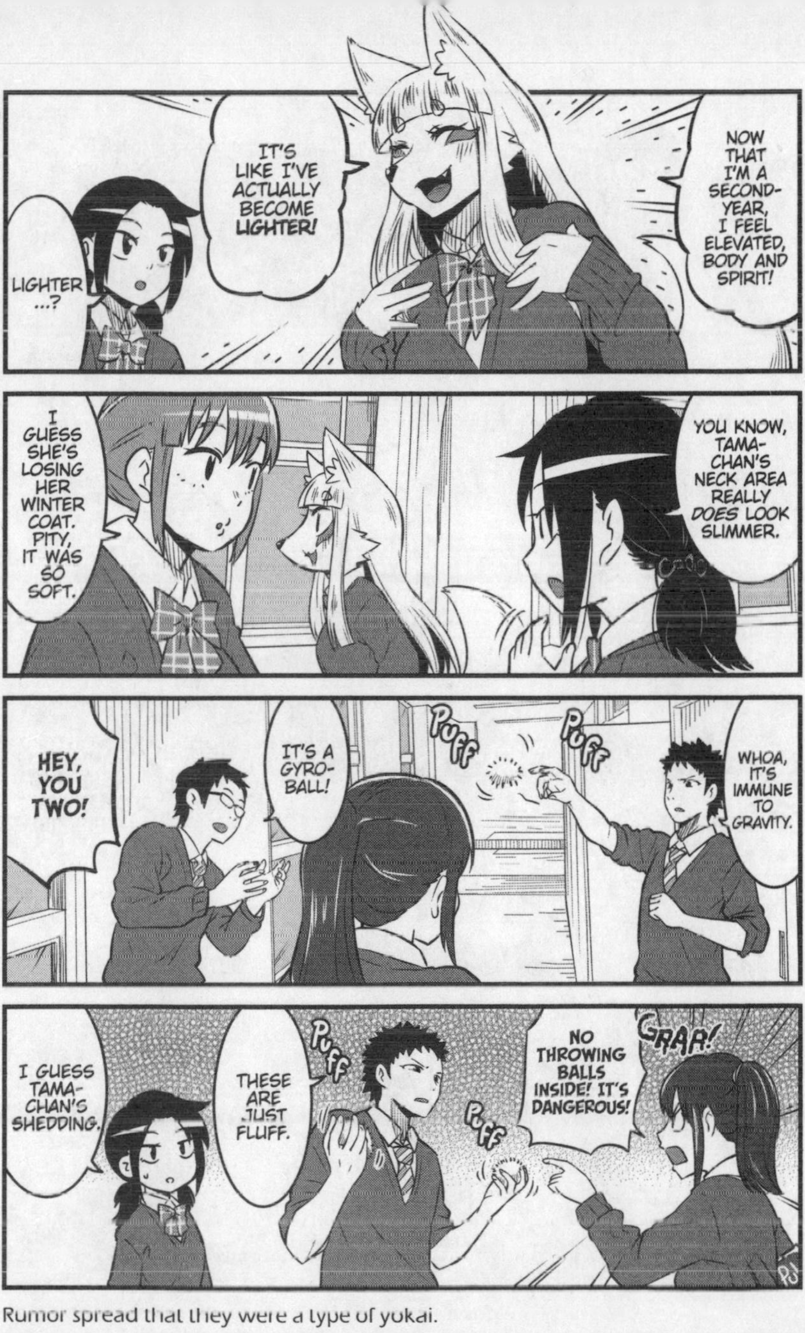
NOW THAT I'M A SECOND-YEAR, I FEEL ELEVATED, BODY AND SPIRIT!
IT'S LIKE I'VE ACTUALLY BECOME LIGHTER!
LIGHTER ...?
YOU KNOW, TAMA-CHAN'S NECK AREA REALLY DOES LOOK SLIMMER.
I GUESS SHE'S LOSING HER WINTER COAT. PITY, IT WAS SO SOFT.
WHOA, IT'S IMMUNE TO GRAVITY.
PUFF
PUFF
IT'S A GYRO-BALL!
HEY, YOU TWO!
GRAR!
NO THROWING BALLS INSIDE! IT'S DANGEROUS!
PUFF
PUFF
THESE ARE JUST FLUFF.
I GUESS TAMA-CHAN'S SHEDDING.

GYROBALL ALSO CALLED THE "MIRACLE PITCH," THIS IS A LEGENDARY UNHITTABLE PITCH USED IN JAPANESE BASEBALL. IT CAN ALSO REFER TO A PITCH THE BATTER KNOWS IS COMING BUT STILL CAN'T HIT.

Rumor spread that they were a type of yokai.

SHEDDING SEASON IN SPRING AND FALL, ANIMALS DROP ONE COAT AS ANOTHER GROWS IN TO BETTER REGULATE THEIR BODY TEMPERATURE IN SUMMER AND WINTER. IT LOOKS LIKE IT'S SHEDDING SEASON FOR TAMAMO AND THE OTHERS.

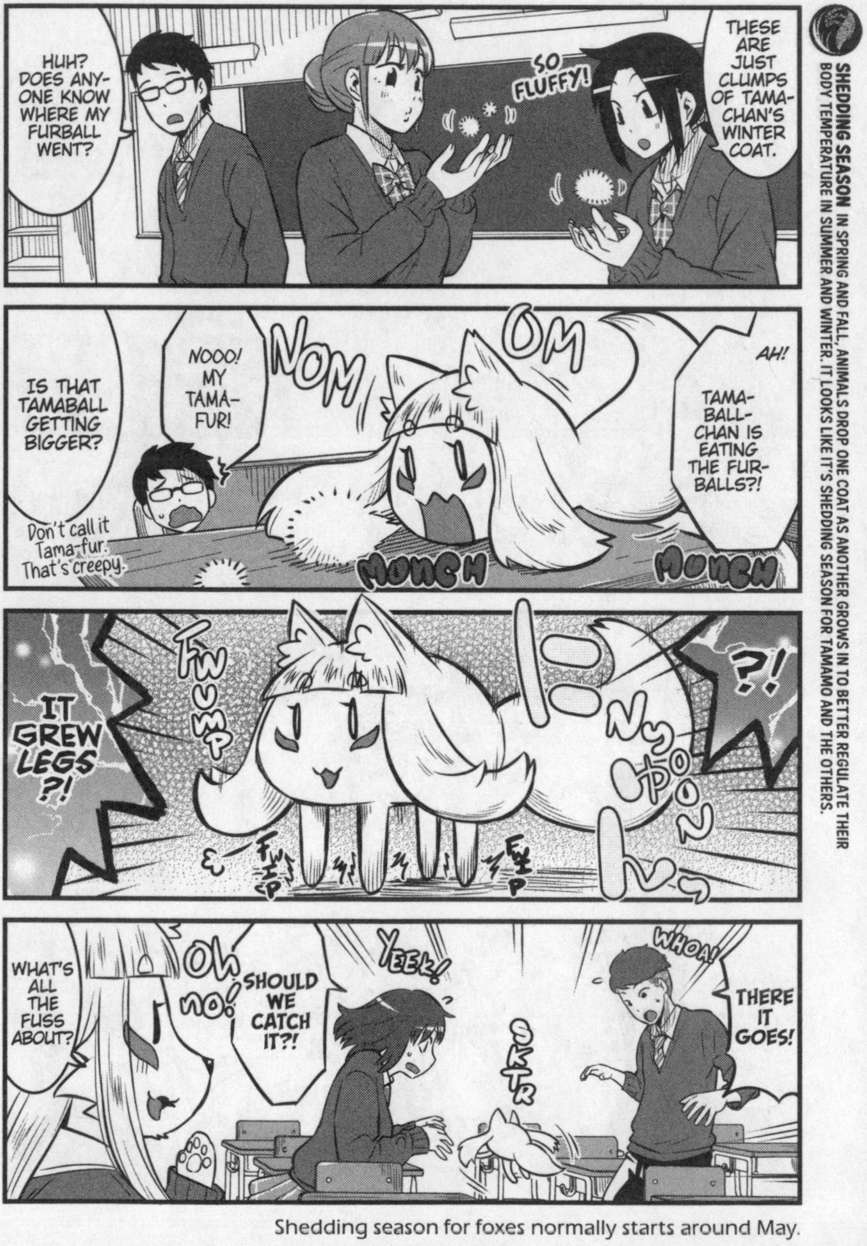
THESE ARE JUST CLUMPS OF TAMA-CHAN'S WINTER COAT.
SO FLUFFY!
HUH? DOES ANYONE KNOW WHERE MY FURBALL WENT?
AH! TAMABALL-CHAN IS EATING THE FURBALLS?!
OM
MUNCH
NOM
MUNCH
NOOO! MY TAMA-FUR!
IS THAT TAMABALL GETTING BIGGER?
Don't call it Tama-fur. That's creepy.
?!
Nyooon
FWUMP
IT GREW LEGS?!
FWIP
FWIP
WHOA!
THERE IT GOES!
SKTR
YEEK!
SHOULD WE CATCH IT?!
Oh no!
WHAT'S ALL THE FUSS ABOUT?

Shedding season for foxes normally starts around May.

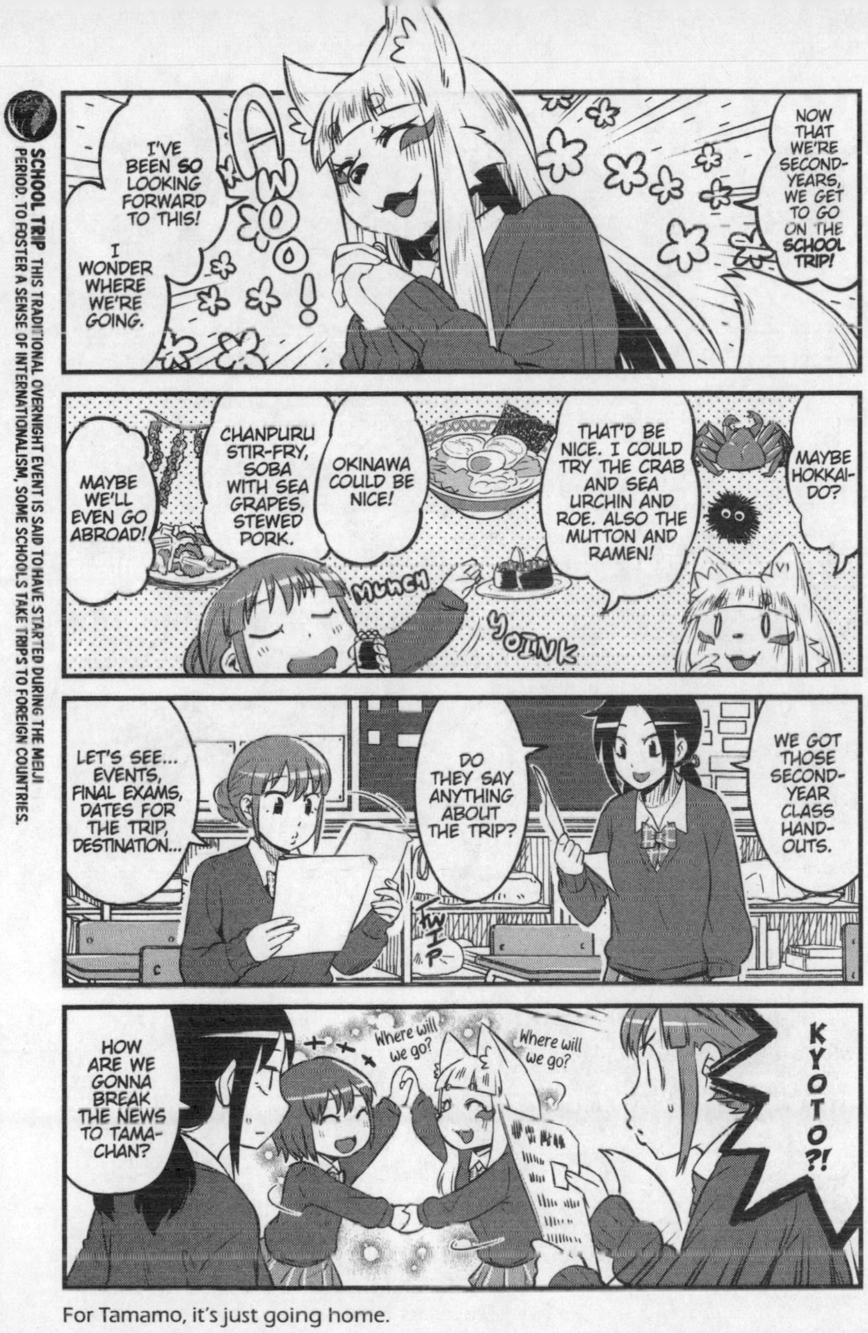
NOW THAT WE'RE SECOND-YEARS, WE GET TO GO ON THE SCHOOL TRIP!
AWOOO!
I'VE BEEN SO LOOKING FORWARD TO THIS!
I WONDER WHERE WE'RE GOING.
MAYBE HOKKAIDO?
THAT'D BE NICE. I COULD TRY THE CRAB AND SEA URCHIN AND ROE. ALSO THE MUTTON AND RAMEN!
YOINK
MUNCH
OKINAWA COULD BE NICE!
CHANPURU STIR-FRY, SOBA WITH SEA GRAPES, STEWED PORK.
MAYBE WE'LL EVEN GO ABROAD!
WE GOT THOSE SECOND-YEAR CLASS HANDOUTS.
DO THEY SAY ANYTHING ABOUT THE TRIP?
TWIP
LET'S SEE... EVENTS, FINAL EXAMS, DATES FOR THE TRIP, DESTINATION...
KYOTO?!
Where will we go?
Where will we go?
HOW ARE WE GONNA BREAK THE NEWS TO TAMA-CHAN?

For Tamamo, it's just going home.

SCHOOL TRIP THIS TRADITIONAL OVERNIGHT EVENT IS SAID TO HAVE STARTED DURING THE MEIJI PERIOD. TO FOSTER A SENSE OF INTERNATIONALISM, SOME SCHOOLS TAKE TRIPS TO FOREIGN COUNTRIES.

NEW CLASS! IT'S A BIT SAD TO BE SEPARATED FROM SOME OF MY FIRST-YEAR CLASSMATES, BUT I CAN STILL SEE THEM NEXT DOOR! HOORAY!

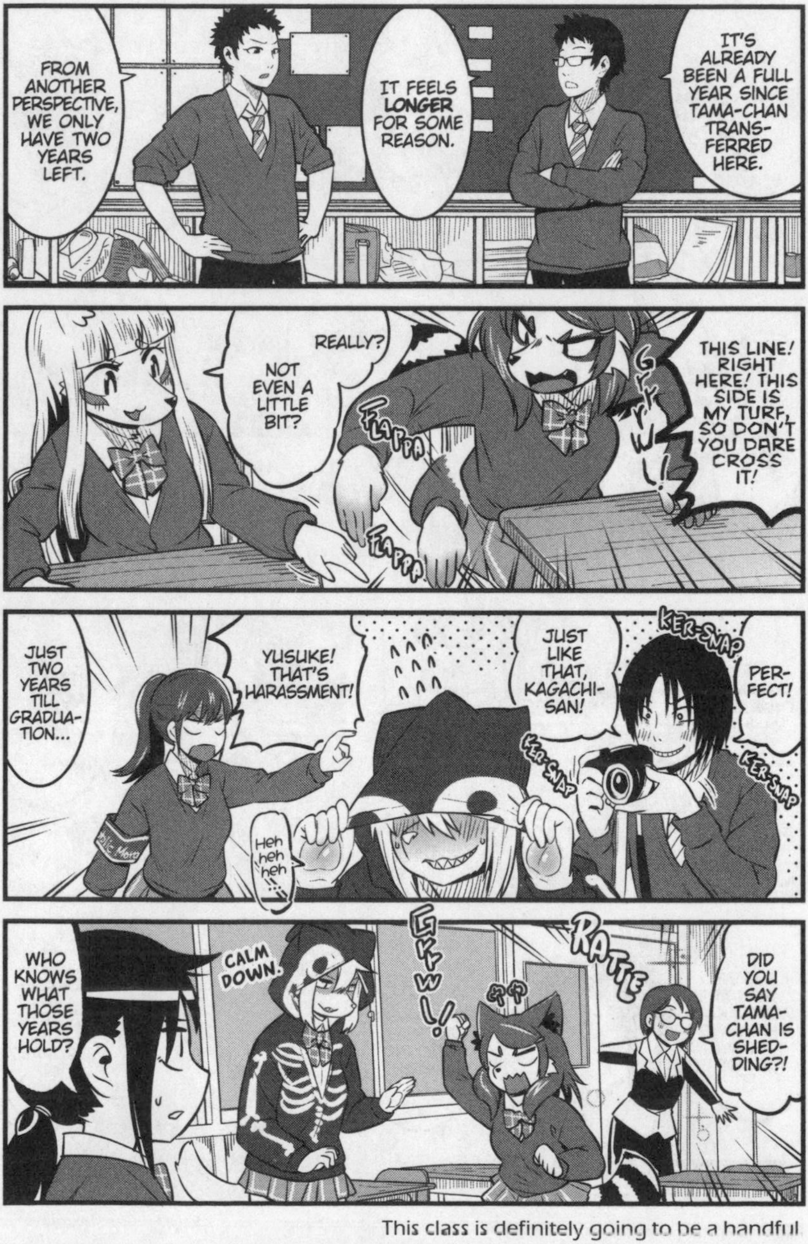
IT'S ALREADY BEEN A FULL YEAR SINCE TAMA-CHAN TRANS-FERRED HERE.
IT FEELS **LONGER** FOR SOME REASON.
FROM ANOTHER PERSPECTIVE, WE ONLY HAVE TWO YEARS LEFT.
THIS LINE! RIGHT HERE! THIS SIDE IS MY TURF, SO DON'T YOU DARE CROSS IT!
GRRRWL!
REALLY? NOT EVEN A LITTLE BIT?
FLAPPA
FLAPPA
KER-SNAP
PER-FECT!
JUST LIKE THAT, KAGACHI-SAN!
KER-SNAP
KER-SNAP
YUSUKE! THAT'S HARASSMENT!
JUST TWO YEARS TILL GRADUA-TION...
Heh heh heh...
DID YOU SAY TAMA-CHAN IS SHED-DING?!
RATTLE
GRRWL!
CALM DOWN.
WHO KNOWS WHAT THOSE YEARS HOLD?

This class is definitely going to be a handful.

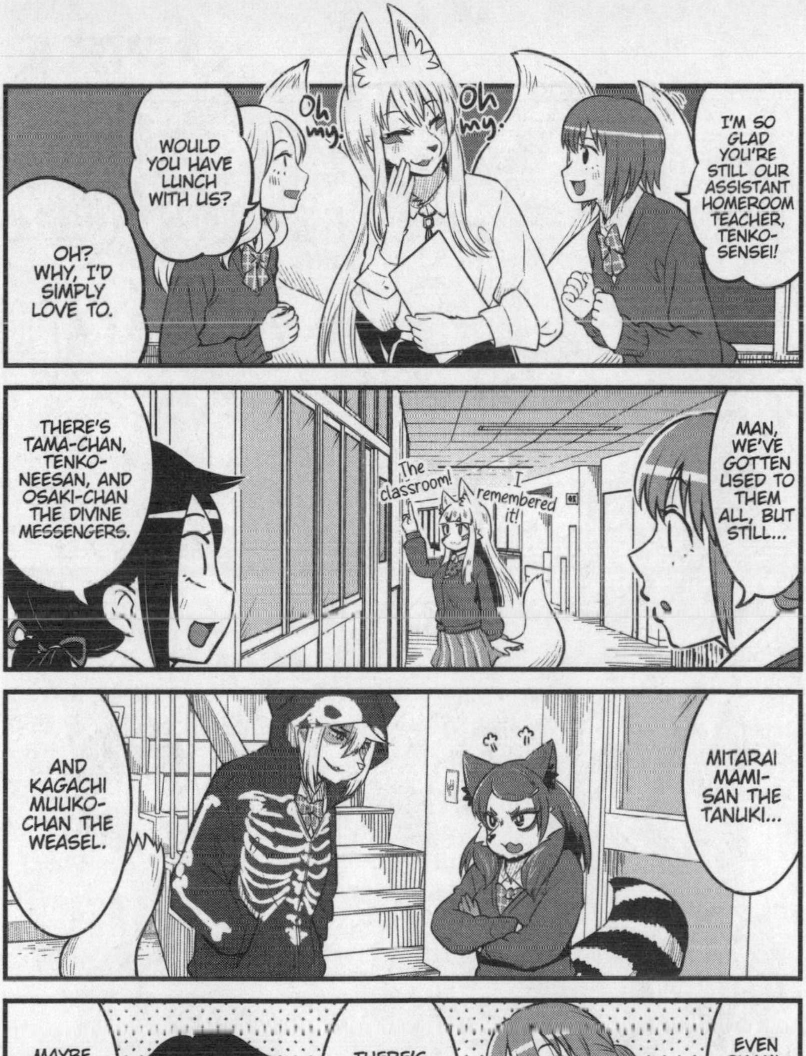
I'M SO GLAD YOU'RE STILL OUR ASSISTANT HOMEROOM TEACHER, TENKO-SENSEI!
Oh my.
Oh my.
WOULD YOU HAVE LUNCH WITH US?
OH? WHY, I'D SIMPLY LOVE TO.
MAN, WE'VE GOTTEN USED TO THEM ALL, BUT STILL...
I remembered it!
The classroom!
THERE'S TAMA-CHAN, TENKO-NEESAN, AND OSAKI-CHAN THE DIVINE MESSENGERS.
MITARAI MAMI-SAN THE TANUKI...
AND KAGACHI MUUKO-CHAN THE WEASEL.
EVEN OKAMI-SAN HERSELF JUST DROPPED IN.
THERE'S A LOT OF SUPERNATURAL BEINGS AROUND HERE.
MAYBE THERE ARE MORE THAT WE DON'T KNOW ABOUT.
CHAPTER 63

CHAPTER 63

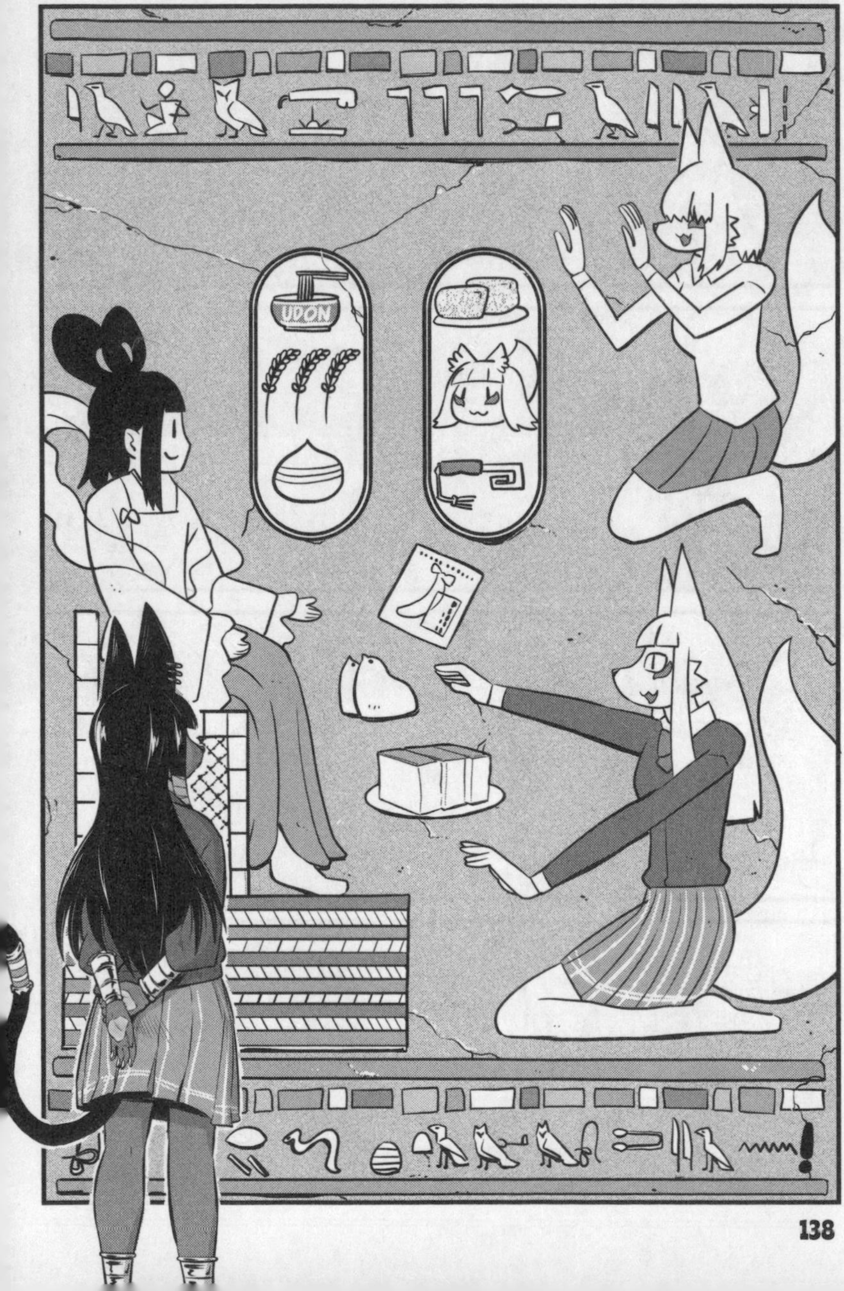
UDON

CLASS PRESIDENT THE CLASS PRESIDENT IS THE DE FACTO LEADER OF THE CLASS. THEY ARE RESPONSIBLE FOR FACILITATING DISCUSSIONS AND ORGANIZING PROJECTS LIKE SCHOOL FESTIVALS.

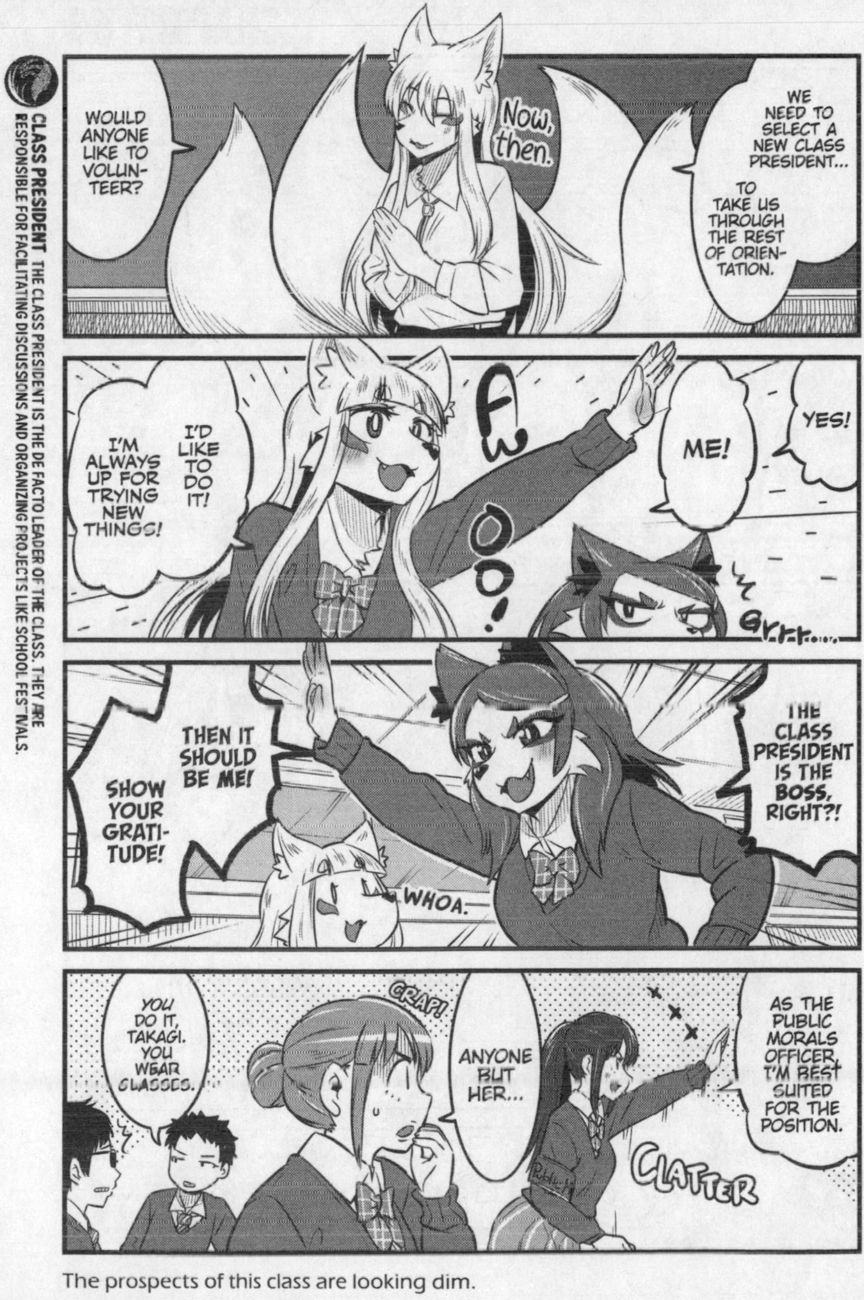
WE NEED TO SELECT A NEW CLASS PRESIDENT...
TO TAKE US THROUGH THE REST OF ORIEN-TATION.
Now, then.
WOULD ANYONE LIKE TO VOLUN-TEER?
YES!
ME!
Fwooo!
I'D LIKE TO DO IT!
I'M ALWAYS UP FOR TRYING NEW THINGS!
Grrr...
THE CLASS PRESIDENT IS THE BOSS, RIGHT?!
THEN IT SHOULD BE ME!
SHOW YOUR GRATI-TUDE!
WHOA.
AS THE PUBLIC MORALS OFFICER, I'M BEST SUITED FOR THE POSITION.
CLATTER
CRAP!
ANYONE BUT HER...
YOU DO IT, TAKAGI. YOU WEAR GLASSES.

The prospects of this class are looking dim.

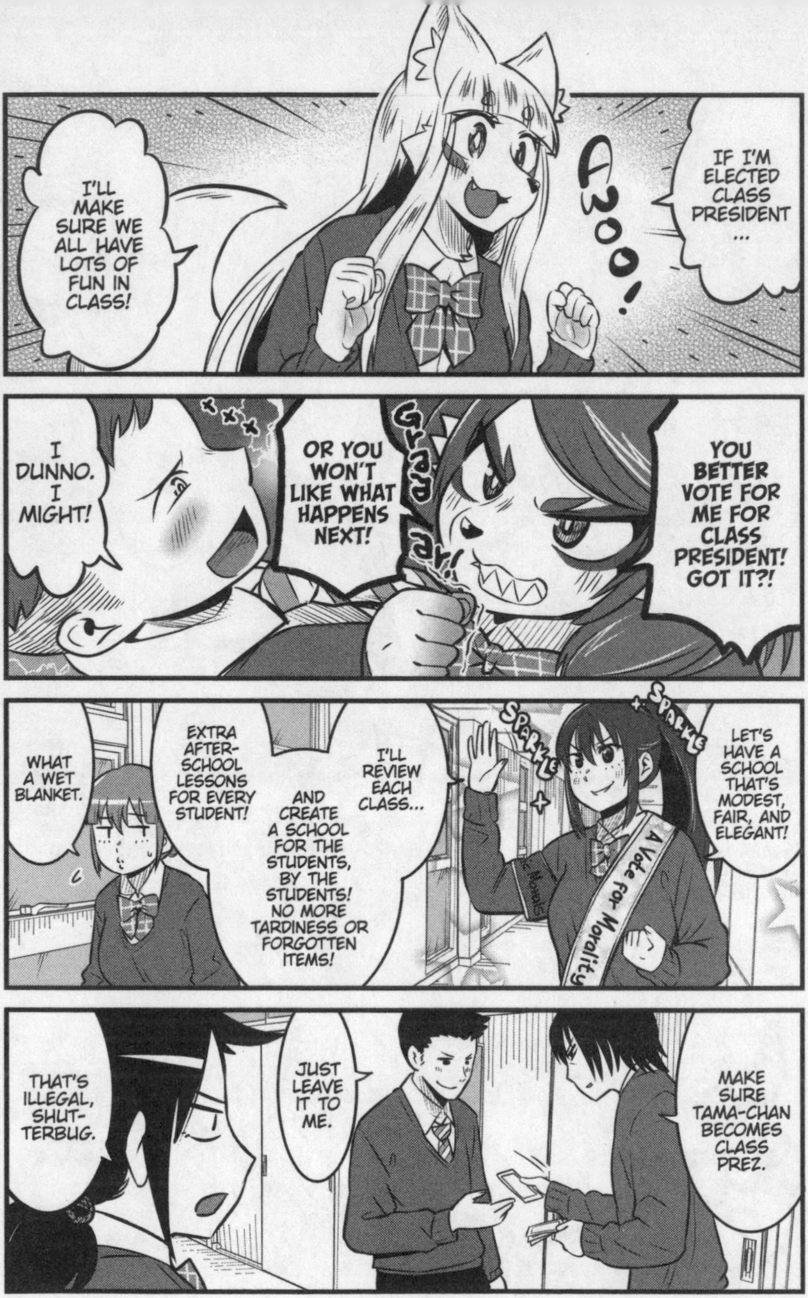
IF I'M ELECTED CLASS PRESIDENT ...
AWOO!
I'LL MAKE SURE WE ALL HAVE LOTS OF FUN IN CLASS!
YOU BETTER VOTE FOR ME FOR CLASS PRESIDENT! GOT IT?!
OR YOU WON'T LIKE WHAT HAPPENS NEXT!
I DUNNO. I MIGHT!
SPARKLE
SPARKLE
LET'S HAVE A SCHOOL THAT'S MODEST, FAIR, AND ELEGANT!
A Vote for Morality
I'LL REVIEW EACH CLASS...
AND CREATE A SCHOOL FOR THE STUDENTS, BY THE STUDENTS! NO MORE TARDINESS OR FORGOTTEN ITEMS!
EXTRA AFTER-SCHOOL LESSONS FOR EVERY STUDENT!
WHAT A WET BLANKET.
MAKE SURE TAMA-CHAN BECOMES CLASS PREZ.
JUST LEAVE IT TO ME.
THAT'S ILLEGAL, SHUTTERBUG.

BRIBES SECRET GIFTS GIVEN TO INFLUENCE SOMEONE'S OPINION OR SUPPORT. SOMETIMES CALLED *SODE NO SHITA* ("UNDER THE SLEEVE") IN JAPANESE, AS THE ACT WOULD BE HIDDEN UNDER THE WIDE SLEEVES OF A KIMONO.

The bribes were pictures of Tamamo, of course.

THE ELECTION I'VE ALWAYS BEEN INTERESTED IN THESE ELECTION THINGS, SO I RAN FOR OFFICE! BASED ON THE MYTHS AND STORIES I'VE READ, I WAS SURE A FOX WOULD WIN.

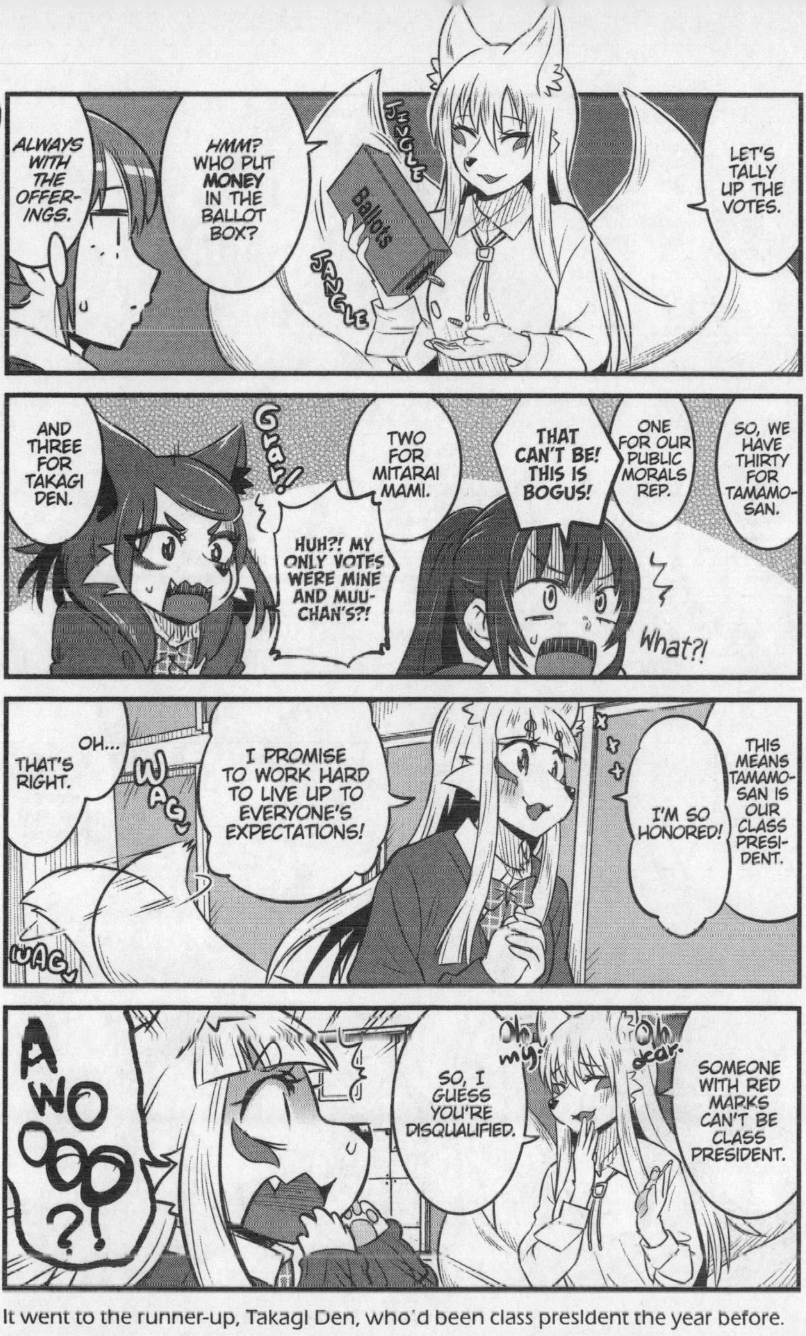
LET'S TALLY UP THE VOTES.
JINGLE
JANGLE
HMM? WHO PUT MONEY IN THE BALLOT BOX?
Ballots
ALWAYS WITH THE OFFERINGS.
SO, WE HAVE THIRTY FOR TAMAMO-SAN.
ONE FOR OUR PUBLIC MORALS REP.
THAT CAN'T BE! THIS IS BOGUS!
What?!
TWO FOR MITARAI MAMI.
Grar!
HUH?! MY ONLY VOTES WERE MINE AND MUU-CHAN'S?!
AND THREE FOR TAKAGI DEN.
THIS MEANS TAMAMO-SAN IS OUR CLASS PRESIDENT.
I'M SO HONORED!
I PROMISE TO WORK HARD TO LIVE UP TO EVERYONE'S EXPECTATIONS!
WAG
OH... THAT'S RIGHT.
WAG
SOMEONE WITH RED MARKS CAN'T BE CLASS PRESIDENT.
Oh dear.
Oh my.
SO, I GUESS YOU'RE DISQUALIFIED.
AWOOOOO?!

It went to the runner-up, Takagi Den, who'd been class president the year before.

TURF TERRITORIAL ANIMALS WILL ATTACK INTRUDERS TO SECURE FOOD OR BREEDING GROUNDS AND TO PROTECT THEIR YOUNG. THE CONCEPT OF TURF AND TERRITORY IS ALSO USED BY HUMANS.

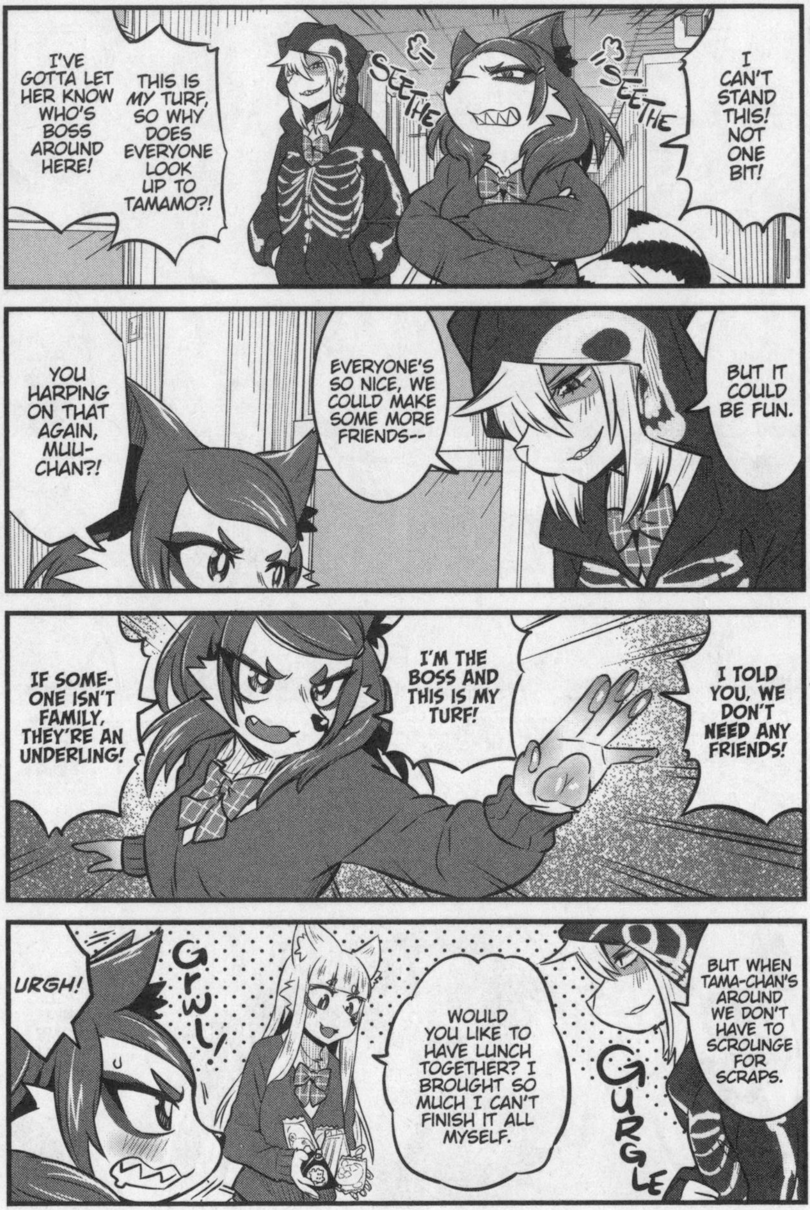
SEETHE
SEETHE
I CAN'T STAND THIS! NOT ONE BIT!
THIS IS MY TURF, SO WHY DOES EVERYONE LOOK UP TO TAMAMO?!
I'VE GOTTA LET HER KNOW WHO'S BOSS AROUND HERE!
BUT IT COULD BE FUN.
EVERYONE'S SO NICE, WE COULD MAKE SOME MORE FRIENDS--
YOU HARPING ON THAT AGAIN, MUU-CHAN?!
I TOLD YOU, WE DON'T NEED ANY FRIENDS!
I'M THE BOSS AND THIS IS MY TURF!
IF SOMEONE ISN'T FAMILY, THEY'RE AN UNDERLING!
BUT WHEN TAMA-CHAN'S AROUND WE DON'T HAVE TO SCROUNGE FOR SCRAPS.
GURGLE
WOULD YOU LIKE TO HAVE LUNCH TOGETHER? I BROUGHT SO MUCH I CAN'T FINISH IT ALL MYSELF.
GRWL!
URGH!

Mami was torn between her pride and her stomach.

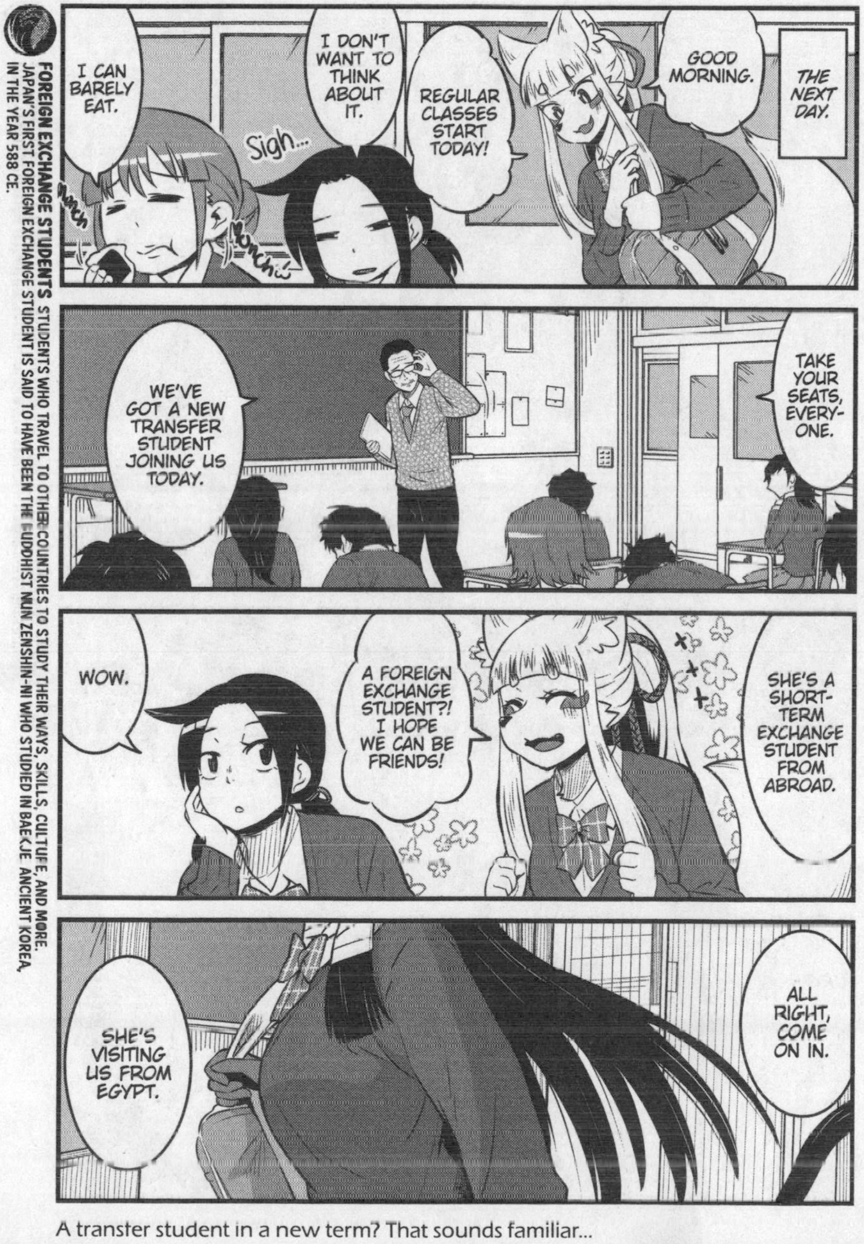
THE NEXT DAY.
GOOD MORNING.
REGULAR CLASSES START TODAY!
I DON'T WANT TO THINK ABOUT IT.
Sigh...
I CAN BARELY EAT.
TAKE YOUR SEATS, EVERY-ONE.
WE'VE GOT A NEW TRANSFER STUDENT JOINING US TODAY.
SHE'S A SHORT-TERM EXCHANGE STUDENT FROM ABROAD.
A FOREIGN EXCHANGE STUDENT?! I HOPE WE CAN BE FRIENDS!
WOW.
ALL RIGHT, COME ON IN.
SHE'S VISITING US FROM EGYPT.

FOREIGN EXCHANGE STUDENTS STUDENTS WHO TRAVEL TO OTHER COUNTRIES TO STUDY THEIR WAYS, SKILLS, CULTURE, AND MORE. JAPAN'S FIRST FOREIGN EXCHANGE STUDENT IS SAID TO HAVE BEEN THE BUDDHIST NUN ZENSHIN-NI WHO STUDIED IN BAEKJE, ANCIENT KOREA, IN THE YEAR 588 CE.

A transter student in a new term? That sounds familiar...

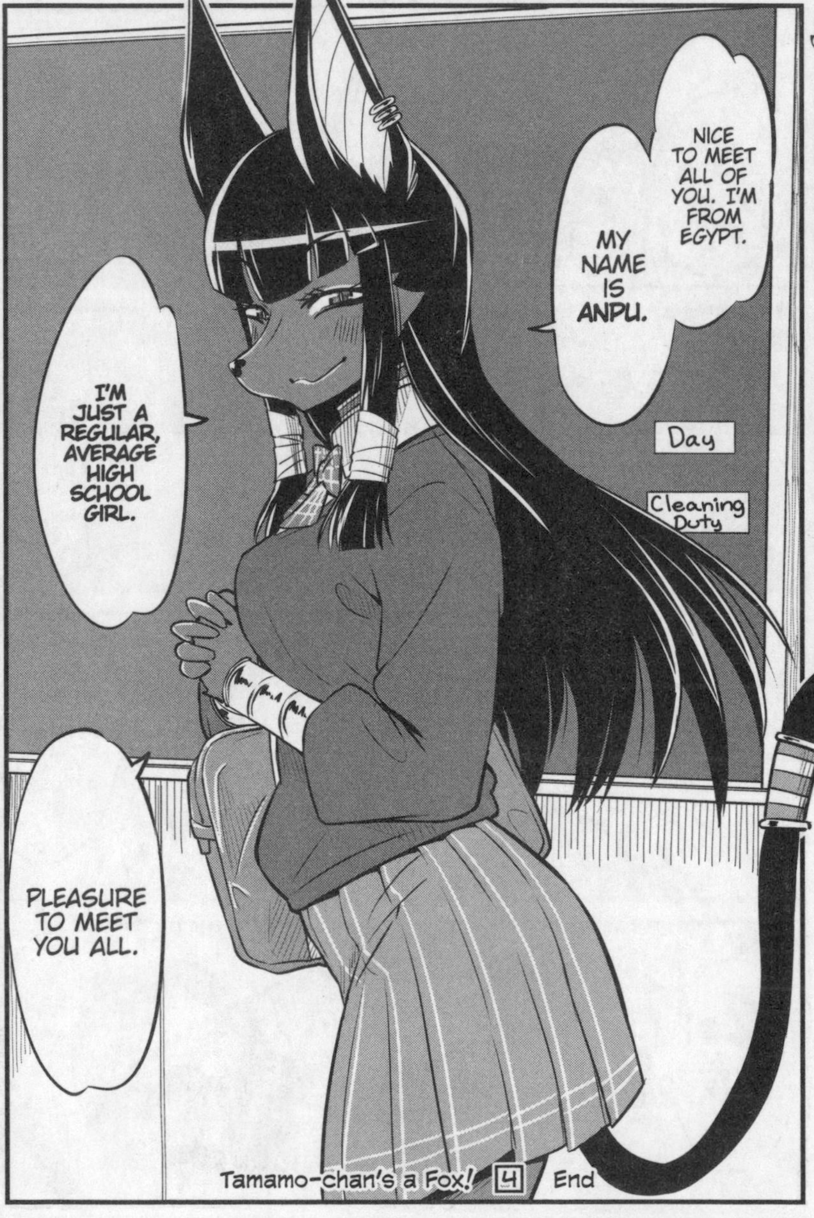
NICE TO MEET ALL OF YOU. I'M FROM EGYPT.
MY NAME IS ANPU.
Day
Cleaning Duty
I'M JUST A REGULAR, AVERAGE HIGH SCHOOL GIRL.
PLEASURE TO MEET YOU ALL.
Tamamo-chan's a Fox! 4 End

A FOREIGN EXCHANGE STUDENT?! NO WAY! SOMEONE LIKE ME COMING HERE FROM ANOTHER COUNTRY...?! IT SEEMS LIKE HER HUMAN DISGUISE HAS FOOLED THE CLASS!

But why is she here...?

Special Thanks

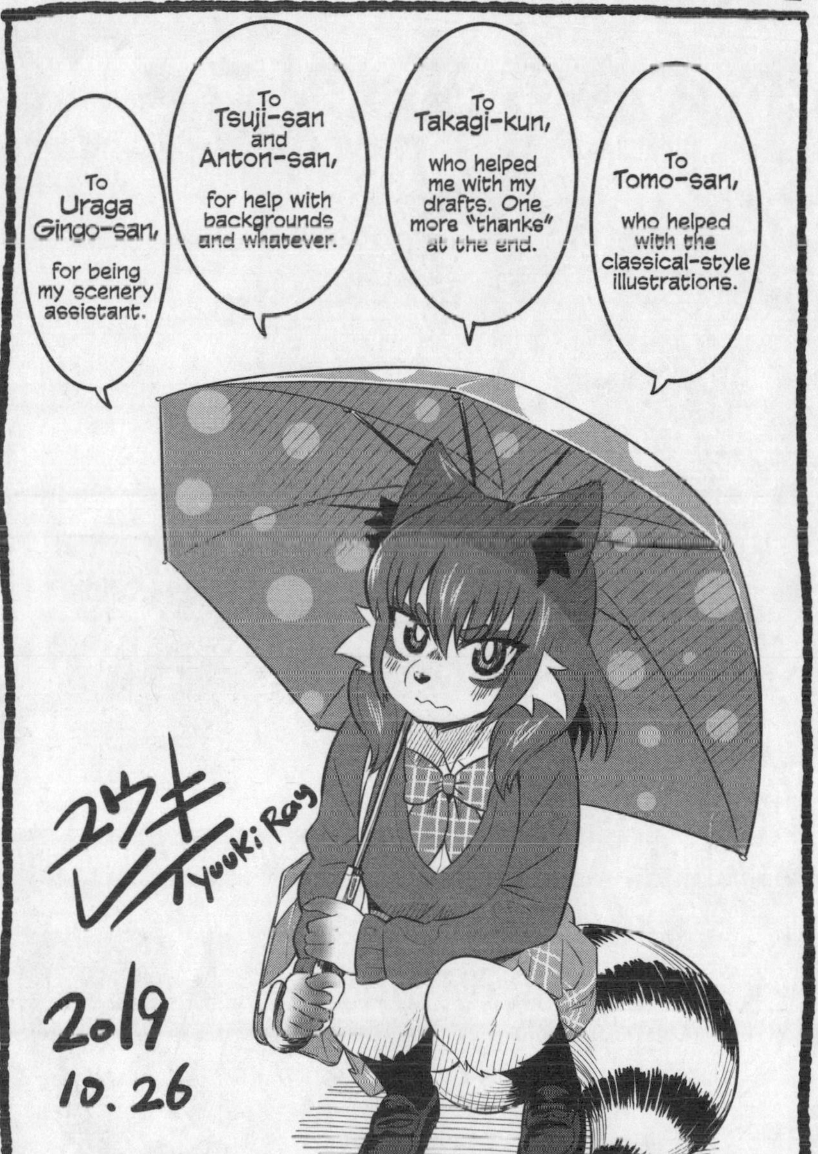
To Tomo-san, who helped with the classical-style illustrations.
To Takagi-kun, who helped me with my drafts. One more "thanks" at the end.
To Tsuji-san and Anton-san, for help with backgrounds and whatever.
To Uraga Gingo-san, for being my scenery assistant.
ユウキレイ
Yuuki Ray
2019
10.26

SEVEN SEAS ENTERTAINMENT PRESENTS

Tamamo-chan's a FOX!

story and art by **YUUKI RAY**

VOLUME 4

TRANSLATION
Wesley O'Donnell

LETTERING AND RETOUCH
Carolina Hernández Mendoza

COVER DESIGN
Hanase Qi

PROOFREADER
Kurestin Armada
B. Lillian Martin

EDITOR
Shanti Whitesides

PRINT MANAGER
Rhiannon Rasmussen–Silverstein

PRODUCTION MANAGER
Lissa Pattillo

MANAGING EDITOR
Julie Davis

ASSOCIATE PUBLISHER
Adam Arnold

PUBLISHER
Jason DeAngelis

OINARI JK TAMAMO-CHAN! VOL. 4
© 2019 Yuuki Ray.
All rights reserved.
First published in Japan in 2019 by Ichijinsha Inc., Tokyo.
Publication rights for this English edition arranged through Kodansha Ltd., Tokyo

Seven Seas press and purchase enquiries can be sent to Marketing Manager
Lianne Sentar at press@gomanga.com. Information regarding the distribution
and purchase of digital editions is available from Digital Manager CK Russell
at digital@gomanga.com.

Seven Seas and the Seven Seas logo are trademarks of
Seven Seas Entertainment. All rights reserved.

ISBN: 978-1-64827-375-9

Printed in Canada

First Printing: January 2022

10 9 8 7 6 5 4 3 2 1

FOLLOW US ONLINE: *www.sevenseasentertainment.com*

READING DIRECTIONS

This book reads from **right to left**, Japanese style.
If this is your first time reading manga, you start
reading from the top right panel on each page and
take it from there. If you get lost, just follow the
numbered diagram here. It may seem backwards at
first, but you'll get the hang of it! Have fun!!

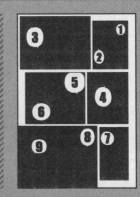